Developing Decision-Making Skills

CONTRIBUTORS

Charlotte C. Anderson

Barbara J. Capron

Edward W. Cassidy

Laura A. Driscoll

Jean Fair

Dana G. Kurfman

John P. Lunstrum

Murry R. Nelson

H. Wells Singleton

Kenneth Weeden

Barbara J. Winston

Celeste P. Woodley

Developing Decision-Making Skills

DANA G. KURFMAN, Editor

47th Yearbook • 1977

NATIONAL COUNCIL FOR THE SOCIAL STUDIES

NATIONAL COUNCIL FOR THE SOCIAL STUDIES

Library of Congress Catalog Card Number: 77-77356
Copyright © 1977 by the
NATIONAL COUNCIL FOR THE SOCIAL STUDIES
1515 Wilson Boulevard, Suite 101, Arlington, Virginia 22209

About the Art

*The unusual mazes that appear as decorative designs
on the cover and before each chapter
in this book
carry through the motif of decision making.
Drawn by artist Vladimir Koziakin,
they are taken from his book* MAZES 6.
*Copyright ©1976 by Vladimir Koziakin,
used by permission of Grosset & Dunlap, Inc.*

Foreword

In 1960, *Social Education* published an article entitled "Decision Making: The Heart of Social Studies Instruction," by Shirley Engle. The article set forth a simple thesis: a main purpose of social studies is to prepare students to become effective citizens; effective citizenship requires a capacity to make sound, thoughtful decisions; social studies instruction should be aimed at improving students' capacities for making good decisions.

This simple but powerful idea has inspired social studies educators for nearly two decades. Alas, the gap between the idea and its successful implementation has proved to be enormous. Among the holes to be filled has been a clear explication of essential decision-making skills and how they can be taught. This Yearbook contributes importantly to filling this void.

This book appears at an ideal time. Once again citizen education has risen to the top of the educational agenda, where it belongs, after years of neglect. Many Americans are concerned about the quality of civic life in the United States and worry about the future of the republic and its institutions. Support for programs to prepare students to fill competently the role of citizens is growing.

The book also appears at a time in which "basic skills" are much on the minds of educators. Public clamor that schools teach "basic skills" has too often directed attention to such skills as reading, writing, and computation, brushing other important skills aside. Sometimes social studies educators have been pressed to justify their efforts in terms of the contribution they are making to "basic skills." It is difficult to imagine any more essential, or "basic," skills than those presented in this book.

It should be noted that this, the 47th Yearbook, is the last of its kind. The Publications Board has recommended, and the Board of Directors has approved, a plan to publish four bulletins each year in place of an annual Yearbook. While some will regret the passing of the Yearbook tradition, I believe that NCSS members will be pleased with the bulletins that have been planned by the Publications Board.

The publication of a Yearbook requires the imagination, energy, and persistence of a great many people. With the exception of the NCSS staff, all commit their time without compensation as a contribution to the profession. I wish to thank and congratulate the editor, Dana Kurfman, the authors, and the members of the Publications Board for their achievement. And finally, a hearty thanks is due the NCSS staff, especially Daniel Roselle, Willadene Price, and Mary Matthews, for making the volume possible.

HOWARD D. MEHLINGER, *President*
National Council for the Social Studies

Preface

This Yearbook continues an NCSS pattern of periodic consideration of social studies skills. The 24th Yearbook in 1953 and the 33rd Yearbook in 1963 each dealt with skills in social studies. This Yearbook maintains that tradition, with decision making as the context within which more traditional social studies skills are treated. Decision making incorporates a number of other threads within the profession, represented by *Effective Thinking in the Social Studies*, 37th Yearbook (1967); *Values Education*, 41st Yearbook (1971); *Controversial Issues in the Social Studies: A Contemporary Perspective*, 45th Yearbook (1975); and *Values in the American Heritage*, 46th Yearbook (1976).

The 33rd Yearbook suggested eight types of skills shared with other subjects, and four considered to be the primary responsibility of social studies. Making rational decisions requires more ability in certain of these skills than others. In particular, such thinking skills as analysis, application, and evaluation are essential for decision making. Equally essential is the ability to obtain and interpret information from different kinds of sources. While highlighting these abilities, it has been necessary to omit such skills as time orientation and writing from this Yearbook.

A discussion of decision making in terms of purpose is provided in Chapter One. This chapter shows how the decision-making process incorporates thinking, information gathering, group process, and social action skills. It also highlights the need to develop the affective characteristics necessary in decision making, and it examines some of the curricular and instructional implications of the process.

The major skills required in effective decision making are treated in Chapters Two, Three and Four. Chapter Two elaborates on thinking skills, such as conceptualizing, generalizing, applying, and evaluating. Each of these skills, as well as being a necessary component of the process, has a role independent of decision making.

Chapters Three and Four focus on the primary types of information gathering needed for decision making and other social studies purposes. Chapter Three is concerned with questioning and observing. In addition, two types of prepared sources, maps and graphs, are treated. Chapter Four highlights reading skills independently of other prepared sources of information. Each of the skills considered in Chapters Three and Four has importance in its own right, aside from its role in decision making.

Most decision-making skills are the same, whether applied by individuals or groups. However, the dynamics of groups introduce significant new factors in the process. Thus, Chapter Five deals with the conditions which are needed for cooperative, equal status groups. It also provides insight into group action skills.

Chapters Six and Seven provide models for teaching decision-making skills in elementary and secondary classes. Useful instructional strategies are also emphasized in Chapters Two through Five. Teachers intending to teach thinking, information gathering, and group process skills will find several well developed teaching-learning exercises in each of these chapters.

The Yearbook concludes in Chapter Eight with a discussion of the complexities of evaluating student attainment of decision-making skills. Skills are carefully defined, and numerous suggestions for their formal and informal evaluation are provided.

DANA G. KURFMAN, *Editor*

Contributors Who's Who

CHARLOTTE C. ANDERSON is an Assistant Professor of Education and Coordinator of the Tutorial-Clinical Program for teacher education at Northwestern University. She served as values consultant for the K-6 Houghton Mifflin Social Studies Series, *Windows on Our World*; and she is currently on the Sexism and Social Justice Committee of NCSS.

BARBARA J. CAPRON is presently teacher in charge and teacher of grade five at Roger Wellington School, Belmont, Massachusetts. She is President of the Massachusetts Council for the Social Studies and has served as SSEC teacher associate and consultant to the ERIC-ChESS Board. Her certificate of Advanced Graduate Credit is from Boston University.

EDWARD W. CASSIDY is presently principal of James McHenry Elementary School in Lanham, Maryland. He received his Doctorate from the University of Maryland. He has served as Visiting Professor of Education at Bowie State College, Maryland, and is a therapist in private practice.

LAURA A. DRISCOLL will receive a Ph.D. in Educational Research and Evaluation from the University of Colorado, Laboratory of Educational Research, in 1977. She was Assistant Director of the Protocol Materials Development Project at the University of Colorado. She has served as a consultant in measurement and evaluation for the California State Department of Education and National Assessment.

JEAN FAIR, Professor of Education, Wayne State University, is a past President of the National Council for the Social Studies and has served on the Board of Directors, as well as on a number of NCSS committees. She has been chairperson of the Steering Committee of the NCSS Project for the Review of National Assessment in Social Studies and Citizenship, and she co-edited the 1967 NCSS Yearbook on *Effective Thinking in the Social Studies*.

DANA G. KURFMAN is K-12 social studies supervisor for Prince George's County, Maryland. He has worked in test development and curriculum evaluation with the Educational Testing Service. He served as evaluation specialist and director of the High School Geography Project, as well as editor of the NCGE Evaluation Yearbook. He also was a member of the NCSS Board of Directors.

JOHN P. LUNSTRUM holds a joint appointment in the fields of Language Education and Science-Human Affairs Education as a professor at Florida State University. He has also been a classroom social studies teacher and guidance counselor, and he has served as co-editor of the Instructional Media Department in *Social Education.*

MURRY R. NELSON, who received his Doctorate at Stanford University, is an Assistant Professor of Social Studies at the Pennsylvania State University. He has also taught elementary and junior high school. He received an M.A. from Stanford University in anthropology and retains an interest in that field as well as in law-related education.

H. WELLS SINGLETON received his Ph.D. from Stanford University and is presently Assistant Professor of Secondary Social Studies and General Curriculum at the University of Toledo. Besides having taught secondary social studies and supervised K-12 social studies programs, he has published articles in various educational journals.

KENNETH WEEDEN, social studies chairperson of Friendly High School, Friendly, Maryland, has done graduate work at the University of Maryland. He is on the county social studies curriculum planning team responsible for the K-12 program of 145,000 students. He has had considerable experience in the teaching of interdisciplinary studies at the senior high school level.

BARBARA J. WINSTON, an Associate Professor of Geography at Northeastern Illinois University, works with elementary and secondary social studies teachers. She served as skills consultant for the K-6 Houghton Mifflin Social Studies Series, *Windows on Our World,* and is active in geographic education. She is currently on the Science and Society Committee of NCSS.

CELESTE P. WOODLEY is Program Development Specialist with the Boulder Valley School District in Colorado, and continuing consultant in social studies to the National Assessment of Educational Progress. She has taught in secondary schools and has been on the faculty of the University of Colorado School of Education. She was director of the Protocol Materials Development Project at the University of Colorado, and has served as chairperson of the Publications Board of the National Council for the Social Studies.

Contents

"Decision making can be defined as the making of reasoned choices from among several alternatives."

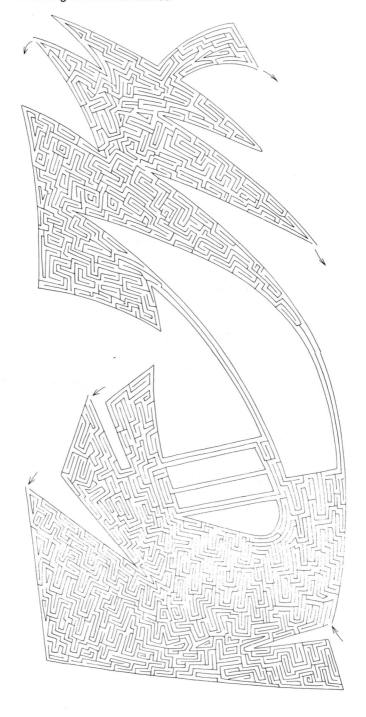

.1.

Edward W. Cassidy and Dana G. Kurfman

Decision Making
as Purpose and Process

The attempt to develop decision-making capability suggests educational objectives different in several ways from the objectives of traditional social studies programs. For example, it will be necessary to highlight such skills as analyzing, applying, and evaluating at the expense of historical knowledge. Even more, this goal implies teaching strategies and learning experiences which are considerably different from those now dominating social studies classrooms. Students will need many opportunities to make decisions and to examine critically the decision-making process.

Decision making can be defined as the making of reasoned choices from among several alternatives. Reasoned choices are choices based on judgments which are consistent with the decision-maker's values. They are also choices based on relevant, sound information. So conceived, decision making is not limited to considerations of public issues, such as for whom to vote, or whether to support high-rise developments in one's community. It includes decisions of a personal nature as well, such as what to do about the threatening person on the playground, whether to buy a car, or which college to attend. The common characteristic of all instances of true decision making, whether they are personal or public decisions, is the existence of alternative courses of action which require judgments in terms of one's values.

This chapter will discuss three major points. One is a rationale for considering decision making as the major purpose of social studies. In this connection, the inadequacy of "knowledge for its own sake" and education in the "basics" will be examined. Then two democratic values will be identified as bases for an emphasis on decision making. Certain misconceptions about decision making will be considered as well.

The second part of the chapter provides an analysis of the decision-making process. Three stages of decision making are considered: identifying decision occasions and alternatives; examining and evaluating decision alternatives; and deciding and reflecting upon the decision. The third section of the chapter develops some of the curricular and instructional implications of decision making for schools. This discussion focuses on skill objectives for decision making, the utilization of traditional content or subject matter, and particularly appropriate experiences for developing decision-making capability.

A RATIONALE FOR DECISION MAKING

Pervasiveness of Knowledge and Basic Skill Objectives

Social studies classrooms have been dominated by attempts to transmit knowledge, often very specific knowledge, about people, places, dates, and institutional structures. Input from the academic disciplines has reinforced this knowledge transmission purpose.[1] In spite of the emphasis on concepts, inquiry, and other new strategies from the social science disciplines, the social studies curriculum has changed little. This should not be surprising, since most of the curriculum input of the past fifteen years has accepted traditional social studies courses, while trying to make them more conceptually sound and consistent with the ways in which modern social scientists work. Instead of facts, the emphasis has been on concepts; instead of bare-bones, fact-finding skills, the emphasis has shifted to inquiry and process skills. But the purpose remains the same: the acquisition of sound knowledge. The ideal is that of the disinterested scholar pursuing truth for its own sake.

There is no denying the importance of knowledge: the more we know, the more sensible our world becomes; the more we know, the more capable we are of enjoying experiences; the more we know, the more likely we are to make sound decisions. But, as the overall purpose of social studies, knowledge attainment is not a sufficiently broad purpose to guide program development or to inspire modern students. Most people, including students, are not primarily "knowers"; they are primarily "doers." The prospect of learning something new may inspire some of us; but for most, knowledge is merely a means to some larger end.

A second characteristic of contemporary social studies programs is their emphasis on basic skills. The accountability movement provides encouragement for this emphasis. Students are expected to do well on tests. The major skills tested are reading and arithmetic.[2] Within social studies, the focus is on reading social studies content, graphs, and maps.

Many teachers in elementary schools are faced with increasing pressure to produce students with increased capability in the three Rs. Consequently, there seems to be less and less time for social studies. Planning social studies units which integrate a number of skills and subjects is difficult under any circumstances, but such units are virtually impossible when there are clearly designated time periods during which work on reading and computational skills is required. Only when time remains can attention be directed to social studies. Even then, priority is often given to measurable skills, such as reading content, graphs, and maps. For accountability proponents, social studies fulfills its purpose if it provides students with rudimentary information-gathering skills.

Learning *only* easily testable fact-finding skills will prove increasingly inadequate for life in the modern world. Much more than fact-finding skills—that is, higher-level thought processes, useful knowledge, and clear values—are needed for students to function effectively. Clearly the purpose of social studies is greater than helping students attain minimal skills. If we do not focus attention on a more compelling purpose for social studies, more and more teacher time will be spent helping just a few more students achieve minimum academic skill levels.

Democratic Values Supporting a Decision-Making Purpose

Decision making can provide such a purpose. Decision making as an educational goal derives its justification from two values which underlie our American social-political system. One of these is belief in popular rule, and the other is respect for the individual. From the democratic value of popular rule comes support for developing skill in making decisions about public issues. From the value of individual dignity comes support for making sound decisions about personal problems.

A major democratic value is popular rule; that is, rule by informed citizens. Most people expect social studies to teach good citizenship. This means many different things, but a necessary characteristic of good citizens is the ability to make sensible decisions about public issues. As Shirley Engle has written, ". . . the social studies are centrally concerned with the education of citizens. The mark of the good citizen is the quality of decisions which he reaches on public and private matters of social concern."[3] At all levels of government, issues continually arise which require people to make up their minds about what should be done, how it should be done, and by whom it should be done.

When people say that democratic government relies on an informed citizenry, this means more than citizens simply having information about the issues. An informed citizenry means that people make enlightened decisions about public issues and about those who contend for leadership. Such citizens are informed with relevant knowledge about issues and also with knowledge about their own values. They are informed with the skills needed to obtain information and to think critically. They are able to make judgments consistent with their values and with their knowledge of the situation.

Individual dignity as a basic value of democracy needs no documentation. It means respect for oneself as a person of worth and respect for other people as well. To the extent we provide our students with decision-making skills, we help them fulfill their individual potential and build the self-esteem on which healthy personalities are based. As people practice making thoughtful decisions and act upon them, they can develop a sense of personal worth. They can also develop an awareness of the values which make them who they are and who they would like to be.

Clearly, democracy in the classic sense of popular rule and individual worth is enhanced by public education which helps people become better decision makers. Thus, democratic values support an emphasis on two kinds of decisions, those focusing on public issues and those focusing on key personal problems.

Some Misconceptions About Decision Making

Most social studies educators tend to think of decision making in a "public issues" context. The work of Oliver and Shaver,[4] among others, has focused on helping students reach sound conclusions about public issues. However, a conception of decision making limited to public issues is inadequate. Personal decision making also finds support in democratic values and must be included in social studies programs. Three additional faulty conceptions of decision making require discussion. These are the beliefs that (1) decision making is just another name for inquiry; (2) decision making is primarily a group process; and (3) decision making requires some sort of overt action.

In the article already cited, Engle urged us "to emphasize decision making at two levels: at the level of deciding what a group of descriptive data means, how these data may be summarized or generalized, what principles they suggest; and also decision making at the level of policy determination, which requires a synthesis of facts, principles, and values. . . ."[5]

When decision making refers to making decisions about meaning and

truth—deciding whether information is correct, deciding how one factor is related to another factor, perhaps as cause and effect—such decisions are part of the inquiry process. Our conception of decision making is restricted to Engle's second level. It always entails a value judgment, whereas scientific inquiry reaches conclusions using criteria of
validity and reliability. Science is concerned with establishing truth,
not with deciding the best thing to do.

If decision making is identified with and restricted to inquiry processes, a curriculum oriented to knowledge and the testing of knowledge
claims would suffice. In fact, it is possible to have a very sound inquiry-
oriented program without providing opportunities for students to
choose between alternatives in terms of their own values. Practice in
making value-laden decisions is necessary to meet both personal and
civic needs.

This is not to deny the importance of inquiry skills. Without such
skills there would be no science and no extension of the frontiers of
knowledge. Clearly, too, inquiry skills are essential in making good decisions. They are needed to obtain reliable information. Even more important, they are needed to project the possible consequences of each
decision alternative. Without inquiry skills there cannot be good decision making, but inquiry skills alone cannot result in good decision
making.

Another misconception is the assumption that decision making is, or
should be, primarily a group process.[6] The fact is that individuals are
called upon constantly to make personal decisions. The essentials of
the process are the same whether a single person or a group makes the
decision. Personal decisions are often made with the advice of others,
but these circumstances of essentially private decision making should
not be confused with group processes. Group decisions require a special kind of interpersonal interplay involving the values and feelings of
several people.

Still another unnecessary association with decision making is the belief that decisions must, or should be, accompanied by overt action.[7]
Certainly, schools have encouraged too much passive behavior. Students should not be encouraged to decide and yet not have the courage
to act on their convictions. Completion of the decision process does
include taking action and reflecting upon the outcomes of the action.
Even while admitting this, it must be acknowledged that many decisions, especially civic decisions, are made tentatively and cumulative-
ly. People make up their minds about many social issues without taking
any overt action. The view that decision making thus is not real or that
the skills involved cannot be practiced without an action follow-
through puts an unnecessary burden on social studies teachers. There

is no need for guilt feelings when teachers help students "make up their minds" even when there is no possibility of overt action.

Thus, the needed kinds of decision making place equal emphasis on public issues and personal problem decisions. Such decision making is distinguished from inquiry by requiring value judgments. It is an individual, personal process as well as a group process. And it does not always require overt action. A systematic analysis of the process itself in the next section will provide the basis for the final section, which considers how social studies programs guided by a decision-making purpose will be different from traditional social studies programs.

THE DECISION-MAKING PROCESS

The decisions of most people are made on impulse, or from habit, or by default—in essence, without much thought. However, a conscious decision presupposes involvement in a very complex process. This section will attempt to provide teachers with an overview of this decision-making process.

The decision-making process has been studied from many perspectives and by many different disciplines. Mathematicians and statisticians have attempted to develop comprehensive decision-making models.[8] Industrial psychologists and organizational analysts[9] have recently focused on the processes which executives should go through in order to make effective decisions. Social studies teachers have examined the decisions made by Presidents and other politicians in an attempt to help students learn from the past. Finally, developmental and career psychologists[10] are currently focusing on the making of personal and career decisions. What, then, should be the focus for the teacher of social studies? The answer has to be a combination of all of the above.

Most authors who write about decision making basically agree about the process. However, there are many differences about the part of the process to emphasize and about the number of steps involved in the process. This chapter incorporates the approaches of a great many authors and practitioners in the field. Three different stages are distinguished: (a) Identifying Decision Occasions and Alternatives, (b) Examining and Evaluating Decision Alternatives, and (c) Deciding and Reflecting on the Decision. Each of these three basic stages is subdivided into several phases which more explicitly define that stage. The proposed model therefore includes a total of nine distinguishable steps. As teachers analyze actual examples of decision making with their students, they may wish to reduce the number of phases to fit the maturity level of their students. The nine phases provide teachers with as much specificity as can be used profitably and practically. The stages and phases thus identified are shown in Figure 1.

FIGURE I

STAGES IN THE DECISION-MAKING PROCESS

Identify Decision Occasions and Alternatives
(a) define the decision to be made
(b) identify the goals of the decision maker
(c) identify available alternatives

Examine and Evaluate Decision Alternatives
(a) examine the probable outcomes of each alternative
(b) evaluate and rank the alternatives

Decide and Reflect on the Decision
(a) select an alternative
(b) implement the plan of action
(c) assess the results of action
(d) consider recycling the process

(left border, vertical) FACTS/GENERALIZATIONS

(right border, vertical) VALUES/FEELINGS

This chart (Figure 1) masks some of the complexity of the process. The descriptions suggest a simplicity and linearity in the process which probably do not exist in "real world," everyday decision making. Decision making seldom follows a nice, singular line or has easily predictable outcomes. While the decision-making process incorporates aspects of the scientific method, it focuses on the choice made by a human being involved in the process. This fact of human choice highlights the uncertainty of the process; for whenever a person is the focus, subjectivity, intuition, individuality, and, particularly, values become involved.

There are two other points which must be considered in referring to the chart. The first point is the interrelatedness of each of the stages and phases in the process. None of the steps really stands as a distinct entity. The process is a series of interrelated and contingent events in which many "mini" decisions are made, each having an effect on the following steps. The second point is that the chart portrays information, in the form of facts/generalizations, and the values/feelings component on the borders of the process. Values, feelings, facts, and generalizations are shown on the borders of the chart because they affect *all* aspects of the process. The point is that decision makers are using data during each of the phases and are also being influenced throughout the process by their feelings and values. The first stage of the process is no less influenced by values, feelings, and information than is the last stage. What one person perceives as an occasion for a decision is certainly influenced by his/her values and the data he/she receives about the situation.

The stages in the process might be examined best in the context of a hypothetical decision which involves the application of as many steps as can readily be depicted without becoming overly complicated and/or cumbersome. The example chosen is from a realm of personal decision making familiar to most teachers.

> The Browns' apartment was being turned into a condominium. They quickly decided that this was the right time to get out of an apartment and into a house. The Browns then felt their decision was to decide which house to buy, so they went out with a real estate agent and looked at some houses. As they began to look at houses, they started to note that the amount of money they felt they could afford really didn't buy much of a house. The Browns also noticed that the salesperson kept showing them houses which were in segregated areas and which were far from shopping and schools. As they continued to look at houses, they quickly gave up the idea of having four bedrooms and a study. The idea of their new house being located on the shore seemed to be disappearing as they became more familiar with the market.
>
> The Browns finally realized that they must set some priorities for themselves in terms of their budget and their values. The Browns felt that they would prefer to live in an integrated neighborhood. They also wanted to be near schools, shopping, and water recreation. The Browns knew that these needs must, of course, be worked into a framework of cost.
>
> After several more trips out with the real estate agent, the Browns' priorities began to take shape, and they finally narrowed their choice of homes to two possibilities.
>
> House A is in a middle income, integrated neighborhood. The house is near schools and shopping. While the house doesn't have four bedrooms, an addition would be a possibility.
>
> House B is also in an integrated, middle income neighborhood, but it will cost $3,000 more than House A. Shopping facilities are quite convenient, but the Brown's children will have a thirty-minute bus ride to school. The house is somewhat smaller than House A, but it does have waterfront privileges.

Which house should the Browns choose?

This fairly typical adult dilemma should help to illustrate the decision-making process which was outlined earlier. Let us examine each phase of the process, using the Browns' situation.

Identify Decision Occasions and Alternatives

The Identifying Decision Occasions and Alternatives stage in the decision-making process is most crucial because it establishes the structure which will be followed throughout the rest of the process. In this phase, the efficient decision maker must: be quick to sense the decisions which need to be made; be sensitive enough to recognize his/her own goals and feelings in relation to the situation; be able to identify viable alternatives in the situation.

(a) Define the Decision To Be Made

It seems safe to say that many people are like the Browns, who rushed quickly to pursue alternatives before they were sure of the problem. The Browns probably jumped over at least two important decisions: (1) Should they buy a condominium or not?, and (2) Should they buy a house or not? The purpose of this step is to emphasize that people must analyze the situation after they become aware that an occasion for decision exists. Clarifying the issues to be decided upon is an obvious preliminary step which is often neglected—to the extent of missing the major issue.

This phase is concluded only when the decision situation has been defined in such a way that the decision makers are clear about the decision to be made.

Information is needed at this phase of decision making, as well as at other steps that follow. The more people know about the situation— that is, the style house they want, how much they can afford, what kind of neighborhood they like, the asking price for a four-bedroom house near the shore—the more effectively they will be able to isolate the primary and secondary questions which need to be decided.[11] If they had sorted out some of this information, the Browns' decision would have been much more clearly defined than "Which house to buy?" It would have been more like "Which house shall we buy in this price range, in this type neighborhood, with these conveniences, etc.?"

(b) Identify the Goals of the Decision Maker

The second phase of the "identifying decision occasions and alternatives" stage is that point at which people identify their goals in relation to the decision situation. In our example, the Browns skipped over this step and had to come back to it. They began identifying alternatives before they clearly identified their goals. It is at this point in the decision-making process that the values of the decision maker begin to come into focus. While values are involved throughout the decision-making process, and really cannot be restricted to one point, it seems that personal values begin to become involved as the decision maker's goals are identified. The Browns had some tangible goals, which they later enumerated. They wanted a certain price range, certain physical characteristics in the house, accessibility to certain services, a certain type of neighborhood, etc. Some of the Browns' goals were influenced by practicality and others by what might be called "personal values."

It is important for the decision maker to be aware of the necessity for explicitly stating his/her goals in objective terms. This specificity will eliminate any internal confusion later on in the process.

This phase can be considered complete when the decision maker has successfully listed, in objective terms, what his/her goals are in this particular decision situation. With clear goals, the decision maker can, later on, observe and assess the results of the process. It is important to remember here that even though a goal is made explicit, it really exists only for this particular decision. Different circumstances may cause an individual to place more stress on some goals rather than others.

(c) Identify Available Alternatives

The final phase of the first stage in the decision-making process follows naturally from the preceding steps. At this point in the process, the objective is to identify as many alternatives as possible. A number of alternatives will provide a wide choice of options for action. If there are no alternatives for what should be done, or how it should be done, there is no possible decision to be made. In our example, the Browns began to identify alternatives very quickly. It was at this point that the Browns' values became a little more obvious. They began to reject certain alternative houses because they did not fit in with some of their values. The final two alternatives were both in integrated neighborhoods. This is obviously a strong value, whereas proximity to school and water were values which could be "traded off."

In other decision-making situations, formulating alternatives may not be as simple or as clear as identifying all the possible houses one might wish to buy. In many situations, alternatives must be created by the decision maker(s). In such instances brainstorming is probably the best method for generating a variety of alternatives. The essence of brainstorming is thinking of as many alternatives as possible while avoiding the evaluation of alternatives until all have been elicited. Early evaluation of alternatives may lead to inhibiting the generation of more creative alternatives or to the premature elimination of a viable alternative.

At this point, creative thinking is needed, as well as critical thinking. The skill of information gathering is also crucial during this phase of the process. The decision maker must be capable of making comparisons with analogous situations in order to determine the possible alternatives which ought to be considered. Unique alternatives may need to be hypothesized for a satisfactory decision to be reached.

Affectively, what is needed is an attitude of openness to new possibilities, while avoiding the inclination to accept the first option that comes to mind. Sensitivity to the timing involved in the decision is also critical. Certain types of decisions allow for time to consider many alternatives, whereas others are more pressing.

It is at this point that information about the situation is helpful in calling forth additional possibilities for consideration. The more we know about the problem before us, the more likely we are to think of creative alternatives which might be considered. The more limited our knowledge, the more likely we are to see only a few alternatives. This phase, and the first stage of the process, is complete when all the possible alternatives have been identified and listed for consideration.

Examine and Evaluate Decision Alternatives

The second major stage of the decision-making process involves thoroughly examining, projecting, weighing, and ranking each alternative. This stage, occurring after the decision has been thoroughly defined and before an alternative is selected and implemented, is really at the heart of making rational decisions. It is during this examining and evaluating phase that we usually say in the vernacular, "I'm thinking things over," or "I'm 'deciding' what to do."

(a) Examine the Probable Outcomes of Each Alternative

After all the possible alternatives have been identified, the next phase in the decision-making process involves tracing the consequences which are likely to follow from each alternative. This step is simply attempting to determine what the likely consequences are of each course of action, until all alternatives and their consequences are identified. Figure 2 shows that alternative A has three probable consequences identified with it, and alternative B has four consequences associated with it. Each immediate consequence may lead to other long-range consequences.

FIGURE 2

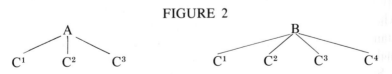

Returning to the example of the Browns, the alternatives identified in

Figure 2 could be houses A and B. For illustrative purposes, selection of house A might have three consequences. (Of course, in a real situation, there would be more.)

1. The Browns would have a house within their means.
2. The Browns would live in an integrated neighborhood.
3. The Browns would be close to school.

Selection of house B might have the following four consequences:

1. The Browns would be financially "strapped."
2. The Browns' children would have to ride a bus to school.
3. The Browns would be able to enjoy water sports and recreation.
4. The Browns would be living in rather "cramped quarters."

Obviously, decision makers should try to project the consequences of an alternative as far as possible. It would be valuable for the Browns to think whether the neighborhoods they are considering would still be integrated five years from now, or if the water near their house would be available for recreation five years hence. It is with this projection of the future consequences of an alternative that maximum uncertainty prevails.

Knowing how to obtain relevant information is a necessary skill at this point in the process. Information may be needed to determine whether, in fact, certain "causes" are likely to have certain "effects." Engaging in this step of determining the most probable consequences for each projected decision alternative requires a high level of thinking. What is called for is the ability to apply what we know in a realistic situation. The skill emphasis here is on testing "if-then" propositions. Under these circumstances, if certain action is taken, what are the most likely consequences?

Knowledge of generalizations and principles derived from the social sciences and from practical experience is of critical importance in accurately predicting the consequence of each course of action. Most useful are those generalizations and principles which allow people to predict what will follow when certain actions are taken in a given set of circumstances or conditions. The more of this kind of knowledge decision makers have, the better they will be at making decisions.

Sensitivity is needed during this phase in order to project or consider how each alternative will affect other people, as well as one's self and one's own values. Respect for the truth is needed, too, even when it points to consequences which arouse negative feelings.

(b) Evaluate the Alternatives

If, in the best of all possible worlds, people could accurately predict the consequences of each decision alternative, they would still have the problem of deciding which set of consequences is most desirable. Using one's values as criteria, the decision maker must judge that one set of consequences is more consistent with the things that he or she values than are competing sets of consequences. This aspect of decision making is the heart of the process.

After a thorough assessment of each alternative, there comes the task of rank ordering the alternatives on the basis of the strengths and weaknesses of each. In the example of the Browns, there were, finally, only two alternatives. Many problem situations will have several decision alternatives. After all the alternatives have been examined thoroughly, they will tend to fall into some sort of order of priority. This rank order will be determined largely by the values of the decision maker. If all options appear equally positive or negative, the alternative presenting the most positive and least negative consequences is probably the option of choice.

The skills required at this point are those involved in making value judgments. This means determining whether consequences are desirable or undesirable from the point of view of the decision maker. The process is complex because people have multiple values which must be applied to multiple consequences. A consequence which is consistent with one value may be inconsistent with another. This is the phase of decision making that forces a clarification of one's values and a reconsideration of their order of importance.

Information is critical at this stage also, but now it is knowledge of one's feelings and values. To the extent that we know how we feel and what we value, we have the needed knowledge. For the Browns, it was important to realize that living near the water was of more importance than living in a crowded house or having their children ride the bus.

An affective requirement of value judgments is a willingness to admit to one's real values. Often what people are supposed to believe and feel needs to be reconciled with what they actually believe and feel. Out of such a reconciliation can come a commitment to one's values and a willingness to live with their consequences.

Decide and Reflect on the Decision

The final stage in the decision-making process is often taken for granted in real life, and yet it is critically important. The steps involved call for the decision maker to choose an alternative, implement the plan, review the results, and, finally, on the basis of the results, determine if the process needs to be re-entered for the purpose of selecting a different or additional alternative.

(a) Select an Alternative

The first step in this third stage is choosing an alternative. This is the integrative step in the decision-making process, where all the information gathering and thinking come to a climax and where a choice is made.

Gelatt et al.[12] cite four different commonly used strategies for deciding amongst alternatives: the wish strategy; the safe strategy; the escape strategy; and the combination strategy. The approach of the decision maker is implied in the name of the strategy. Using the wish strategy the decision maker chooses the alternative he/she desires most—come what may—regardless of the consequences. The decision maker who plays it safe seeks to avoid taking any risks and chooses an alternative which is most likely to succeed—even if it is not the most highly desired alternative. The escape strategy is often utilized by those who tend to be more pessimistic. This approach selects an alternative for what it avoids rather than for what it can bring. The most desirable alternative in this case is that one which insures an escape from negative consequences. Finally, the combination strategy selects the alternative which seems to have both the highest probability of success and the highest desirability for the decision maker. This final strategy is probably the most reasonable approach for most people.

A plan for implementing the chosen alternative is often implied in the description of the alternative. Drucker[13] suggests that an alternative is not viable unless it includes plans for its implementation. Once the Browns selected either House A or B, implementing that choice would seem to follow logically. Using a different example, if a high school senior finally decided to attend U.C.L.A., he would need a plan to follow through with this selection. If there were no plan, then the process would end with the choice, and the senior would not have done anything about applying, registering, scheduling courses, and the like.

The plans which need to be developed at this point call for the ability to use the data collected when the consequences of the chosen alternative were being projected. These data then need to be synthesized and ordered in a step-by-step plan for achieving successful implementation of the alternative of choice.

(b) Implement the Plan of Action

Implementing the action plan which was developed in the previous phase is basically a mechanical process. The step calls for simply acting upon the plan. What makes the step noteworthy is, first, that taking action is difficult for many people, and, second, that overt action is not necessary or appropriate for every decision.

People will very often go through a decision-making process right up to this point and then not act because of fear of the unknown, or of failure, or of certain consequences. What is needed in these instances is a strong sense of commitment to take the required action. It is possible to go through the decision-making process and attempt to avoid actually coming to grips with the decision by not taking overt action. Anyone who has bought a house, like the Browns, knows that when it comes to signing that contract, there is a definite sense of insecurity. This insecurity exists despite all the hours of weighing alternatives and predicting outcomes. With decisions such as buying a home, selecting a college, or changing jobs, it is usually fear of the unknown which slows or stalls taking action. In other, more personal decisions, the action indicated in the plan may call for behavior which is contrary to the decision maker's usual lifestyle.

Many times people make up their minds about what should be done in preparation for acting when the occasion arises. Many, if not most, political decisions are made with little expectation of taking immediate action. People think through their positions about foreign policy and domestic issues and reach tentative decisions about what they want to have happen.

In fact, people make numerous decisions while holding action in abeyance. The process of decision making outlined here cannot be undertaken with any degree of effectiveness without time for the rational consideration and development of alternatives. If all decisions were left for the moment of action, instinctive reactions, rather than rational decision making, would be the basis for the action taken. Thus, many of the significant decisions we make are indeterminate with respect to overt action. Action can be the final step in making a decision, and ultimately it must be; but this only accentuates the need for many instances of rational decision making before a time of action is upon us.

(c) Assess the Results of Action

It is only after the decision has been implemented that people can reflect upon both the process they have been through and the product or outcome of that process.[14] Outcomes of the decision-making process are usually fairly easy to assess. Did the alternative achieve its intended results? Do the Browns like their new house? Do you like your new job? However, there are some decisions which must wait for a time until additional data are obtained. Will the decision to vote for Jimmy Carter have good or bad outcomes? There will probably never be a totally satisfactory answer. A good outcome for one person, a draft evader who receives amnesty, might be perceived as a very bad outcome by a disabled veteran.

Besides assessing the outcomes of a decision, people can also reflect on the three stages of the total process in order to assess how well each phase or step was executed. After this examination, it is entirely possible that one might say, "Well, the outcome was not satisfactory to me; but in terms of my values at that time, I did do a good job with the process."

Successful completion of the decision-making process requires a careful completion of the previously listed phases. This review, coupled with a knowledge of the outcomes, will provide feedback regarding this particular decision-making occasion. Feedback which comes after having followed the process through means that, as Tyler[15] says, "We can't lose. We'll either celebrate our success or celebrate our failure." In other words, even if the outcome of one's decision is not what one had hoped for, the individual still gains information. The information can be as esoteric as insights into the meaning of life itself, or as basic as the realization that one did not consider an obvious alternative.

This review of the process is often neglected, especially when the outcome of a decision is favorable. If everything works out the way we wanted, then we seem to be content to "leave well enough alone." However, it is important, for two reasons, to examine the process even after a good outcome. First, the good outcome could reflect a good process to apply in the future. Second, even a good outcome could reflect a poor process which could be remedied in the future. It is important to remember that some apparently great decisions have been due to luck rather than to excellent process!

(d) Consider Recycling the Process

This last phase of the decision-making process could have been included with the previous one but was separated for the sake of emphasis. It is important to remember that most decisions are not irreversible. If the outcome is not to one's liking, one can usually "go back and do it again." Since the decision-making process is really cyclical, a review of the process may cause one to consider re-entering the process to choose a different alternative. For example, if the Browns chose House B and the outcome was that their family turned out to be unhappy, they might re-enter the process and look at other houses.

When this final step is applied automatically by the decision maker, then the approach has become a way of life in which decisions are systematically analyzed, applied, reviewed, and re-enacted when necessary.

It should be apparent that the decision-making process outlined in this chapter is not rigid and lock-step. The phases flow one from another and even back and forth. Each step in the process can take on a different appearance as additional information is gathered or as values become more clearly identified. Decision makers are often forced to retrace their steps in light of new circumstances.

Finally, we need to recognize that while the process, as it is outlined here, is definitely time-consuming, the return for that investment of time is more effective decisions. What ultimately follows from more effective decisions is a greater sense of independence and an increase in control over one's environment.

CURRICULAR AND INSTRUCTIONAL IMPLICATIONS

Once there is commitment to a decision-making purpose and an understanding of the process, the curricular and instructional implications of that purpose and process must be delineated. The major curriculum implication is a shift from learning content to attaining the skills and affective characteristics required for effective decision making. The major instructional implication is a need for student opportunities to practice and reflect upon decision making, using varied social studies content or subject matter.

Primacy of Skill Objectives

Most educators are familiar with the phenomenon of curriculum add-ons. Everyone seems to be thinking of new things to do; no one suggests what to take out of the curriculum in order to make way for the new program. Fortunately, a decision-making curriculum can be implemented using existing social studies subject matter. Such a curriculum does, however, require a restructuring of objectives, a reformulation of priorities, and an emphasis on certain skill objectives and related affective objectives at the expense of knowledge attainment objectives.

A decision-making social studies program de-emphasizes "knowledge for its own sake" while focusing on the knowledge needed to decide upon critical issues of the past, present, and future. As students become more aware of how knowledge operates in making decisions, they should become more conscious of its usefulness. Thus, a decision-making focus does not diminish the importance of knowledge; instead, it should heighten the value students place on the kind of knowing which serves their purposes in resolving personal and social problems.

Two types of skills are needed for effective decision making, whether practiced by individuals or groups: thinking skills and information-gathering skills. An analysis of the three stages of the deciding process elaborated in the preceding section leads to the identification of three major thinking skills: (1) analysis-synthesis, required during all three stages of the process; (2) application-prediction, required during the second stage; and (3) evaluation-judgment, required primarily during the second stage, but also during the third stage. Information-gathering skills are of two types. Needed information can be obtained directly by (1) asking questions, (2) observing, and (3) listening. It can be obtained also from prepared sources by (1) using mapped information, (2) using graphs and tables, and (3) reading written communications. Each of these six information-gathering skills may be needed during all three stages of the process.

All of these skills have value independent of their contribution to decision making. Analysis and application skills are needed to verify the truth of propositions. Information-gathering skills are needed to satisfy curiosity, enjoy reading, and understand the meaning of maps and graphs. Thus, even in social studies programs without any commitment to decision making, there will be attempts to develop these skills, particularly the information-gathering ones.

The decision-making skills noted above require support for certain affective characteristics. The use of thinking skills in making decisions requires persons with positive attitudes about themselves, tolerance for ambiguity, and—when action is taken—a willingness to accept the consequences of their actions. Moreover, if thinking is to result in socially acceptable decisions, individuals must demonstrate respect for other people, as well as for themselves. Gathering the information needed for decisions requires confidence in using varied sources of information. Effective information gathering may, in some circumstances, also depend upon empathy for people in other cultures and circumstances.

When groups, rather than individuals, make decisions, more emphasis is placed on some skills and affective characteristics than is the case when individuals make decisions. In particular, asking, listening, and summarizing skills are highlighted. Moreover, effective group work requires sensitivity to the purposes and feelings of others. This means a willingness to hear others out and to provide the emotional support needed for self-confidence.

Skills are often listed separately from "objectives" or "learning outcomes" in commercial materials and curriculum guides. However, in a decision-making curriculum, certain skills are the primary objectives. Thus, information gathering and thinking skills are major categories for listing objectives or expected learning outcomes. In the following list of decision-making skill objectives,[16] no claim is made for completeness. This listing provides a nucleus of decision-making objectives which can be clarified and expanded as understanding of the decision-making process increases.

DECISION-MAKING SKILL OBJECTIVES

Direct Information-Gathering Skills
  A. Asking questions
     1. Asking who, what, how
     2. Reformulating questions
  B. Observing
     1. Using all senses
     2. Interpreting cues
     3. Deciding which senses to use
     4. Making inferences
  C. Listening
     1. Paying attention
     2. Paraphrasing
     3. Asking clarifying questions

Skills for Gathering Information from Prepared Sources
  A. Reading
     1. Clarifying the purpose
     2. Identifying word meanings
     3. Recalling or recognizing
     4. Summarizing and inferring
  B. Using maps
     1. Interpreting symbols
     2. Determining directions
     3. Determining distances
     4. Selecting appropriate maps
  C. Using graphs and tables
     1. Identifying title and axis variables
     2. Extracting facts
     3. Drawing inferences

Thinking Skills
  A. Analyzing—Synthesizing
     1. Identifying the elements in the occasion for decision
     2. Comparing with analogous decision occasions
     3. Defining the issue(s) to be decided

4. Identifying two or more possible decision alternatives
5. Identifying values of the decision maker(s)
6. Formulating a plan of action

B. Applying—Predicting
1. Applying information from analogous occasions
2. Recalling relevant "if, then" generalizations
3. Predicting the probable immediate and long-range consequences of each alternative

C. Evaluating—Judging
1. Judging the desirability of projected consequences
2. Evaluating each alternative in terms of consequences
3. Comparing alternatives in terms of strengths and weaknesses
4. Evaluating the chosen alternative in terms of its actual consequences

Providing a Sequential Development of Skills

Students will not become effective decision makers through the one-shot efforts of a few teachers. Significant educational attainments take time to develop. To help students develop skills, teachers must build on the work of one another. The group of teachers who make up a school staff has the responsibility for coordinated skills development. In fact, each school system—if it intends to achieve continuity from elementary schools, to middle schools, to high schools—does, too. This requires development of a sequential K-12 skills program in which teachers at each grade level have clear responsibility for emphasizing certain decision-making skills and affective objectives, while their colleagues have responsibility for emphasizing other skills and affective outcomes.

A school plan for decision making requires some sequential ordering of thinking and information-gathering skills, so that students grow in overall decision-making capability as they proceed through school. Although there is little evidence to support one sequence over another, this does not deny the need for some sort of sequential pattern. Teachers in different grades and courses want a sense of the specific skills and levels of skill development to which they should attend. If all teachers are expected to assume responsibility for all skills, the result is likely to be no sense of responsibility at all.

One way to arrange for sequential skill development is for teachers of different grades to agree upon one or two sets of skills as their primary responsibility. Thus, at each elementary grade, teachers could be responsible for developing general decision-making capability. At the same time, they could take responsibility for one of the skills listed under each heading. For example, third-grade teachers might assume responsibility for the skills of observing, evaluating, and using maps, whereas fourth-grade teachers would assume primary responsibility for asking questions, analyzing, and reading. This does not mean that a third-grade teacher concentrating on evaluation skills would ignore analysis and application skills. It would mean only that the third-grade teacher's priorities would be the development of specific observing, evaluating, and map skills. If different types of thinking and information-gathering skills were repeated periodically, students would go through several cycles in their K-12 experience. Each cycle would provide a more advanced level of skill experiences. The main thing for a school staff to do is to plan for the teaching of skills in a recurrent and systematic way at gradually more sophisticated levels.

Even with a plan for sequential development of decision-making skills, teachers need help in finding out where students stand with respect to each of the component skills. Undoubtedly, students progress at different rates. Thus, during the second cycle of gathering information from graphs and tables, some students will be at a very elementary level, whereas other students will be at a very advanced level. In order to move students along on several skills at their own pace, teachers need diagnostic data on each student.

The major reason for failing to diagnose students' levels of attainment is a failure in data management. Scoring, recording, and interpreting data on individual students is an overwhelming task for most teachers. Another difficulty in managing diagnostic data is arranging the data so they can be used in guiding students to appropriate skill-development exercises. Finally, most schools have failed to find manageable ways of transmitting diagnostic data from one grade level to another. Schools must find ways of correcting these data management problems.

Thus, a school system and a social studies program dedicated to the development of decision-making capabilities need to define their objectives carefully, develop a grade-by-grade plan for their sequential development, and provide teachers with the diagnostic help they need to work with individual students. Only then will appropriate learning experiences be provided to meet the decision-making needs of all the students the school system seeks to serve.

Classroom Conditions Needed to Develop Decision-Making Skills

Among the classroom conditions needed for decision making are (a) an open atmosphere, (b) opportunities for decision making using varied subject matter, (c) provision for analysis of the process, and (d) opportunities for systematic individualized instruction on thinking and information-gathering subskills.

A classroom atmosphere which encourages expression of diverse viewpoints is essential for decision making. Decisions are never right or wrong; they are more or less appropriate in terms of a particular situation and an individual decision maker's values. The "right or wrong" approach to knowledge attainment may have its place in some learning situations, but it will not work for decision making. Moreover, an open atmosphere is necessary for fostering such related affective objectives as self-confidence, tolerance for ambiguity, and a willingness to accept the consequences of one's actions.

There is controversy regarding students' freedom to act out decisions in the school and community environment. That is, to what extent does the need for an open classroom atmosphere justify freedom of action in implementing individual or group decisions? Some decision-making experiences must certainly extend through the action stage. Yet, schools have a responsibility to establish some parameters for legitimate action.[17] The viewpoint of this chapter is that there are occasions when decision-making skills and affective characteristics can be developed without overt action. The elementary and middle school years probably require more controlled decision making than would be necessary in senior high schools. Even in senior high schools, certain types of overt action may stir up such public opposition as to threaten the total decision-making program. Then teachers face a decision between the total program and continuing to encourage certain types of direct action.

Providing numerous opportunities for decision making *is* a necessary condition for developing the requisite skills. Fortunately, most traditional social studies content provides occasions for students to either (a) make decisions, (b) role-play decisions, or (c) analyze the decisions of others.[18] When students make decisions about how to spend their allowances, select a summer job, or plan a career, they are directly involved in the process. When they simulate the role of another person in a controversial behavior situation or in a corporate management team, students are a step away from reality, but nevertheless they can develop their decision-making skills. Even when observing or reading about the behavior of another person making decisions, students can analyze the process and become more conscious of the skills which are involved.

The skills of decision making which have been described can be developed in a number of social studies subject matter contexts. In addition to "teachable moments," units and even courses which center on personal behavior and controversial issues are particularly appropriate. Such content can be organized so that students make tentative decisions; i.e., "make up their minds" about personal problems and key public issues. Economics and government courses also provide numerous occasions for making decisions about contemporary issues and for role-playing simulations.

Of course, decision making need not be restricted to a consideration of such contemporary social and personal issues. Decision making can also be a major emphasis in history and geography courses.

Among other things, history is a recording of important decisions and their probable consequences. By looking at the decisions of historical personages and by evaluating the effectiveness of these decisions, students can be involved in analyzing the decision-making process.[19] History teachers can raise such questions as: "What were his/her alternatives?" "What did this leader take into account in reaching her/his decision?" More evaluative questions include: "Could the decision situation have been defined in another way?" "What should have been done in these particular circumstances?" "How should it have been done?" "Why should it have been done at all?" "Would you have done what he/she did?"

A critical examination of decisions which have already been made will help students understand the process better. Although many historians frown upon "what if" treatments of history, these can be motivating and can provide practice in developing decision-making skills. By having students decide what they would have done in particular historical circumstances, they can have realistic simulated decision-making experiences.

Decision-making experiences are also appropriate in geographic studies. People in other places and other cultures make decisions very comparable to those made by American youngsters and American communities. These decisions can be looked at in terms of the particular cultural context involved, including the probable values of the decision maker, as well as the alternative values open to people in that culture. Geography also includes the making of location decisions,[20] particularly on the location of certain kinds of economic activities. Other geographic decisions deal with resource utilization or preservation, land-use problems, and urban planning.

Most makers of simulation games are careful to point out the need for "debriefing" sessions following the exercise. These sessions serve to bring out the main points of the simulation game and help students to become more aware of the process they have experienced. Providing time to examine decision-making experiences, whether the experience was real, simulated, or just observed and analyzed, is another necessary condition for developing awareness of the decision-making process and the skills called for in the process. Students need more than experiences with decision making. The educational payoff is in becoming self-conscious about the process itself.

A final condition for attaining decision-making skills is the opportunity to practice those subskills most in need of development. Certain of the subskills—perhaps reading, using maps, and using graphs/tables—lend themselves to systematic instruction. Many teachers have mini-units which provide directed study and practice for their classes. Even when this approach is not used, it is essential that teachers provide opportunities for individualized study and practice of selected subskills. Even though exercises are more readily available for some of the nine skills identified on pages 19-20 than others, teachers can develop learning centers for skills usually ignored, such as observing, analyzing, and evaluating.

Teachers willing to provide opportunities for directed study of decision-making subskills, opportunities to make decisions and to study the process itself, and a classroom climate conducive to different viewpoints can establish the instructional conditions to develop decision-making capability. They are helped when guided by a careful formulation of objectives and bolstered by the cooperative efforts of fellow-teachers following a sequential plan for developing the skills.

The decision-making process which has been outlined in this chapter is not an easy one to teach. It is also not an easy process for students, or anyone, to learn. The process is time-consuming and calls for expending a great deal of energy. Nevertheless, Tolbert[21] cites research to show that, while it is difficult, the process can be taught to students, even elementary-age students. Computer systems, programmed instruction, and simulation have all been used effectively to teach students decision-making skills.

The curricular implications of teaching decision-making skills range from the obvious to the very profound. Teaching decision making does not call for new building designs or a total revamping of curricula. It does require a special climate in which there is opportunity to examine alternatives, make decisions, and, at times, suffer the consequences. Educators must be prepared to foster such a climate, even though questioning, creativity, and action can sometimes be difficult to live with. The payoff will be high school graduates who know what they value, are able to support those positions, and can apply them to real life situations with confidence.

FOOTNOTES

[1]See Lee Ehman, Howard Mehlinger, and John Patrick, *Toward Effective Instruction in Secondary Social Studies* (Boston: Houghton Mifflin Company, 1974), pp. 44–45. All of Chapter One provides insight into social studies content emphases and student attitudes toward social studies.

[2]Sharryl Hawke, Christine Ahrens, and Irving Morrissett, *State Accountability Activities and the Social Studies: A Nationwide Survey, A Proposed General Accountability Model, and Some Guidelines*, SSEC Publication No. 175 (Boulder: ERIC Clearinghouse for Social Studies/Social Science Education and Social Science Education Consortium, Inc., 1975), p. 33.

[3]Shirley H. Engle, "Decision Making: The Heart of Social Studies Instruction," *Social Education* 24 (November, 1960), p. 302.

[4]Donald W. Oliver and James P. Shaver, *Teaching Public Issues in the High School* (Boston: Houghton Mifflin Company, 1966).

[5]*Ibid.*, p. 301.

[6]This viewpoint has been popularized by Fannie Shaftel and Ronald Lippitt. See Fannie Shaftel and George Shaftel, *Role Playing for Social Values: Decision-Making in the Social Studies* (Englewood Cliffs: Prentice-Hall, Inc., 1967), and Ronald Lippitt, Robert Fox, and Lucille Schaible, *Social Science Resource Book* (Chicago: Science Research Associates, Inc., 1969).

[7]James Banks argues this viewpoint forcefully. See James A. Banks, *Teaching Strategies for the Social Studies: Inquiry, Valuing, and Decision-Making* (Reading, Massachusetts: Addison-Wesley Publishing Company, 1973), pp. 480–518, and James A. Banks, "Liberating the Black Ghetto," *Teaching About Life in the City*, Richard Wisniewski, editor, 42nd Yearbook (Washington: National Council for the Social Studies, 1972), p. 172.

[8]W. Edwards, "Dynamic Decision Theory and Probabilistic Information," *Human Factors* 4 (1962), pp. 59–73.

[9]Herbert A. Simon, "Administrative Decision Making," *Public Administrative Review* (March 1965).

[10]Anita M. Mitchell, G. Brian Jones, John D. Krumboltz, eds., *A Social Learning Theory of Career Decision Making* (Palo Alto: American Institutes for Research, 1976).

[11]In their book, *Educational Evaluation and Decision Making*, Daniel L. Stufflebeam, Walter J. Foley, William J. Gephart, Egon G. Guba, Robert L. Hammond, Howard O. Merriman, and Malcolm M. Provus stress the importance of this first step. They use the example of President Kennedy's decision to quarantine the waters around Cuba. They point out that a decision process did not begin until Kennedy was made *aware* that there were missile bases being built in Cuba. (Daniel L. Stufflebeam, et al., *Educational Evaluation and Decision Making* [Itasia, Illinois: Phi Delta Kappa, Inc., 1971], pp. 50–51).

[12]H. B. Gelatt, Barbara Varenhorst, Richard Carey, and Gordon P. Miller, *Decisions and Outcomes: A Leader's Guide* (New York: College Entrance Examination Board, 1973).

[13]Peter Drucker, *The Effective Executive* (New York: Harper & Row, 1967).

[14]Gelatt et al. (*op. cit.*, p. 33) note the significant distinction between process and outcome. The notion here is that there are good and bad processes, and that there are outcomes which are satisfying and some which are not. The quality of the outcome is not always indicative of the quality of the process, and vice versa.

[15]Forest B. Tyler and Margaret Gatz, "The Development of Individual Psychosocial Competence in a High School Setting," *Journal of Consulting and Clinical Psychology* (in press 1977).

[16]A much more complete listing of social studies skills can be found in Eunice Johns and Dorothy McClure Fraser, "Social Studies Skills: A Guide to Analysis and Grade Placement," *Skill Development in Social Studies*, Helen McCracken Carpenter, editor, 33rd Yearbook (Washington: National Council for the Social Studies, 1963), pp. 310–327. Eight types of skills which are a definite but shared responsibility of social studies are identified, as well as four types of skills which are the major responsibility of social studies.

[17]James Banks (*op. cit.*, p. 172) discusses the alternative courses of action a sixth-grade class in a black ghetto school might take regarding a school board proposal for forced bussing. He notes that "possible action may include presenting their case before the school board, threatening to boycott classes if their school is closed, and planning a march downtown to dramatize their grievances." Some of these actions would be considered questionable in most school circumstances. In any case, other possible actions—e.g., coercion of unwilling students by the class majority—would surely be outside the parameters of legitimate action.

[18]This threefold distinction of student roles, from more to less direct involvement in the process, was suggested by observations made in Chapter Eight.

[19]An excellent example of historical decision-making analysis is applied to Jefferson's and Madison's policies on the impressment of American sailors in Jack R. Fraenkel, "Teaching About Values," *Values of the American Heritage: Challenges, Case Studies, and Teaching Strategies*, Carl Ubbelohde and Jack R. Fraenkel, eds., 46th Yearbook (Washington: National Council for the Social Studies, 1976), pp. 192–193.

[20]A number of learning experiences involving geographic decision making are described in *Experiences in Inquiry: HSGP and SRSS*, The High School Geography Project and Sociological Resources for the Social Studies (Boston: Allyn and Bacon, 1974). See especially the materials on "Metfab," "School Districts for Millersburg," and "The Game of Farming."

[21]E. L. Tolbert, *Counseling for Career Development* (Boston: Houghton Mifflin Co., 1974), p. 164.

"Concepts thus help to simplify, to reduce confusion by making some sense out of the multitude of matters in everyone's environment."

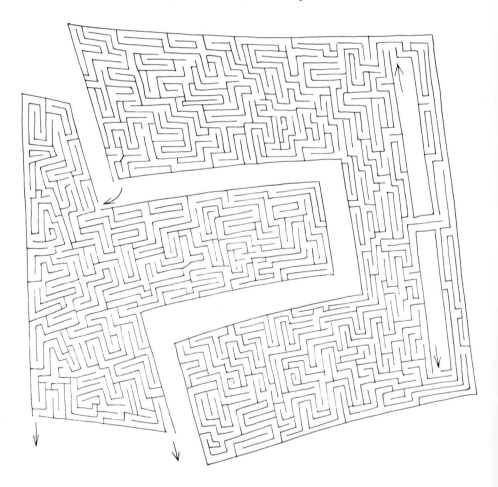

.2

Jean Fair

Skills in Thinking

The basic importance of "thinking" in social studies education is acknowledged almost everywhere. Statements of long-range goals and sets of objectives almost invariably recognize its worth. Some teachers and some schools have been doing admirably well for years at developing young people's abilities. Even more teachers now see how to go about it, as studies of the processes of social education are translated into curricular programs and instructional strategies. New doors are open at a time when society's need for thinking citizens becomes ever more!

Nevertheless, for many young people in many classrooms, opportunity for thinking is sparse. Conventional curricular programs and instruction are not organized for much of it. The heavy hand of custom makes social studies learning largely a matter of acquiring knowledge, and, all too often, merely information about standardized subjects and "current events." Only the intellectually able or mature, the knowledgeable or well-off, are supposed to be capable. Teachers who see thinking as only cognitive cannot connect it to values. It is still hard for many teachers to devise ways of encouraging thought.

In the hope of being helpful to teachers and schools, this chapter takes off from a set of positions.

1. All students can learn skills in thinking, although the quality of thinking will differ among individuals.
2. Thinking can be taught.
3. Students learn to think by practicing thinking. They cannot learn to think by having someone else do it for them.
4. Knowledge, although a requisite tool, does not automatically result in thinking. Nor must all the knowledge needed for some act of thought be learned before thinking can occur. Thinking, however, is necessary for sound concepts and generalizations.

29

5. Students must think about something. What they think about should be worthwhile, not made up solely for the practice of thinking skills.
6. Thought need not be separated from values, and rarely is.
7. Thinking is a large term. Teachers must aim for more specific abilities.
8. Identifiable skills in thinking ought ordinarily to be learned in context with other learnings. Decision making is the preferable context. Occasionally the development of specific abilities requires special practice outside of any larger context.
9. Instructional strategies for promoting identifiable abilities are available and workable.
10. Teachers can learn to use these strategies.

The basic definition of thinking, and one this Yearbook draws on, is still that of John Dewey.

> Active, persistent, and careful consideration of any belief or supposed form of knowledge in the light of grounds that support it, and the further conclusions to which it tends, constitutes reflective thought.[1]

Dewey's formulation has been followed by a host of analyses and inquiries which, in turn, have resulted in a proliferation of terms: to reflective thinking have been added problem-solving, inquiry, critical thinking, Socratic method, discovery, inductive and deductive thinking, intellectual abilities, scientific method, analysis and clarification of issues, convergent and divergent thinking, values clarification, and decision making. Most of these terms represent conceptual frameworks for relating specific abilities within some process. These frameworks cannot be reconciled here. This Yearbook relies upon the framework of decision making.

This chapter focuses on skills in thinking needed for the process of decision making and some few instructional strategies it implies: first, for building up the concepts and generalizations which serve as tools for use, and then upon their application and integration in the stages of decision making.

SKILLS IN BUILDING TOOLS OF KNOWLEDGE

Conceptualizing

Conceptualizing is among the most basic of all skills. It is a process (or the processes) by which students arrive at some concept. Schools ought to see that students acquire knowledge in a form that enables them to retain, revise, and enlarge upon what they have learned, and to use their knowledge in the social world around them.

A concept is an abstraction, given a label or a name, of some set of particulars—events, conditions, objects—which have some common attributes. Once learned, concepts enable people to make meaning out of the otherwise unorganized particulars of their social world. Concepts thus help to simplify, to reduce confusion by making some sense out of the multitude of matters in everyone's environment.

Concepts are matters of definition; they do not wait upon verification by evidence. To be sure, some definitions do better than others, and are worth more than others in accounting for the particulars of the social world. Because concepts developed in the scholarly fields are the ones likely to have power, they underlie the social studies curriculum. Still, concepts identified by scholars or included in curricular plans are not students' concepts until students have actually formulated these concepts for themselves. Students' own early formulations will lack the fullness and shaping which can come with use in experience. Scholars, too, continue to develop their knowledge by revising old concepts and constructing new ones. Students should learn to expect to modify and enrich their own concepts.

Teachers, students, and parents sometimes fear that facts will be neglected for concepts. Facts are verifiable items of information. Facts, of course, though capable of verification, may be as yet unverified. What is more, "facts" may be contrary to known evidence, even though believed to be true and "factual." It is out of these items of information that concepts are abstracted; the abstractions cannot be made except from particular items of information. Students need a rich fund of facts. While students may recall small items of fact without conceptualizing, students cannot conceptualize without facts. Conceptual learning is enhanced when the information students are expected to learn is chosen with an eye to building significant concepts.

Concepts are not merely cognitive constructs. Teacher and students have to recognize that such concepts as "social class," "democracy," and "market system" call forth feelings. Moreover, some concepts are abstractions of items of information about value-laden behavior and feelings: "honesty," "love," and "justice," for example.

Concepts are often talked about as "vocabulary" or "terms." To do so emphasizes the name or the label, rather than the abstraction. It is possible to formulate a concept without knowing the conventional term or name for it, and also possible to verbalize the conventional name without having conceptualized. To see concepts simply as "vocabulary" tends to obscure process, although to see them as terms does recognize their significance. Conceptualizing is more than learning words. It requires the actual construction of some abstraction by which instances can be distinguished from non-instances and meaning can be made out of bits of experience.

Young people are more likely to develop concepts when teachers and instructional materials make systematic plans for doing so. Planning requires identifying concepts to be learned. It also requires instructional strategies which reflect the process of conceptualizing. Two sorts of broad *instructional strategies* are spelled out here, discovery and exposition. Discovery is also illustrated in a set of instructional materials. Suggestions then follow for what an expository strategy might look like in roughly the same material.

Discovery means that students begin with the particulars, the instances for which they find some common attributes, some criteria by which to classify the instances and rule out non-instances. These instances may come from a book, a film, observation, or any number of sources. Discovery as a strategy does not imply that students will find what no one has ever thought of before. They may, but it is not likely. Seven steps in a discovery strategy are indicated on the left. Teaching questions to facilitate each step are noted on the right.

STEPS	QUESTIONS
1. Enough is said to give the process focus.	What can we make out of all this information?
2. The instances, the particular points of information, are collected from any of several sources. Teachers must elicit enough from students so that all find meaning in at least some of the items. Some points may be supplied or drawn from previous study or personal experiences.	What did you find out? Notice? See here? What do you recall about this? Do you know of other similar points?
3. Students themselves group points of information on the basis of common attributes. What students put together may or may not be what the teacher expected. Teachers may direct attention to points to be grouped, or even ask whether some concept will offer a helpful grouping. Making more than one grouping with some overlap in points is likely to encourage flexibility.	Which of these points can be put together? How are they alike? Different? On what grounds? What are the criteria for grouping these points? What are their commonalities?

STEPS	QUESTIONS
4. Students give a label or a name to their categories. If they do not know a conventional label, the teacher can supply it.	What do we call this category? What is the usual term or label for this group?
5. Students see that some grouping(s) can be subsumed by another, perhaps one previously studied.	Can any group here fit under some other? Is this set an instance of this larger concept?
6. Students make the meaning of the concept explicit.	What have we said this concept means? Will you list the characteristics of? Write a statement of?
7. Perhaps after Steps 4 and 5 and surely at some later times, students ought to see new instances, modify, and enlarge upon the concept. Students continue to build and use it.	Does anyone know of another instance? Should the statement of the concept be changed? What does this concept offer to this new situation?

A second instructional strategy is expository. Students begin from the statement of the concept which includes points of information, instances and non-instances, and perhaps even distinctions from other concepts. The statement may come from a book, a lecture, a film, or any number of sources. That students can repeat the statement of the concept at the outset does not necessarily mean that they have actually conceptualized. They may, but it is not likely. Five steps in an expository strategy are indicated on the left. Teaching questions to facilitate each step are noted on the right.

STEPS	QUESTIONS
1. The statement of the concept comes at the outset. Students read or listen to comprehend.	What is this statement about? What points does it make?
2. Students are asked for particular points of information, instances or non-instances of the concept in the statement. Students may contribute similar points of their own. Teachers must elicit enough from students so that all find meaning in at least some of the items.	Which points are instances of the concept? Not instances? On what grounds? Do you know of other similar examples? What are their commonalities?
3. Students see that some grouping(s) can be subsumed by another, perhaps one previously studied.	Can any group here fit under some other? Is this set an instance of this larger concept?

4. Students restate the concept in their own words.	In your own words, what does this concept mean? Can you list the characteristics of this concept?
5. Perhaps after Step 4 and surely at some later times, students ought to see new instances, modify, and enlarge upon the concept. Students continue to build and use it.	Does anyone see another instance? Should the statement of the concept be changed? What does this concept offer to this new situation?

The instructional materials that follow employ a strategy of discovery. They are taken from *Conflict and Change: Themes for U.S. History*, a set of seven lessons, in total some ten to twelve class sessions, designed to be integrated with appropriate topics in an eleventh-grade United States History course organized chronologically.[2]

The first lesson is included in full. In a column at the right of the text of this lesson are annotations pointing out steps of the discovery strategy as they appear in the materials.

Conflict: What Is It?

Conflict is an important part of everyone's life. In one form or another, we experience it every day. But if we were to try to say exactly what the word means, we would have trouble defining it. Even social scientists, who specialize in the study of conflict, disagree over the meaning of the term.

Instructional materials set focus for students. *(Step 1)*

What is conflict? Is it good or bad? What does it have to do with violence? Can it be useful—or should we try to avoid all conflict? How has conflict operated through history? How does it operate in our lives today?

These are a few of the questions you will be dealing with in this study. There are no set answers. In fact, your major task will be to find your own answers. You will be studying stories and cases from America's history. But you will find that much of what you learn about conflict can be applied to many other situations—including events in your own life.

ACTIVITIES

1. To begin, see what you and your class can figure out about conflict from these short newspaper items.

Offers familiar instances. *(Step 2)*

- *This was supposed to be a classic conflict between State and Ridgeville, but it ended in the most lopsided football game of the season.*
- *The next step in the conflict between Apex Manufacturing and the union is likely to be a strike.*
- *In October, the conflict between Israel and the Arab countries again erupted in violence.*
- *In the egret's struggle for survival, the bird finds itself in conflict with the demands of human society.*

What does each quotation suggest about the meaning of the word *conflict?* Make a list of ideas you come up with. (For example, conflict can involve two teams in a sporting event.)

Asks for common attributes of instances.
(Step 3)

If you run into trouble with this, try asking yourself: What kind of event or situation is being described? You can begin then by saying that a football game can be a conflict, and go on from there. Two other useful questions would be: Who is involved in the conflict? What is the conflict about?

Some people believe conflict and competition are the same. Do you agree?

Asks for another category, discriminating and/or subsuming.
(Step 5)

Within a few minutes, your class should be able to make a good-sized list of statements that help describe conflict. It would be a good idea to keep this list going throughout the study, adding to it any new discoveries you make about the subject.

Asks for flexible statement of concept.
(Step 6)

2. For more practice, try to substitute the word *conflict* in the following sentences:

Further instances or non-instances to be categorized by their criteria.
(Step 7)

- We had quite an argument trying to decide where we would go on our vacation.
- Jake had a problem—he liked both girls and wanted to take both of them to the dance.
- The American people face a choice between increasing production or saving the environment.
- The range war ended when the homesteaders decided to move farther west and search for new land.

3. As mentioned at the beginning, all of us face conflict every day of our lives. Usually, though, these situations seem so mild and normal that we don't even notice them. Make a list of conflicts you have experienced within the past

Asks for more instances from students' experiences.
(Step 7)

week. (The events might be as simple as a conflict over whether or not to do your homework.)

*You might think about these questions as you make
your list. How did you know you were involved in a conflict (anger, argument)? What was the conflict about?
Who was involved? Did you resolve it? How?*

Compare your list with others in the class. Can
you discover anything new to add to the list of statements about conflict?

Asks for additions to
common attributes and
perhaps reformulation
and reinforcement.
(Step 6)

By now it should be clear that conflict exists in
our daily lives in a great many different ways. To
explore the subject in more detail, you can now begin to analyze some episodes from this country's
history. During the study, look for other cases in
your textbook that illustrate conflict.

Points to future use and
additional instances.
(Step 7)

Note that the above illustration of a discovery strategy does not follow the suggested steps to the letter. Step four, in which students label
their categories, was not used because "conflict" appears throughout
the material. Moreover, some steps were repeated. The point is that
suggested strategies can be used with considerable flexibility by teachers developing lessons to help students build important social studies
concepts.

The lessons in the illustration above might have been based on an
expository, instead of a discovery, instructional strategy. Had it been
so, students would have been given several paragraphs stating clearly
the meaning of conflict. The same four examples might have been included, along with some further instances and non-instances according
to the attributes of conflict which were described. Students might also
distinguish and/or subsume conflict and competition. They might be expected to contribute other examples of conflict out of their experiences, before stating the concept for themselves. In conclusion, students would be urged to look for other examples in their history
course, just as in the discovery strategy.

Whether the strategy is discovery or exposition, students need opportunity to enrich and use their concepts. Such opportunity is built
into the six lessons which follow the one quoted above. These lessons
on "Conflict and Change" offer case studies, a script, and contrasting,
firsthand accounts of conflicts. They fit in such usual United States history content as the Constitutional Convention, Native American Indians and white settlers, nineteenth-century abolitionist and feminist
movements, labor and management, the organization of the NAACP,

and international affairs. Students will consider conflicts over both ideas and tangible gains; such types of conflict resolution as win-or-lose and compromise; and ways of expressing and regulating conflict.

Moreover, the seven related lessons on "Conflict and Change" exemplify a discovery strategy for building up a *conceptual framework* for "conflict resolution." Conceptual frameworks can be put to use to deal with new and complex problems. The last lesson, specifically, points students towards resolving conflicts arising over maintaining living standards and yet protecting the environment, and towards using the framework in decision making.

Within such lessons as those of "Conflict and Change" are opportunities not only for conceptualizing, but for developing other thinking skills which build meaning.

Interpreting

Interpreting is going beyond, making more meaning out of what is given in some communication, doing more than comprehending or grasping what is actually explicit. In the narrowest and most usual sense, interpretation is making some modest extension of meaning: seeing relationships among explicit points or inferring directly from the information in a communication.

Interpretation can be conceived more broadly. When a communication is complex, or when students are expected to relate points from a few sources, perhaps even from a previous study, interpretation may even be thought of as hypothesizing, proposing a generalization in need of further testing. Much of the hypothesizing which goes on in the everyday affairs of classrooms is short, close to data, and usually confirmed by the teacher or some student; however, sometimes it is even left as a matter of speculation. No extensive or systematically planned testing follows.

Teachers and students ought to raise questions habitually calling for skill in interpreting, as they use one communication or another in and out of the classroom. These kinds of questions promote this skill:

1. What is the topic? (Classify.)
2. What is the major point? (Distinguish major from minor points.)
3. Will you summarize what was said? (Summarize when the communication itself has not done so.)
4. Which points are alike? (Compare.)
5. Which points are different? (Contrast.)
6. Which points are causes? Which effects? (Recognize cause-effect when they are not so labelled.)

7. What trend can you see? (Note trends.)
8. What is likely to happen next? (Extrapolate, extend the data.)
9. Is this sub-point likely to fit into the points presented here? (Interpolate.)
10. Is the event, condition, person, or group, typical of the whole class? (Sample.)
11. Are the author's credentials sufficient to allow you to believe what is said? (Recognize authority.)
12. What was the purpose or intention of such and such? (Infer a purpose.)
13. How might you explain this matter? (Hypothesize.)

Interpreting also shades into analysis in the sense that students see how to take a communication apart and develop the habit of looking for relationships.

Analyzing

Analyzing is still another skill for increasing meaning. Analysis is a matter of breaking some communication down into its parts, seeing the relationships among these parts, and understanding the principles by which the communication is organized.

What is meant by "breaking down" becomes clearer by looking at types of analytical questions such as these:

1. What are the key points, the key issues, the key concepts? (Identify major elements.)
2. Which are statements of fact and which of value? (Distinguish facts from values.)
3. Which are statements of hypotheses and which of supporting evidence? (Distinguish hypotheses from evidence.)
4. What are the assumptions, stated or unstated? (Recognize assumptions.)
5. Which of these points supports (or does not support) the hypothesis, conclusion, or judgment? (Recognize logical consistency.)
6. Which are statements of hypotheses and which of warranted generalizations, conclusions, judgments? (Distinguish hypotheses from conclusions.)
7. Which of these points is off-subject? (Recognize irrelevancy.)
8. Are any of these points examples of faulty reasoning? (Recognize logical fallacies.)
9. What is the overall tone or style of this communication? (Recognize an overall principle or feeling.)

10. Will you identify the basic point of view in this communication? (Recognize a bias or frame of reference.)
11. What kind of organization is used in this communication? What is the form of the argument? (Distinguish organizing principles.)
12. What techniques or devices are used to persuade, create a feeling, organize an argument? (Relate techniques to organizing principles.)

Several of these analytic questions ask that key distinctions be drawn. None, it is worth noticing, refers to the oft-cited distinction between fact and opinion, because that distinction is not useful. Simply stated, a fact is anything verifiable, be it a discrete bit of information or a broad, powerful, and productive generalization. An opinion, on the other hand, may have any one of several meanings: a matter capable of verification, but still a matter of speculation; a matter of value, of "ought" or "should"; or any statement of belief made off the top of one's head. What students should learn is to distinguish (a) hypotheses from generalizations; (b) facts, including generalizations, from values; and (c) verified facts from facts contrary to known evidence. All of these are analytic skills for which some capability in generalizing is required.

Generalizing

Generalizations, like concepts, are abstractions. Generalizations, too, can account for the particulars of many social phenomena—objects, events, conditions. Generalizations are broadly applicable. A rich fund of generalizations, like a store of concepts, reduces the disorder and confusion in otherwise isolated bits of experience. Generalizations increase the possibilities of managing what is encountered in the social world and making worthwhile decisions.

Generalizations are verifiable, unlike concepts which are definitional in nature. Generalizations depend upon the support of evidence and, until they are verified, are better conceived as hypotheses yet to be tested. Moreover, even knowledge tested in the scholarly fields is subject to reformulation.

Consequently, students must learn, on the one hand, to take generalizations seriously; they represent the best knowledge available. On the other hand, students must also learn to see their limits, the extent to which they can describe, explain, or even predict. Students also have to hold generalizations as tentative, subject to revision by new formulation and new evidence. That learning task is far from easy. Young people all too often believe either that anything "in the book" is true or that everything in social studies is just a matter of opinion.

Scholarly fields have formulated numerous generalizations. Curricular plans ought to make them available to students. Students, however, must go through the process of formulating generalizations for themselves. Just as it is possible to have grasped the meaning of a generalization without stating it succinctly or well, so also it is possible to repeat the words of some generalization without having grasped its meaning. Curricular plans ought to focus on some manageable number of powerful generalizations and allow time for extensive and structured opportunities to learn them. Moreover, frequent questions which encourage small-scale hypothesizing and/or examining evidence in support of purported generalizations develop not only skill but the significant expectation that broad ideas are what count.

An instructional strategy to encourage generalizing can in some circumstances require only a short time, a class session or two, or even part of one.

The process of generalizing may also be the structure for a more extensive inquiry demanding several weeks of work, just as did developing a conceptual framework for conflict resolution. When generalization is the framework for extensive study, it will require skills in conceptualizing, interpreting, and analyzing, and the ability to synthesize.

Synthesis is putting together some collection of information and ideas so as to form a whole. Merely reordering what are already recognized as the parts of a whole is not synthesis. Synthesis requires an integration which is in some degree new, fresh, unique. Although creativity is much to be desired, it cannot yet be defined as a skill. Still, synthesis carries some flavor of the creative, the original. When students are asked to propose an hypothesis to account for a sizable collection of data, they are most likely asked to synthesize. To do so may require an intuitive leap, a flash of insight—or something less than that. On the one hand, learning opportunities ought to encourage the creative, intuitive leaps. On the other hand, the process of generalizing by students should not be considered tantamount to rediscovering the wheel. Generalizations already abound in the disciplines. The point is that students have not yet learned them. What students ordinarily do in hypothesizing is synthesizing in the sense of forming a tentative whole new to them. That others may have already proposed and tested that hypothesis does not deny that students are doing so. When students propose a plan for testing an hypothesis, they are also synthesizing. That others have used similar methods matters only in the sense that students can reap the benefit of that work.

An instructional strategy of *discovery* is essentially the same for generalizations to be developed in a class session or two or in a several weeks' study. The outline emphasizes steps in generalizing, with only cursory attention to the process as a curricular framework for extended study.

STEPS	QUESTIONS
1. Some focus directs students' attention on lack of organization, something left hanging, an expectation of a task to be done.	What can we make out of all of this? Is there some generalization we can develop out of this?
2. Students examine two or more communications about which it is sensible to ask like questions. Comprehension comes first. Students develop awareness of what is incomplete, incongruous, unordered.	What does this point mean? Which points are alike? Which different? What are the key points, concepts, issues? What does this concept mean?
3. Students attempt to express or describe the data, account for what occurred, propose hypotheses. Teachers' clarification or cues may help, but students must do the proposing.	How might we explain or describe all this? What hypothesis can you propose?
4. Students test out each hypothesis, one at a time, to see whether it can be supported by the data at hand. Students may have to identify more and needed evidence, make a plan for collecting it, collect it, and interpret it. Hypotheses may be reformulated.	What evidence do we need? What does this evidence mean? Do we need more evidence? Is any off-subject? Unaccounted for? Suppose we take this hypothesis. Does it square with the evidence? Is there a better, modified hypothesis?
5. Students draw a conclusion that an hypothesis can be supported (or cannot). They recognize its degrees of certainty or limits in use. Students state the generalization.	Can we accept this hypothesis? How certain can we be of it? Will you state the generalization?

Retrieval charts promote generalizing. One from Lesson 7 of "Conflict and Change" is quoted on page 42. At the outset of collecting facts for that chart, a teacher might point students' expectations toward generalizing from it. Once the chart has been completed, either by individuals or by dividing the task among small groups, the teacher might start the ball rolling by saying something like this: "Look at the column on U.S.-Canada border disputes. Is there some general statement you can make which may account for all the information there?" Should a student propose that U.S.-Canada border disputes were always resolved peacefully, a teacher (or other students) must accept it temporarily but

RETRIEVAL CHART

KEY QUESTIONS	U.S.– Canada Border Disputes	Spanish- American War	World War I	World War II	Cold War Conflicts	
1. What issues started or signaled conflict?						Aspects of the conceptual framework, translated into analytical questions. Offers chart for organization, analysis, and presumably generalizing.
2. What decisions or events made things worse?						
3. Were any attempts made at compromise? With what results?						
4. How was the conflict expressed?						
5. What methods were available to solve the dispute without violence? Were any of these tried? Did they succeed or fail? For what reasons?						
6. If violence occurred, why do you think nonviolent solutions were abandoned?						
7. How was the conflict resolved?						
8. If violence was involved in settling the dispute, did this lead to new conflicts?[3]						

call for testing against evidence. Is that hypothesis consistent with American action during the War of 1812? Revised hypotheses are proposed and tested until students can state something like this: "U.S.-Canada border disputes were mostly resolved by withdrawing, compromise, and negotiating, so nobody fights about them now."

Should the teacher focus upon the last of the key questions and the information in its row across, such questions as these might be appropriate: (a) What proposal can you make which accounts for all the information in that row? (b) If violence always leads to violence, how can you explain the information in the Cold War column? (c) Will someone look up the Punic Wars for whatever light they shed on this matter? (d) Is the point about whether the Russian people really want Communism on target here? (e) If we can't buy our first hypothesis, then what modification might we accept? (f) What have we said? What is the generalization we can accept on violence and new conflicts?

In this lesson, several generalizations can be developed, not just one. Those that are simpler come first. Students who can handle a high degree of abstraction and complexity may even manage, from the chart as a whole, generalizations like this: As long as major nuclear powers recognize a no-win situation, they are more likely to resort to other ways of resolving conflicts than all-out war.

A second broad strategy for generalizing is *expository*. It would follow these steps.

STEPS	QUESTIONS
1. Students study some communication(s) which explains or describes several points supporting generalization.	What is the big idea here?
2. Students must comprehend the information. They will probably need to conceptualize, interpret, and analyze.	What are the key issues, concepts, points? How is this point related to that? What does this concept mean?
3. Students grasp the argument. Interpretation, analysis, and perhaps evaluation are all in play.	Which is the hypothesis? Which the evidence? Which the conclusion? Will you summarize the argument? How certain can you be of this generalization?
4. Students should use the generalization in a fresh example or two.	Here's another instance. Will this generalization account for it also?
5. Students state the generalization in their own words.	Will you state the generalization in your own words?

In place of the retrieval chart on American history, teachers might have presented an article on, let us say, Cold War conflict. By citing a number of issues or events causing conflict, along with decisions or events which made matters worse, by explaining what major nuclear powers might expect from full-scale war, by describing how conflicts were from time to time expressed and methods employed to reduce them, and so on, the article might have built up the generalization that as long as major nuclear powers recognize a no-win situation, they are more likely to resort to other ways of resolving conflict than all-out war. Students using the article would follow the steps of the outline above until they could state the generalization for themselves.

Perhaps to be conceived as a third strategy is a *combination* of both *discovery* and *exposition*. Students may practice some of the steps in the discovery strategy. Still, for any number of reasons, they may have too little evidence or time to support or deny a hypothesis. The active practice is worthwhile, although students may not arrive at a generalization they can count on. Then an article, a film, or some other communication, the results of someone else's more rigorous generalizing, may confirm their hypothesis. The steps in using such a communication will be a brief version of those in the expository strategy. In none of the strategies can steps be rigidly followed. Students will inevitably move back and forth, one to another.

No one instructional strategy is best. Students will profit from experience with all of them. Discovery strategies are especially useful when the emphasis is on forming hypotheses, testing against evidence, and developing an expectation of figuring things out. Expository strategies are especially useful when the emphasis is on acquiring a fund of significant generalizations or generalizations needed quickly to carry on some process. For example, some of the information needed to fill in the retrieval chart on "Conflict Among Nations" is actually lower-level generalization.

SKILLS IN USING KNOWLEDGE

The first section of this chapter considered skills in developing meaning and knowledge, tools basic both to further knowledge and to sound decision making. This section focuses upon use of these tools.

Applying Knowledge

Application is a skill more commonly endorsed than developed in classrooms. Perhaps because acquiring knowledge has long and properly been a major goal of social studies education, many classrooms emphasize knowledge as if there were no tomorrow. There is a tomorrow. Students will need ability to apply their knowledge in tomorrow's experiences. There is also a today, about which the same statement can be made. It is obvious enough that students cannot apply knowledge they have never learned; it should be obvious that they can acquire knowledge, at least temporarily, that they are not capable of using. "Covering the material" is not the end-all of social studies education. Skill in developing powerful knowledge ought to go hand in hand with skill in applying it. When they do, students will come to expect their interrelation. Less common will be the feeling that "social studies doesn't do any good."

In its broadest sense, application may be synonymous with problem-solving, testing hypotheses, or even decision making. At the end of the sequence on "Conflict and Change," for example, students are to use the conceptual framework for conflict resolution in a new problem. Applying as a part of decision making is illustrated later in the sequence on "Political Decision-Making."

Application is discussed here in a narrower sense. When students are applying, (a) they are dealing with some comparatively new or unfamiliar situation, (b) on which they bring previously learned knowledge to bear (c) with the purpose of explaining, describing, or predicting what will occur, what is to be expected or looked for.

In the course of applying, students will surely flounder when they have next to no information about the unfamiliar situation, or when the available information lacks meaning for them. Matters current or famous, or in the textbook, for example, are not necessarily understood by students. The particulars of the new situation have to "be there" for students before they can see which features to make salient. Students will also flounder when they are asked to apply some concept, generalization, or criterion they have not actually grasped, something about which they can at most recite words. Social studies materials ordinarily carry heavy conceptual loadings and verbal accounts of social affairs. "Covering" this material often results in scanty meaning and so in ineptitude in applying. Students must have mastered the information they are expected to apply.

Students unaccustomed to making applications may be bewildered by requests to do so. Surely, they feel, the answers must be given somewhere, in a book or by the teacher. The students' job is finding, not figuring out. When teachers take these expectations into account, they can find ways to clarify the tasks, offer support, and change the expectations.

Applying often occurs in learning situations colored by feelings and values. In the course of applying, students have to put aside momentarily what should or ought to be, what they hope or want to be the outcome. Feelings and values prevent students from seeing all the significant aspects of the new situation; delete portions of reality; block the retrieval of ideas to be applied; and augment resistance to undesired but probable outcomes. What is more, application is frequently practiced in the context of decision making where values are inextricably involved. It is not that applying should occur in situations separated from valuing; far from it. Separation lures everyone into the common and erroneous belief that "once we know the facts, we will see the right course of action." Critical values are thereby obscured and ignored. Teachers and students ought to raise questions about whether some expected outcome is desirable. But they must also distinguish "what can be expected to happen if . . .," from "what ought to happen" according to their values. This ability to be objective is all the more difficult to learn because application shades into the skill of evaluation.

Confusion often arises over the question of whether concepts can be applied. By conceptualizing, people have attributed commonalities not only to objects, but to conditions, events, even processes. When people state these attributes—that is, define the concept, and especially complex concepts—they are likely to state lower-level generalizations (and other concepts). Generalizations, conversely, may be characterized as statements showing relations among concepts. What is concept can hardly be disentangled from what is generalization in the give-and-take of everyday classrooms. Perhaps it will reduce confusion to say that concepts cannot predict in the strict sense of the word. They can, however, be brought to bear in a comparatively unfamiliar situation. They enable students to recognize a new instance of the familiar. They are part and parcel of the generalizations used to describe, explain, and predict the knowledge to be retrieved to apply.

Projecting consequences is an aspect of applying of particular importance for decision making. Students will project consequences, more or less certain, depending on the type of generalization. Powerful, explanatory, if-then generalizations yield highly probable consequences. Generalizations which describe or those which explain only within narrow limits yield consequences which are largely suggestive, less certain, "iffy," but still consequences.

Consequences, in turn, have consequences. In many classrooms, learning tasks in applying are insufficiently pursued. Teachers and students project immediate consequences without following through on further consequences. Some of these further consequences will be unexpected and, without careful attention, unnoticed; these are often called "side-effects." In many learning tasks, applying ought to be thought of as projecting trains of consequences, maybe even several trains.

As with other thinking skills, an instructional strategy for learning to apply has to fit the process. The steps in a strategy occur in the following order, though with movement back and forth among steps. In simple cases, Steps 1 and 2 seem to occur simultaneously.

STEPS	QUESTIONS
1. Students face some situation comparatively new or unfamiliar to them. They must comprehend, perhaps interpret and analyze.	What does this situation mean? What might happen?
2. Students retrieve relevant knowledge, concepts, and generalizations, with an eye to projecting consequences.	What will explain this?
3. Students project consequences and explain causal relations. Students must search for comprehensiveness and logical consistency. They must also avoid logical fallacies, off-subject points, and what is desired.	What outcome do you expect? Why? Are these points consistent with that outcome? Off-subject? In error logically? Have you left some points unaccounted for?
4. Students state conclusions and their degree of probability.	What is your conclusion? How certain can you be of the outcome?
5. Students often project further consequences of consequences by repeating the process.	If such and such can be expected, what results will follow from that?

Teachers will more often than not need to exert strong influence to help students make applications. Loosely structured discussion, perhaps in small groups, may help at the stage of retrieving relevant knowledge, but Step 3 requires structuring, cueing, support, probing, and keeping thoughts on track.

Practice in applying, built into curricular sequences, is illustrated later in this chapter. In most classrooms, less systematically planned opportunities occur frequently. They are worth capitalizing upon. The examples here may suggest others.

1. The class is currently studying minority groups and means of improving their status. The matter of their influence in government has come up. The class has also studied the workings of the Congress. The teacher (or a student) asks this question: "Suppose black

people in a largely black congressional district want more influence in the House of Representatives. And suppose that two candidates, both about equally capable and both black, are running for that district's representative. One is the incumbent. He has served eight years. Which of the two, once elected, is likely to have more influence in the House of Representatives?"

2. The class is discussing yesterday's TV news reports about the rate of inflation. The teacher asks, "If this country should have a high rate of inflation, whose incomes are the more likely to be hurt: those of old people who live on pensions or those of steel workers who belong to a union that bargains collectively?"

3. The class has studied group behavior. Some time later an informal discussion is going on about an outing on which the children have gone. A group of girls got into a predicament; by spending all their money right at the outset of the affair, none of the girls had anything left for what was needed later in the day. The teacher asks, "Why do you think all five of them got into that fix? Why not expect at least one of them to act differently?"

4. The class has worked its way through a unit on the legislative branch of the federal government and is now studying the executive branch, most particularly the powers and responsibilities of the President. Several examples of what recent Presidents actually did have already been discussed. The teacher asks, "Suppose the President impounds funds appropriated by Congress for highway construction. The President maintains that the federal government cannot afford to spend that money. A state sues on the grounds that it did not receive the money for highways to which it was entitled. What would you expect the Supreme Court to rule?"

Evaluating

Application is hard to distinguish from evaluation because logical consistency is called for in both. The distinction between evaluating and decision making is also fine. The latter is often conceived as more complex, requiring more examination of values and formal relation to evidence, and carrying a greater commitment to take some action.

Since evaluation obviously implies the use of values, values need some definition here. Values are standards by which things are judged good or bad, proper or improper, desirable or undesirable. Because values are abstractions, rather than concretes which can be pointed out, people take statements of value as representing actual values. Such statements are couched in terms of "should" or "ought to be." But statements are not values themselves, and disentangling the two is often hard.

Values are not the same as emotions: feeling elated, confused, or angry, for example. Yet values are often deeply laden with feeling, and what arouses emotion gives clues to someone's cherished values. Nor are values merely matters of idiosyncratic, personal taste. Whether someone prefers peanut butter sandwiches or hamburgers, or blue or green, is not a matter of much consequence; it makes little difference. Values, in a sense, make all the difference.

Values are learned in the personal circumstances in which everyone grows and lives. On the one hand, these circumstances must be unique ones for every person; on the other, these circumstances must be part of a complex, changing culture. Because values are so learned, young people—indeed, all people—are often unclear about, perhaps even unaware of, the values they hold. One aspect of evaluation, then, must be the identification and recognition, even clarification, of the value standards to be used.

Of course, it is possible to evaluate by some standard recognized though not held. It may be helpful learning to consider such a question as this: "If you take efficiency as the criterion, what is your judgment of this set of procedures?", even though students are unwilling to accept that criterion. However, most evaluation is carried on by values actually held. Because of the circumstances in which values are learned, young people have some general values which conflict when applied to particular situations. Thus, resolving inner value conflicts becomes a major aspect of the valuing process and decision making.[4] The point remains here, however, that evaluation requires the use of some standard(s).

Evaluation is characterized below, not broadly as synonymous with decision making, but narrowly, as within that process. Students will need to evaluate arguments, books and articles, films, and other communications, be they students' work or that of others. These are the types of questions which foster evaluation:

1. By what standards, values, criteria are you judging? (Identify value standards.)
2. Which value are you holding most important? (Prioritize values.)
3. What do you mean by the value you have stated? (Clarify value.)
4. Do these points belong in this consideration? Are these points consistent with one another? Are all the appropriate points accounted for? (Test for internal consistency.)
5. To what extent are these data correct and reliable? (Estimate the worth of data.)
6. What warrants do you have for your judgment? (Relate evidence to standards.)
7. What is your judgment? (Make judgment explicit.)

THE ROLE OF SKILLS IN DECISION MAKING

Thinking skills, including application and evaluation, are better learned in some larger context: building conceptual frameworks, building generalizations, and decision making. A conception of thinking as a mere collection of separate skills is inadequate, even though there will be times in any classroom when students need to practice some one skill or another. Skills are not essentially ends in themselves; if they are to be conceived at all as products of social studies education, it is only in the sense of products to be used. Skills, values, and knowledge ought to be learned ordinarily in the context of decision making because they are required for it. That statement can be turned around: skills, knowledge, and values have implications for action, and action has consequences. Inept thinking and misunderstanding of the social world lead to what is unforeseen and unfortunate, just as fuzzy and ill-considered values lead to what is unwanted. To come closer to the outcomes they want, to the realization of worthy values, young people must learn to decide.

Chapter One considered the process of decision making as a whole. Here attention goes to where thinking skills fit into that process, and how the development of any one skill depends upon the others. Decision making requires a shuttling back and forth among several stages, all requiring thought. These stages are listed next, along with required skills in thinking.

STAGES	SKILLS IN THINKING
1. Recognizing and clarifying the decision to be made, the issues to be decided.	Bringing knowledge to bear on the situation. Simple analysis of the situation, raising questions.
2. Proposing alternatives, two or more courses which might be chosen.	Analysis in the sense of identifying key concepts, issues, value conflicts. Synthesis in the sense of proposing hypothetical courses of action.
3. Tracing the probable consequences of each of the alternatives.	Interpreting data. Analyzing data. Developing requisite concepts and generalizations. Application in the sense of projecting or predicting consequences for each alternative.
4. Recognizing values at stake and evaluating consequences.	Evaluation of each set of consequences. Prioritizing and qualifying values.
5. Settling upon a choice, ready to follow as the occasion requires.	Evaluation as making the judgment. Application.

The sequence of an actual curricular plan will make plainer the roles of thinking skills, knowledge, and valuing in the stages of decision making. The plan has been used successfully with middle-grades children who are often, but improperly, believed to be not quite ready to engage in the process. Of course, children in the middle grades cannot carry on decision making at the more abstract levels to be expected of capable high school students. This plan, then, may also be described as providing activities colloquially called "easy."

Citizenship Decision-Making: Instructional Materials, Grades 4–8, contains four mini-units designed to supplement social studies instruction in intermediate and junior high schools (grades 4–8).[5] The units are made up of short, self-contained lessons. The lessons are designed to use forty minutes per day and to take from one to three days to complete. The lessons may be used as a sequence of activities interspersed throughout the school year or taught as four units requiring about three weeks' consecutive work for each unit.

The first example is drawn from Unit I. At the outset, students are to develop an awareness that they do make decisions from among alternatives in their everyday lives. Then students focus on the concept of political decisions as decisions about rules. Children use cases, fill in logs, make charts, role-play, read stories, and do other activities. Similar activities follow to develop concepts of positive and negative consequences of choices and goals. By Lesson 9, students make their first try at "climbing a decision tree," an outline of steps in making decisions. In the following exercise, their second try, annotations on the right provide comments about the strategy used and its relation to the decision-making process.

Developing the Lesson

STEP 5

Ask if the students would like to try climbing another decision tree. Assuming class interest is somewhere between enthusiastic wall climbing and Rip Van Winkle apathy, use the "Decision Tree, Staying After School" example. This may be shown via overhead projector, or the tree with empty signs may be traced on the chalkboard so you may fill spaces in as you climb. If you use the transparency, cover it with paper and expose the picture after completing each step, as you did with Sir Lottalance. Advise your students they are to put themselves in the place of the student in the story "Staying After School."

Explanation for teachers. Focus for a second round of conceptualizing the process. The strategy is largely expository, although with some discovery.

They may imagine the student is themselves, as the object of the exercise is to familiarize students with the parts of the decision tree so they can climb to the top in their own decisions.

Staying After School

You are very interested in getting home from school on time. Your club or troop is going on a trip which you have been looking forward to for weeks. Today the health department is giving hearing tests to everyone. The whole class looks like jet pilots with their earphones on. The health people have warned that there must be absolute quiet. If the class is disturbed, everyone will have to stay after school to finish the hearing test properly.

You look up. One seat ahead in the next aisle is Weird Wembley. Weird Wembley about to disturb the class! Weird Wembley is a terrible decision maker. He acts first and is always surprised by the consequences. What can you do—you don't want to miss the trip!

An open-ended case for students. Content drawn from their everyday experience.

STEP 6

Raise the paper on the transparency so the "Occasion for Decision" sign is exposed, or fill it in if using the chalkboard. Ask the students what alternatives could be used to climb the tree. Elicit the three illustrated, or more if you prefer. Three are used on the transparency to avoid oversimplifying decision making and to help students think in terms of several alternatives.

A blank decision tree provides structure. Simple analysis.

STEP 7

Ask the students to climb higher into the branches of the tree to look at the consequences of the students' alternatives. Ask:

- What would be a good or positive consequence of telling the teacher about Weird Wembley?
- What would be a bad or negative consequence of telling the teacher?
- What would be the consequences of doing nothing?
- What would be a negative consequence of stopping Weird Wembley?

Students project consequences. Distinguish fact and value. Doing nothing is an alternative, not an escape.

WHAT THE DECISION TREE MIGHT LOOK LIKE ONCE COMPLETED

DECISION TREE
STAYING AFTER SCHOOL

- What would be a positive consequence of stopping Weird Wembley?

Weigh the consequences, and place the class goal high in the tree.

Concluding the Lesson

STEP 8

The following exercise may be an individual or small group exercise, at the discretion of the teacher. The objective is to have students use a decision tree to illustrate political decisions they may face, such as:

Students extend concept with content from everyday experience.

- Deciding what to do with friends one afternoon
- Deciding where to go on a field trip
- Deciding to join (or quit) Scouts or a club

Ed. Note: *Seven others are omitted here.*

In Step 8 students work through the decision-making process again by filling in the spaces of decision trees. Then they compare their trees to extend and enrich their concepts and skills. They are asked also to look for the use of a value, the pursuit of happiness, as they "climbed the decision tree." Further instructional options and activities follow, along with a bibliography of stories for correlation with reading and literature. The last lesson contains activities which summarize what is to be learned in Unit I.

In this first mini-unit, children are engaged largely in conceptualizing a process, "political decision making," and its constituent stages, each a sub-concept. After children grasp these by "doing them" one by one, they are asked to formulate, again by "doing" in the lesson above, at least the rudiments of the process. In many classrooms the lack of a concept of process means that real decision making never gets off the ground, or degenerates into a recitation of contrasting positions or an exchange of off-the-cuff opinions.

A concept of the process serves as an analytical framework by which children see how to take an amorphous matter apart and how to get a grasp on it. In that sense, children here also engage in simple analysis, structured by the diagram of "climbing a decision tree." They are to recognize that a decision must be made and break it down into alternative courses of action. Students do project consequences for each alternative, unreliable as they may be. They must be plausible, however, with some fit for the reality of the situation; consistent, that is, and on-subject. Even a gross distinction between facts and values is called for when children identify positive and negative consequences and are asked to find evidence in what they did for valuing "a person's right to pursue happiness." Skills in analysis are in play in recognizing both elements and organization.

Unit II, Skills in Making Political Decisions, begins with a review of the concept of "political decision." Then students move on to identifying eight basic values: well-being, affection, enlightenment, skill, rectitude, wealth, power, and respect—values to be conceived as rules, goals, and resources, and all to be used in climbing decision trees for two open-ended cases. Next students turn to conceptualizing three ways of group decision making: consensus, authority, and voting. Again they try them, one at a time, and decide which to use at what time. In succeeding activities children (a) decide such issues as whether parents should have to pay for property their children damage; and they actually vote, going through the state's voting procedures; and (b) engage in an exercise simulating decision making by such government officials as the "Director of Public Welfare (County)." In these and a variety of other activities, children consider both consequences *and* explicit values. A summary lesson requires use of the concepts, values, and process.

Unit III, Skills in Judging Political Decisions, focuses on the evaluation of consequences of political decisions: groups affected and how; and judgments by the eight basic values. Decisions are drawn from many areas: family, friends, school, city, state, and nation. In the beginning, building "decision chains" on five issues using interview data provides structure. Next students organize information on diagrams: (1) for each political decision, such as outlawing handguns or opening up school baseball to girls, children list (2) several groups affected and (3) the effects on each group. Then children act out a court trial involving freedom of speech for students. Role cards supply procedures, evidence, and Constitutional principles; a student jury must decide. At the end of this mini-unit, students are asked to judge several more political decisions, again with the needed knowledge largely supplied by cases and helped by the Decision Tree diagram (enlarged below to ask for feelings, students' values, and a statement of evaluation). (See p. 56.)

In Unit IV the focus shifts from effects of decisions to Skills in Influencing Political Decisions. Out of numerous examples—some in cartoons—children are to conceptualize five methods of influencing political decisions: authority, power, reward, affection, and information. The second lesson of Unit IV follows here. After some short review activities (Step 1), students are to decide which method to use.

Developing the Lesson

STEP 2

Advise the students that it takes skill to know which method of influence to use. They are going to have a chance to act out five ways of influencing a political decision. In each case, one of them will play the role of the teacher or principal; the others will play the roles of students in trouble trying to influence a decision. On the basis of their role playing they will fill out a giant Decision Tree on the chalkboard to see the positive and negative consequences of their alternatives.

On the chalkboard, draw a large Decision Tree—see diagram below—but leave all spaces blank.

Explanation for teachers. The strategy is primarily discovery interlaced with exposition.

A blank decision tree provides structure.

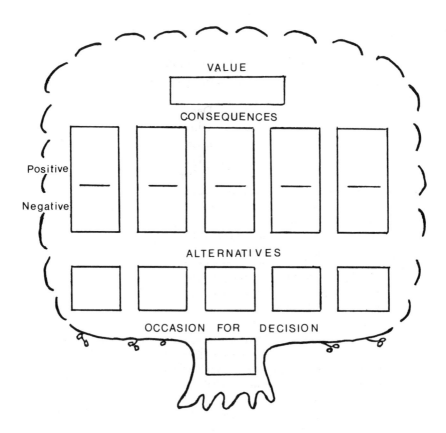

Read or pass out a reproduced copy of the "School Scenario."

School Scenario

Dick and Roger were upset. Molly was walking up the aisle between their desks when she tripped. Both boys laughed. The teacher said they couldn't go out for recess for a week for tripping Molly! The boys claimed Molly fell over her own feet. The teacher said they had better work quietly or they would also stay after school for disturbing the class. They went straight to the authorities—their parents. But their parents told them the teacher had the authority to keep order in the class so students could learn. Dick's mother suggested they examine alternative means of influencing the teacher's decision.

A case for students, out of their everyday experience.

STEP 3

In the Decision Tree on the chalkboard, write "No Recess" in the "Occasion for Decision" space. Ask the students what five alternatives they might have. Fill in the words "Authority," "Power," "Reward," "Affection," and "Information" in the Alternative spaces on the Decision Tree as the students suggest these methods.

Use of key concepts to propose courses of action.

Advise the students they will have strategy cards to give them ideas for each method of influence, but they will have to make up their own roles and perform a skit showing the rest of the class *how to use* each particular method of influence. Choose people who can ad lib to play the roles of the principal, Roger, and Dick. Give them a copy of the "Authority Strategy Card," and have them go into a corner for four minutes to read the card and practice their skit. If your real principal knows about the lessons and is a bit of a "ham," you might invite him or her to ad lib the role of principal.

Interpretation.

While they are rehearsing, tell the others that they have worked with Decision Trees before, but a review of values might help them here. Remind them that values are preferred events around which people organize their actions. On the chalkboard, list:

Students identify most wanted value by which to evaluate consequences.

Well-Being	Rectitude	Skill
Affection	Wealth	Respect
Enlightenment	Power	

Discuss with them which of these they might want in this instance—Wealth? Skill? Enlightenment? etc. (probably well-being).

Call the role players to center stage. Remind the students that one attempt to use authority—the boys' parents—has already failed. Now they will be asked to judge the use of authority for its positive and negative consequences. Let the skit unfold.

Since you have a copy of their strategy card in the lesson, you can make sure they cover all points.

> Students are to avoid omissions in consequences.

Discuss with the class:
1. Would this work?
2. What are the positive/negative consequences of this alternative in this situation?

Fill in the consequence space above "Authority" in the Decision Tree.

> Children project consequences of one course.

Step 6

Divide the class into four groups. Each group will put on a skit based on a strategy card showing how its method would be used to influence the *teacher*. In each skit, one of them will play the teacher and two will play Roger and Dick; the others will be Roger and Dick's friends. Pass out a strategy card to each group and send groups to the four corners of the room to rehearse. Move from corner to corner, coaching, getting "rehearsals" started, making sure they read the cards. Encourage the "teacher decision-makers" to be firm but reasonable. Make sure each skit is clear and well-rehearsed.

> *(See pages 59–60 for strategy cards.)*

Step 7

1. Have everyone sit down.
2. Go through a skit.
3. Discuss whether it could work and its positive and negative consequences.
4. Write these on the Tree on the chalkboard.
5. After identifying positive and negative consequences of this method, go on to the next skit.

> Children evaluate consequences of each alternative.

Remember, in judging whether a method would work, students will be judging whether or not it will help them achieve their value at the top of the Tree.

> Several rounds of practice extend concepts.

Concluding the Lesson

STEP 8

When the Tree is filled, discuss:

1. Is one method better (more positive consequences) than the others?

2. Is one method loaded with more negative consequences than the others? (Society tends to use police power against the naked use of power.)

3. Is a combination of methods useful? (Help students synthesize their own tactical solution.)

4. How could learning how to influence political decisions *several* ways be helpful to Native Americans today? to Afro-Americans? to Ohio Students? to Teachers? to You?

Children make trade-offs and settle upon a choice.

Concepts extended by more instances.

AUTHORITY STRATEGY CARD

Students—Convince the principal:

• To pass a rule saying teachers should be fair to students.

• To make teachers give students a chance to explain.

• To ask your teacher to give you another chance to behave.

Principal:

Be firm, ask them what right they have to try to influence a teacher. The decision is up to you.

REWARD STRATEGY CARD

Students—Convince the teacher:

• If you can go to recess you will be perfectly behaved.

• If you can go to recess you will study, listen, not talk.

• If you can go to recess you will tell everyone how much you're learning from your excellent teacher.

• If you can go to recess you will help keep the class in order.

Teacher:

Be firm, get what you want from them. The decision is up to you.

INFORMATION STRATEGY CARD

Students—Convince the teacher:
- Punishment is not as good as rewarding good behavior.
- You have been well-behaved and excellent students.
- Asking Molly what happened could show you did not trip her.
- You have learned not to laugh at others' mistakes.

Teacher:
Make your own decision after hearing all they have to say.

AFFECTION STRATEGY CARD

Students—Convince the teacher:
- You're proud to be in that teacher's class.
- Your teacher is a sharp dresser—you want to be one, too.
- We have a great school—teachers are tough, but fair, here.
- Your teacher knows exercise is important to growing students.

Teacher:
Be firm. But remember, your students are only children. The decision is up to you.

POWER STRATEGY CARD

Students—Convince the teacher you will make an offer the teacher can't refuse—let you go to recess or you will:
- Demonstrate in the halls and streets, protesting unfairness.
- Sign a petition to the board asking for removal of the teacher for cruelty and unfairness.

Teacher:
Remind them threats are illegal—their parents and police will not take kindly to the idea they are threatening an employee of the government. The decision is up to you—don't let anyone push you around.

The lesson above is followed by one on using information to influence. Children are to map out the potential effects of decisions on several groups, identify alternatives and their consequences, supply relevant information, and, if necessary, focus public attention and enlist allies, again for several cases, some of which they may develop themselves. This last unit concludes by a summary lesson of many sorts of activities: using pictures, puzzles, games, and fill-in exercises, even individual decision making on whether to recommend the Citizenship Decision-Making Units for next year's students.

A careful look at this exemplary lesson and the sketch of mini-units preceding it shows students still "climbing decision trees," but more capably than in the earlier illustrative lesson.

The concept of decision making is still the analytical framework, the means of getting a hold on a problem; but intervening lessons gave children special practice in using each of the stages. By the lesson reprinted directly above, students can recognize and break down an occasion for decision by bringing relevant and more sophisticated knowledge to bear: the concepts of ways of influencing decisions, straight out of political science, and the scenario information with all the meaning it conjures up from their own lives. More knowledge and more skill enable children to handle not just two or three alternatives, but five.

Even before projecting consequences, students are to select, out of the eight they have by now dealt with, one relevant value they want most as their goal and their standard for judging. Children in the middle grades are probably less able than older students to clarify the relations between value issues specific to particular situations and larger, more abstract value conflicts. The degree of differentiation and abstraction needed to handle value conflicts in public issues is not expected here. No extensive probing of inner value conflicts is called for. But the analytical skill of distinguishing values from facts is clearly in play.

The distinction is facilitated by children's role playing the use of one means of influence or another. Here what is verifiable is right before their very eyes, and much of it will not be what they wanted. Although role cards supply information, students must use their skills in interpreting, making more out of what is explicitly there, in order to make their skits happen.

Knowledge is developed because it is needed for projecting consequences. Nonetheless, its use hardly takes on the character of applying if-then generalizations as more mature students might do. Some defensible generalizations may be put in operation from the role cards, and their results duly observed; but the emphasis here is not on developing or applying tight generalizations and, so, on obtaining highly probable predictions. Children project only what could happen. Since tracing consequences of consequences is complex, it is not asked for, although some will probably occur.

Were the decision situation more complex and the students more mature, more evidence would have to be gathered about what could be expected. Then the skills of finding information, interpreting, and generalizing before applying would be in more extensive use. Teachers and students must exercise some care at this stage. Too much information cannot be digested, and time runs out. Real decision making gets short shrift while knowledge becomes all-important. Generalizations are worth developing and needed in the process. Reliance primarily on process produces snappy, superficial choices. By picturing a sample of defensible choices, teachers can identify the skills and knowledge actually required. The lesson included here has attempted to do just that.

The diagram of the Decision Tree continues to offer support. Because it encourages children to see several consequences for each of several alternatives, children are less likely to make shallow choices by leaving things out. In keeping focus clear, the diagram steers students away from irrelevant material and pushes them toward consistency between each alternative and its consequences. The diagram also makes plain that no wholly desirable consequences can be had. Children have to make tradeoffs among positives and negatives, giving up a little positive to avoid more negative, with the chosen value as the standard for judging.

While the model made visual by the diagram provides structure, it is hardly rigid. In the lesson above, for example, while students are using concepts for analysis, they are also building them up in role-playing and projecting consequences. In the unit as a whole, practice emphasizes one stage of the model after another, but as moving around among stages of a whole.

One last point about this illustration. Throughout the four mini-units children role-play the events, the particulars from which concepts are to be abstracted. Such experience is not only direct; it is actual manipulation of concrete events. Children themselves "make it happen," albeit with role cards and other props. Out of these experiences, concepts develop, symbols of the actual. When students can manipulate symbols instead of actual events or objects, they have left what Piaget called the stage of concrete operations and have moved into the stage of formal thought. In this latter and qualitatively different stage, students can deal with classes of events, conditions, and objects and form relationships between abstract generalizations.

While the stage of formal thought is reached by many children at about eleven or twelve years, it does not occur inevitably. Nor is it reached "across the board," as some pervasive change in all of thinking. It occurs, instead, in areas of thought on a raggedy front, collo-quially speaking. The stage of formal thought in any area is not reached unless the stage of concrete operations has preceded it. Only after the manipulation of concrete events and objects has been sufficient for de-veloping symbols can their manipulation in formal thought go on.[6]

No wild claims are made here that this unit, or any other like it, will sweep children into some stage of formal thought beyond their years. But the frequent use of role playing; the nearly direct experience in nu-merous cases from everyday life; and the opportunities for additional, optional activities needed by some children for mastery are all worth noticing. Such activities do have appeal. The sheer variety adds spice. Chances to get in the act make for widespread participation and in-volvement. But seen in the light of theory in cognitive development, such activities take on increased significance.

That point can be applied to strategies for junior and senior high school students, indeed for adults. Students may need some practice in concrete operations before they can engage in formal thought. Passing one's twelfth birthday is no guarantee of capability. Role playing, act-ing out scripts, simulation exercises, and out-of-school participation, along with the less direct opportunities in anecdotal accounts, stories, drama, and cases, enable students to develop skills in abstract thinking and decision making which they could not otherwise make their own.

LEVELS OF DIFFICULTY AND SEQUENCE

When teachers look at curricular plans and strategies for thinking, they sometimes say, "It may be great, but my kids can't do that." Al-though teachers may be right, they do well to ask what is meant by "can't" and "that." Do students lack the skills? Or is it the content or the climate that gets in their way? What makes learning experiences in thinking easy or difficult, do-able or not do-able by young people? Some suggestions for answering may help.

1. The sheer quantity of matters to be dealt with makes for com-plexity and difficulty. Two points of view to compare or interpret, for example, are easier than three or five. It is harder to project consequences for four courses of action than for two. A great mass of data is harder to organize for evidence than is a small.
2. What is more abstract is more difficult. Students can develop their skills when the level of abstraction in the content is reduced to the level they can handle, or when sufficient time and practice go to raising the level of abstraction they can handle. The first point

above notwithstanding, material which is "shorter" and "less" is not necessarily easier. "Longer" because illustrations are fuller promotes handling the abstractions. What is too abstract depends upon what students themselves can manage, and not on what is in a textbook or a curricular plan. So does what is not abstract enough.

3. Fine distinctions are more difficult than gross ones. It is easier to differentiate related situations or arguments when particulars are clearly different. It is harder to distinguish what is "probably true" from "true" than what is "true" from "false." It is harder to project consequences when trends must be separated from if-then outcomes, and harder to put a finger on the most significant attribute of a concept than on mere attributes. Precise and explicit statements of concepts, generalizations, and value judgments demand more than those less clearly formulated in words; the former may be ultimately more desirable, but in many situations the other kind will do.

4. Relying solely on print for grist for the mill makes thinking more difficult. Activities to foster thinking offer opportunities to improve skills in reading. Reading and thinking skills go hand in hand. But thinking can occur without reading—and reading without thinking. Even those who can read whatever they are asked to read need ample, direct experience. Films, art, role playing, simulation exercises, actual participation or observation—all such forms of communication, used when they are needed, reduce the difficulty.

5. It is easier to develop skills in thinking about matters which students see as closely related to their own lives. Although it is likely that social studies curricula ought to include more of the behavioral sciences or more of studying the community, the recommendation here is not for what is geographically close or even needed this afternoon. The point is simply that it is harder to think about what is believed to make no difference.

6. Providing structure, cues, and props makes thinking easier. Structure may be a conceptual framework, a sequence of steps in a process, a sense of direction in a task. It is harder to use when it must be kept only in mind, and easier when it appears in a diagram, a retrieval chart, a set of questions or directions in a study guide, an outline on the board or transparency. However, structure has been made by people for people; people, including students, are not made for structure. Rigidity gets in the way of thinking. Generalizing, applying, and decision making are made easier by clear delineation at the outset of key concepts, principles, and values. Young people can learn to interpret more readily when material to

be interpreted is already available, and to see what is evidence when at least some of it is at hand. Teachers' questions in the form of cues enable students to carry on tasks they could not otherwise do. But cues are cues and are not the same as "the answer."

7. The emotional loading makes a difference. When a problem area is overloaded with feeling, students are too threatened to think their way out of it. Teachers can shift to a similar issue in a situation arousing fewer hackles with the hope of coming back to the earlier one. A problem that taps no feeling at all offers no challenge. Both "too hot" and "too cold" make for difficulty. Challenge means that the matter at hand is right for students.

8. Thinking skills are easier to learn when students expect to learn them. From years of schooling when such was not the case, many students expect to get the answer from a book, a film, or the teacher. Making clear by word and deed that students are to figure things out for themselves makes it easier for them to do so.

9. An open classroom climate encourages thinking. Condemnation and hoots of laughter produce students afraid to make tries. Inept thinking is better greeted with questions that call for testing it out. Students pressure each other, and all but the most intrepid feel some urge to conform. More than one proposal is often required, and by one tactic or another teachers must get them and keep them out on the floor. A closed and threatening climate makes for needless difficulty.

10. Carefully planned sequence is more likely to promote competence. Strategies must jibe with some defensible process. Teachers have to see what students must have mastered before they can move on to what is more complex. Mastery may require special practice on building up needed concepts and generalizations, for example, or skills in interpretation or application, or clarifying values. Never simple or certain, sequence well done reduces difficulty and fosters success.

These suggestions do not mean that "easy" is "good." "Challenging" is "good." Learning opportunities appropriate for students' capability levels are likely to result in achievement.

Teachers and other curricular planners give a good deal of attention to grade placement of thinking skills and to development of long-range K-12 sequence.

The question of which skills should be assigned to which grade levels is probably the wrong question to ask. A better question asks how much abstraction and complexity students at any grade level can handle, or how much concrete or nearly concrete experience students must have for any skill. Moreover, development of the several skills in thinking go hand in hand, one with the others—and with other skills in social studies as well. Convenience may warrant emphasis on one skill or another at some grade level, but the emphasis is more likely to be productive as an aspect of building conceptual frameworks, developing generalizations, and decision making. In such contexts the usefulness of the subskill can be made apparent. Some suggestions may translate this point into broad outline.

1. In the primary grades, children are barely into the stage of concrete operations. They need many opportunities to manipulate concrete objects and events. Children need experience in comparing and contrasting; ordering before and after and cause and effect, and differentiating these pairs; distinguishing true from false, and true from valued; identifying topics and important points. (These abilities are basic to all the skills identified in this chapter.) Children can begin to build rudimentary concepts and low-level generalizations, although labels and statements will be implicit or imprecise. Differentiations will be gross. Content must come out of the everyday experience of an as yet small social world. The quantity of information must be small, learning sequences short, and practice frequently repeated, although perhaps in seemingly different activities. Young children need much in the way of structure, cues, and props.

2. Middle grades children are well into the stage of concrete operations. They still require opportunities for concrete manipulation of objects, events, and conditions, although pictures, films, anecdotal accounts, and the like can increasingly represent realities. Concepts and generalizations can be abstracted from concrete experiences, although labels and statements will be somewhat imprecise. Differentiations will be gross, although more can be made. Except for applications of what will be sketchily referred to here as formal logic, children can develop aspects of all of the thinking skills at least in rudimentary form, but only in proper circumstances. Repeated, though not identical, opportunities for dealing with small quantities of material are needed. Sequences must be short and broken into manageable parts. Clear structure, props, and cues are helpful.

3. Junior high school students are in transition to the stage of formal thought. Since many can manipulate symbols only in some few areas, more concrete or nearly concrete experiences are needed than are commonly provided. Students can develop many aspects of thinking skills; they can, for example, formulate more explicit concepts, test generalizations, infer, make simple judgments of logical consistency, see the relations between more specific and gener-

alized values, and relate values to empirical evidence. They can, that is, when the quantity of data and the length of the sequence are moderately sized, and when opportunity has been ample for mastering concepts and generalizations. Structured sequences can allow for their growing ability to organize for themselves.

4. High school students have ordinarily reached the stage of formal thought at least in many areas, although concrete or nearly concrete experience is needed far more often than is ordinarily recognized. Students can develop thinking skills with considerable precision in explicit, abstract statements, distinctions in degrees of certainty, logical consistency, and complexity. Structure, cues, and props are needed, although students can structure shorter segments of longer sequences for themselves. Emphasis on comprehending great masses of material in which abstract concepts and generalizations are often buried means less development of thought. Students can comprehend larger "amounts" than they can think about or with. Inadequate development of skills at earlier grade levels hinders what could otherwise be developed in high school.

One last statement should be made. Teachers ought to evaluate achievement of skills in thinking. What is evaluated has a powerful influence over what teachers will teach and what students will learn. When the chips are down, both students and teachers know what counts. Even informal assessment methods have the virtue of making plain to all hands—teachers, students, parents, and administrators—that development of thinking skills is to be taken seriously. And, indeed, it is. On it depends much of the welfare of students and society.

BIBLIOGRAPHY

Banks, James. *Teaching Strategies for the Social Studies*. Reading, Massachusetts: Addison-Wesley, 1973.

Bloom, Benjamin S. et al. *Taxonomy of Educational Objectives: the Cognitive Domain*. New York: David McKay, 1956.

Ehman, Lee, Howard Mehlinger, and John Patrick. *Toward Effective Instruction in Secondary Social Studies*. Boston: Houghton Mifflin, 1974.

Fair, Jean and Fannie Shaftel, editors. *Effective Thinking in the Social Studies*. 37th NCSS Yearbook. Washington, D.C.: National Council for the Social Studies, 1967.

Fraenkel, Jack R. *Helping Students Think and Value*. Englewood Cliffs, New Jersey: Prentice-Hall, 1973.

Hunt, Maurice and Lawrence Metcalf. *Teaching High School Social Studies*, 2nd edition. New York: Harper and Row, 1968.

Metcalf, Lawrence, editor. *Values Education*. 41st NCSS Yearbook. Washington, D.C.: National Council for the Social Studies, 1971.

Oliver, Donald and James Shaver. *Teaching Public Issues in the High School*. Boston: Houghton Mifflin, 1966.

Raths, Louis, Merrill Harmin and Sidney Simon. *Values and Teaching*. Columbus, Ohio: Charles E. Merrill, 1966.

Taba, Hilda. *Teachers' Handbook for Elementary Social Studies*. Palo Alto, California: Addison-Wesley, 1967.

FOOTNOTES

[1]John Dewey, *How We Think* (New York: D.C. Heath, 1933), p.9.

[2]Excerpted and adapted from David C. King, *Conflict and Change: Themes for U.S. History*, Intercom #76 © Center for Global Perspectives of the New York Friends Group, Inc. Teachers at all grade levels will find materials published in *Intercom* helpful. Reprinted with permission.

[3]*Ibid.*

[4]One widely used formulation of the valuing process is found in Louis Raths, Merrill Harmin, and Sidney Simon, *Values and Teaching* (Columbus, Ohio: Charles E. Merrill, 1966). Readers who compare that process with that of this Yearbook on decision making will see many commonalities, although a difference in emphasis.

[5]Roger LaRaus and Richard C. Remy, *Citizenship Decision-Making*. These materials have been developed by the Citizenship Development Program at the Mershon Center, Ohio State University, with support from the Mershon Center and the Ohio Department of Education. A national version of the materials is being published by Addison-Wesley Publishing Company, Inc. Besides the basic set of lessons, there are further optional activities, including many which integrate social studies and language arts. Copious explanations are offered to teachers. Schools will find the materials useful as they are and as models.

Political decisions are defined as collectively binding decisions about the management of groups. Thus, political decisions (a) make rules for groups; (b) allocate things group members think are desirable or important; (c) set goals for a group; (d) are also decisions about how to act toward a group's decisions. All of us make decisions, attempt to influence, and are affected by political decisions. For more information about this approach to decision making, see Richard C. Remy, "Making, Judging and Influencing Political Decisions: A Focus for Citizen Education," *Social Education*, Vol. 40:6 (October, 1976), pp. 360–66.

[6]Hilda Taba, "Implementing Thinking as an Objective in Social Studies," *Effective Thinking in the Social Studies*, Jean Fair and Fannie Shaftel, editors, 37th NCSS Yearbook, Volume 37 (Washington, D.C.: National Council for the Social Studies, 1967), pp. 29–31. Taba drew upon the ideas of both Piaget and Bruner.

"All prepared sources share one characteristic. They are designed to communicate information by means of language, such as printed words, numbers, pictures, or abstract symbols such as dots or lines."

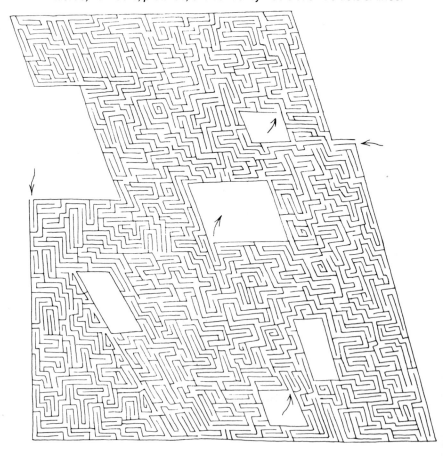

.3.

Charlotte C. Anderson and Barbara J. Winston

Acquiring Information
by Asking Questions,
Using Maps and Graphs, and
Making Direct Observations

We are committed to fostering enlightened, confident, and socially responsible decision makers. In shaping this discussion and designing instructional strategies, we have made three implicit assumptions about the processes of developing this kind of decision maker.

Assumption 1—*Students can become more enlightened decision makers as they develop skills to acquire information.* The process of deciding is abetted as one becomes better able to gather information from a wide variety of appropriate sources.

In Chapter One, the Browns' decision-making occasion (buying a house) created several instances where skillful information gathering would have been helpful. They would be aided, for example, by an ability to ask pertinent questions of the realtor *and* of the residents in the neighborhoods they considered. Knowing how to phrase productive questions and being able to select the most knowledgeable person or persons to answer such questions would help the Browns to make an enlightened decision.

The Browns also would benefit from an ability to gather information by using direct observation (using their eyes, ears, and other senses) as they toured each area. Skillful direct observation might add a great deal of information that the Browns could not gain by asking questions of others.

Finally, it is noted that the Browns did not consult any documents as they struggled with their decision. Gathering data from maps, tables, charts, and other media communicating information about their potential choices might further assist the Browns to make an enlightened and gratifying decision.

Skills acquiring information help foster rational choices. If we want to be skilled at acquiring information on those crucial decision-making occasions we all face, we need considerable practice over long periods of time. If we want our students to gain skills in acquiring information, we must provide repeated opportunities for them to develop these skills. Therefore, we focus in this chapter on building skills in the three basic ways children (and adults) acquire information: (1) by asking questions and interviewing; (2) by extracting information from prepared sources; (3) by making direct observations.

Assumption 2—*Students will experience increasing self-confidence as they become skilled decision makers.* Confidence or self-respect develops hand in hand with increased competencies and feelings of efficacy. The student who can skillfully acquire information and thus move toward a rational decision is bound to feel good about himself or herself. In turn, growing self-respect reinforces and promotes learning and helps the student to seek, rather than avoid, decision-making occasions. The disposition to seek such occasions is the forerunner of selected, active participatory behaviors we associate with citizenship.

Thus, while this chapter focuses on ways to help decision makers build information-acquisition skills, it also attempts to foster their increasing self-respect. This is accomplished by designing learning tasks at which students can succeed while becoming more competent. Such tasks are found in the illustrative learning experiences throughout the chapter.

Assumption 3—*Students can learn to make socially responsible decisions if learning experiences include a conscious integration of skills and affective development.* Students respond emotionally or psychologically to any experience. Such responses shape both what the student *can* do and determines what he or she *will* do. Therefore, teachers need to think consciously about the affective outcomes they desire and subsequently seek these in given learning experiences.

As we suggest ways to promote enlightened and confident decision makers by building students' information-gathering skills, we will attempt to portray ways in which learning experiences designed for such purposes can also integrate affective development and thus help to promote greater social responsibility among our students. To serve this end, we have identified a specific set of positive affective outcomes regarded as especially vital in a social studies curriculum. These are given and defined at the close of the next section.

It should be noted that attention to self-respect and social responsibility is not exclusively associated with the development of information-acquisition skills. Rather, pertinent discussion in this chapter will be limited to that context.

OVERVIEW OF SKILLS AND AFFECTIVE OBJECTIVES

Asking Questions and Interviewing

As soon as children are able to string words together, they begin to ask questions. Social scientists and other researchers also utilize this technique to gather information. In all instances, those who are skilled at gathering information by asking questions and interviewing are able to (1) identify what they want to know, and why; (2) effectively frame questions that are productive means to obtain information; (3) make rational decisions about who can best answer their questions; (4) make rational decisions about how to best communicate their questions.

Extracting Information from Prepared Sources

Children also learn by extracting information from media such as graphs, charts, diagrams, maps, globes and other models at reduced scale, photographs, drawings, paintings, case studies, reference books, television, radio, recordings, tapes, films, slides, filmstrips, and all the other things prepared for the purpose of communicating information. Children who are skilled users of prepared sources will: (1) be able to conceptualize the parts of a medium and their functions (e.g., map parts include a key, symbols, direction indicator, scale—each with a different function); (2) master the operations necessary to use media to extract facts—that is, simply identify what is shown—and to extract information that is, in fact, not shown; (3) be able to evaluate alternative media in order to select the most useful for a given purpose.

Using Direct Observation

In many ways the child experiences a world which is a microcosm of a larger world. Hence, children can learn a great deal from making direct observations. These observations are fed through receptors— eyes, ears, nose, mouth, and skin. They allow children to obtain information through sensory behaviors such as seeing, hearing, smelling, tasting, and touching.

Children who are skilled observers will be able to: (1) utilize all their senses; (2) evaluate the strengths and weaknesses of each for given purposes; (3) make rational decisions about which sense to use or trust under different circumstances.

Fostering Information-Acquisition Skills

All healthy children obtain information by asking questions, using prepared sources, and observing. These are natural behaviors. Our aim is to help the child become *skillful* at these behaviors. Students can be regarded as skillful only when they are able to acquire information from a wide range of sources which they can select intelligently and use both comfortably and productively.

Children will become increasingly skillful if teachers consciously provide experiences designed to meet that end. Experiences can be organized around the following general guidelines:

1. In order to develop skills in acquiring information, children must learn specific strategies. We have called these strategies *basic and transferable operations*.[1] An example may be helpful. Suppose an individual decides to bake a cake. He or she will assemble the ingredients and utensils and preheat the oven. This strategy or set of steps will be followed, perhaps in a variable order, if the baker makes cookies, or pies, or bread. The steps are the basic and transferable operations people have learned to use when they bake things. There are basic and transferable operations that can be applied to acquiring information. These operations, if systematically developed and mastered, will allow students to use any of the methods and media to acquire information accurately and efficiently.
2. Skills development must be carefully and continuously monitored so that children do not practice erroneous operations.[2]
3. Once skills are introduced, children should have intermittent practices to use learned operations. This will ensure that skilled behavior patterns become established and natural.[3]
4. Skills in acquiring information should be developed in conjunction with their counterparts—skills in reporting information. Tandem consideration serves two purposes:
   a. If teachers and students are to evaluate weaknesses and strengths in reading and extracting information from a table or other media, provision must be made for students to report this information in some appropriate manner. Information acquisition may be effectively measured by simply answering a question about information in a table (e.g., given a table showing beef consumption in the U.S. over the period 1960–1976, the child will

identify the year in which the most beef was consumed). The child who observes and records the technology in the office of the school nurse can report findings by drawing a picture of the nurse's office, writing a story about the things the nurse does with her tools, or telling the class of the findings. A child who interviews the principal can describe what he or she has learned about the principal's role to a class investigating the social organization of the school. Thus, some type of information reporting can often accompany information acquisition.

b. Information acquisition and information reporting are productively developed in tandem for another reason. Learning to decode information recorded in some media may proceed most effectively with concurrent experiences in encoding data in similar forms. Table-reading is reinforced with table-making; graph-reading is reinforced with graph-making; map-making and map-reading should go together when it is practical and productive to do so. Consider this example. A child can observe a familiar environment (e.g., the classroom). The teacher may later take a slide photo of that scene and ask the children to sketch a picture map from the projected slide. Thus, the children have invented their own symbols; they have had an initial encounter with reduced scale; they have had a simple mapping experience in a way that seems more meaningful than if the steps were reversed. It should not be inferred that this is always possible or practical. But the point remains that if it seems natural and within the range of the child's abilities and past experiences to encode information while he or she is learning to decode, one behavior will reinforce the other.

Developing Intended Affective Outcomes

In the introduction to this chapter we suggested that students can make socially responsible decisions if learning experiences include a conscious integration of skills and affective development. Here we identify and explicate specific and positive affective outcomes that we regard as vital in a social studies curriculum.

Selected affective outcomes seem to group neatly into the following four categories.

Self-Awareness

Children demonstrate self-awareness when they are able to:
- *define* their physical appearance, feelings, attitudes, values, beliefs, and actions.

- identify the *sources* of their feelings, attitudes, values, beliefs, and actions.
- explain how they *affect* the world around them.
- evaluate their *impact* on the world and identify ways they can *change* undesirable behaviors.

Respect for Others

There appear to be certain psychological orientations that inhibit a person's ability to respect other people. These inhibiting factors include an inability to empathize, and tendencies toward egocentric, ethnocentric, and stereotypic perceptions. Children demonstrate respect for others when they are able to:

- *exhibit empathy*. That is, they can imagine themselves as another person and explain how the world looks from that alternative perspective.
- *decrease egocentric perceptions*. They recognize that others experience the world differently than they do; consider the welfare of others; and recognize their interdependence with others.
- *decrease ethnocentric perceptions*. They do not use their own groups as standards by which they judge all others, but can explain the legitimacy of behaviors growing out of alternative group membership.
- *avoid stereotyping*. They do not make universal and closed generalizations about others.

World-Mindedness

This category includes respect for both human life and other life forms on planet Earth. It is the capacity, on the one hand, to view one's self as a member of the global society of humankind. And it is an ability, on the other hand, to view humankind as part of the planet's overall ecological system. Children demonstrate increasing world-mindedness when they:

- define themselves as human beings and describe commonalities they share with all human beings.
- define themselves as part of the community of life and describe their dependence on and responsibility for other life and the support system that sustains life.

Tolerance of Uncertainty

In this category we subsume affective responses that enable people to tolerate and cope constructively with an uncertain world. Major uncertainties in this world include conflict, diversity, change, and ambiguity. Children demonstrate tolerance of uncertainty when they exhibit:

- *tolerance of conflict*. They perceive conflict as inevitable and natural; identify sources of conflict; describe alternative ways to manage conflict.
- *tolerance of diversity*. They perceive diversity as inevitable and natural; respond to diversity by defending or promoting desirable differences and condemning or reducing undesirable differences.
- *tolerance of change*. They perceive change as inevitable and natural; recognize change; adapt to change in their own lives; and promote change for the general welfare.
- *tolerance of ambiguity*. They recognize it is not easy to determine what is fact nor what is good. They are willing to examine many alternatives before arriving at a conclusion. And they recognize there are times when *no* conclusion is warranted and when no single conclusion can be defended.

Many of these affective outcomes have been consciously integrated into the illustrative learning experiences in this chapter. Some affective outcomes are excluded because the particular strategies we chose did not lend themselves to a given affective development. In no way do we intend to suggest that some of these affective dimensions should be of less concern than others.

ASKING QUESTIONS

One way to acquire information is to get other people to tell us what we want to know. A major way to do this is, of course, to ask questions.

Basic and Transferable Operations in Asking Questions

Three-year-olds, doctors, tour guides, and social scientists all must make the same decisions in order to ask *effective* questions. These decisions are basically four:
   (1) What do I want to know?
   (2) Whom should I ask?
   (3) What should I ask?
   (4) How should I ask?
The initial step is to define the purpose clearly; i.e., what do I want to know? A clearly defined purpose will serve as a benchmark to evalu-

ate responses to each of the remaining decisions. For example, "*Whom* should I ask? If I ask those people, will they be able to tell me what I want to know?" "What should I ask? If I ask these questions, will they be effective in finding out what I want to know?" etc.

We have suggested four decisions that recur in question-asking situations. In any given instance, there may be others. Any alert five-year-old recognizes that it is a good idea to wait until Dad is in a good mood to ask a favor. In these instances, "when" becomes a salient issue!

Skillful question-askers are people who recognize the decisions to be made and then are able to make the kinds of decisions that give them the information they want.

An Example of a Lesson on Asking Questions

In the following example of an exercise on asking questions, it will be useful to think about these things:

1. Find the points in the lesson where the basic and transferable operations are utilized. Note how they are developed in this example.
2. Identify the intended affective outcomes in the lesson. The exercise is designed for *self-direction* for a group of eight students. Fourth or fifth graders should be able to handle this easily.

Asking Questions

Form a group of eight to do the following exercises:

GATHERING YOUR INFORMATION
1. Suppose you want to know these two things:
   A. Do more people in our class like reading, math, science, or social studies?
   B. Why do people like each of these subjects?
2. If you want to know this, you have two decisions to make. You must decide: (1) *whom* to ask and (2) *what* to ask.
3. *Whom should you ask?*
   Should you ask?
   a. the teacher
   b. the principal
   c. kids in the room next door
   d. each person in our class
   e. the class president
   f. one-half the class
   Discuss the advantages and/or disadvantages of asking each of the above people.
   Whom have you decided to ask?_____

4. *What should you ask?*
   What you should ask depends on what you want to know.
   Write down the two things you want to know here:
   I want to know: A. _____
                        B. _____
   Look at the questions below. *Discuss* why each is or is not good to help you
   find out the two things you want to know.
   a. Do you like hot dogs?
   b. Do you always do your math work on time?
   c. Why is that your favorite subject?
   d. Do you like math better than reading?
   e. Which subject do you like best: reading, math, science, or social stud-
      ies?
   f. What is your favorite subject?
   g. Why is math your favorite subject?
   Pick the two best questions.
   What questions have you decided to ask? Write them down here just as you
   would ask them:
   A. _____
   B. _____
5. *How should you ask?*
   Choose one of these two ways to ask your questions:
   A. Use prepared questionnaires on which all classmates record their own
      answers.
   B. Use oral interviews; that is, let each member of the group interview four
      or five classmates. (Be sure all classmates are interviewed!) The group
      members should ask the questions and take notes on their classmates'
      answers.

REPORTING YOUR INFORMATION
1. *Prepare a report of your findings.*
   A. Make a bar graph like this one showing how people answered question
      5A.

	Favorite Subject
Reading	
Math	
Science	
Social Studies	
	1 2 3 4 5 6 7 8 9 10 11 12 13 14 . . .
	Students

B. Divide your group into four pairs. One pair can prepare a report on why people like reading best. Another pair can do the same for math, another for science, another for social studies.

When the reports are ready, present them to the rest of the class. Think about how you answered the questions. Why doesn't everybody feel the same way you do?

IDENTIFYING AND APPLYING YOUR QUESTION-ASKING SKILLS
Four things to decide in order to ask effective questions:
  (1) What do I want to know?
  (2) Whom should I ask?
  (3) What should I ask?
  (4) How should I ask?
Think of something that interests you. Go through the four steps to find out about it.

Analysis of Intended Affective Outcomes in this Lesson

This lesson helps children increase their *self-awareness* as they are asked to identify a favorite subject and reflect on why they feel this way. In other words, they focus on the source of this attitude. This is a good opportunity for the teacher to explore with the children the effects or impact of these attitudes. For example, is there any correlation between how well a student likes a subject and how well he or she performs? Then, of course, strategies for change can be discussed; i.e., what can be done to help me like and/or achieve in a subject I currently neither like nor achieve in?

Decreasing egocentrism and *tolerance of diversity* are fostered as children focus on the choices others have made that are different from their own. The more time children spend focusing on the reasons others give for differing choices, the greater the affective payoffs. In this way children will see not only that differences exist, but that these differences grow out of differing perceptions and experiences. Thus, they will come to accept the legitimacy of these kinds of differences.

Tolerance of ambiguity is fostered by having the children struggle to select "good" questions. By discussing the merits and demerits of each question with others and experiencing the process of achieving consensus, they are encouraged to recognize that the "right" way is not always easy to discover.

Sequencing Considerations

Very young children can profitably explore the issues involved in good question-asking. Early lessons should include exercises in which children are asked to choose the best person to ask for specific information. For example, if one wants to know how to fix a bicycle, which of these people would be the best to ask: a nurse, a postal worker, a person who repairs bicycles? Other lessons should include exercises in choosing the best question out of several. More advanced exercises would have the children formulating and evaluating their own questions and deciding whom to ask.

Practicing by *actually* posing different questions to different people and evaluating results will sharpen the children's ability to frame good questions. The disappointment and the frustration of not getting the desired information are more influential in getting a child to reframe a question than is a teacher's judgment, "That is not a good question." The child should, of course, have repeated opportunities to reshape questions and, thus, experience success in this venture.

After students have had the kind of experience identified in this lesson, they should be ready for a more formally constructed question-asking exercise. They could, for example, interview children in other classrooms. In this case, the children would also need to consider the best means of gathering the data—assign each student five people to interview? construct questionnaires?

Older students will be ready to consider the problems of sampling. When the total universe of people from whom one wants information cannot be reached, then the decision "Whom should I ask?" presents a special problem. What proportion of a total population who could supply this information will be enough for me to reach a warranted conclusion?

As students work in many and varying kinds of question-asking experiences, they will begin to recognize there are some consistent guidelines for determining *whom to ask* and *what to ask*. These seem to be the more obvious:

Whom should I ask? Someone who—
1. has the information
2. is accessible to me
3. I can communicate with
4. is unbiased (is likely to give "straight" information)

What should I ask? Questions that—
1. will be understood by the respondent
2. will elicit the responses that meet my objectives
3. will not shape answers because of my biases

Teachers could simply present students with these guidelines at the outset. However, if the students are aided in discovering them for themselves, the guidelines will be far more meaningful. As children gain experience in asking questions informally and in formal interviews and surveys, they will become more and more proficient in analyzing each new question-asking situation. In these analyses, their guidelines will emerge.

EXTRACTING INFORMATION FROM PREPARED SOURCES

All prepared sources share one characteristic. They are designed to communicate information by means of language, such as printed words, numbers, pictures, or abstract symbols such as dots or lines. The skillful child understands the differences among the media, can use most media with comfort and efficiency, and can identify which will be most useful under selected circumstances. If we want students to develop skills related to these objectives, we must provide learning experiences to serve those ends.

In the following pages we have focused on students' use of maps, graphs, and tables as prepared sources. These media are used frequently as sources of information in social studies. Additionally, considerations regarding their use are in many ways more complex than those involving other media. This focus has allowed us to devote detailed attention to related skills and affective development.

USING MAPS

There are four map skills that we regard as basic: (1) using symbols; (2) using directions; (3) using scale; (4) selecting appropriate maps to serve given purposes. Lessons to build these skills can also integrate specific and intended affective outcomes. Although we will focus on the four skills above and selected affective outcomes, we recognize that such lessons also provide opportunities for children to practice comparing, inferring, classifying, hypothesizing, analyzing, and other thinking skills. These learning experiences also can offer students decision-making occasions and practice in reporting information.

Basic and Transferable Operations in Using Maps

Using Symbols

In one way, symbols on maps are like all other symbols—they stand for real things. Map symbols are different from other symbols, however, in that their *location* on a map stands for the location of real-life objects on Earth. Children must develop these conceptual understandings before they can undertake the operations necessary to use symbols on maps.

The operations involving the use of map symbols include (1) using the key or legend to find out what a symbol stands for; and (2) locating the symbol on the map to find out where the real-life object or situation is located on Earth.

Using Directions

Directions on maps are representations of directions on Earth. Just as children learn to use the key to decode symbols, they should learn to use the compass rose or direction indicator to orient themselves to directions on a map.

Using Scale

Symbols as representations of objects or areas on a map are usually smaller than life size. Such representations are not unlike a child's drawing of his or her family, a tree, or the school. This is a somewhat simplistic but essential introduction to matters of scale. Most pictorial representations (and maps are also these) have to shrink large objects to fit on small pieces of paper. Objects and areas on maps are reduced to specific proportions that are shown in scale notations (e.g., 1 in. = 1 mile, or $\frac{1\,cm}{10m}$). Students must learn to refer to the scale on a map in order to calculate represented earth distances.

An Example of a Lesson on Using Maps[4]

In the following example, it will be useful to think about these things:

1. Find points in the lesson where the basic transferable operations are utilized.
2. Identify the intended affective outcomes in the lesson.

This lesson can be used by fourth graders. Note that instructions are addressed to students.

Using Maps

LEARNING THE PARTS OF MAP A
1. A good title will tell you the information you should be able to find in a map. What information do you expect to find in Map A?
2. Where would you look to find the meaning for each symbol? Find the symbol for *desk* in the key. Now find it on the map. Draw the symbol for *water fountain*. For *copying machine*. Now find them on the map.

3. Where is north on this map? How do you know? Is the copying machine on the east or west side of the map? Is the coffee machine on the north or south side of the map? On what side of the map is the typing paper closet?
4. Work with a partner to answer these questions:
   a. About how many centimeters on the map do you measure between the water fountain and the coffee machine?
   b. How many meters on Earth would this distance be?
   c. What part of the map helped you answer these questions?

Using Map A

Write answers to these questions.
1. How far does the person in Office B have to walk to get a cup of coffee?
2. How far does the person at Desk 2 have to walk to get paper for typing?
3. Which office, A, B, or C, is closest to the copying machine?
4. Is office C north or south of office B?
5. In which direction would you walk to move from the meeting room to office B? From office B to office C? From C to A?

LEARNING THE PARTS OF MAP B
1. What information do you expect to find out in this map? What part of the map did you use to answer this?
2. Draw the symbol for the airline office. Now find it on the map. Find the bank on the map.
3. Is the hotel on the north or south side of the park? What did you use to find this out?
4. What is the distance on Earth from the east edge of the map to the west edge of the map? How do you know?

Using Map B

Write the answers to these questions.
1. Every morning Maria, a woman who works at the airline office, takes letters to the post office. What is the direction Maria walks in as she goes to the post office?
2. How far does she walk from the office to the post office?
3. Sometimes Maria takes the subway to her home. She walks from her office through the park to the subway. In what direction does she walk? How far does she walk?

MAKING DECISIONS: CHOOSING USEFUL MAPS
1. What does Map A tell you about the airline office that Map B doesn't tell you? What does Map B tell you about the airlines office that Map A doesn't?
2. Does either Map A or B tell you these things? If Mexico City is in the western hemisphere? What is the latitude of Mexico City? How many people live in Mexico City? What is its climate like?
3. Use maps A and B to fill in the chart below. The first is done for you.

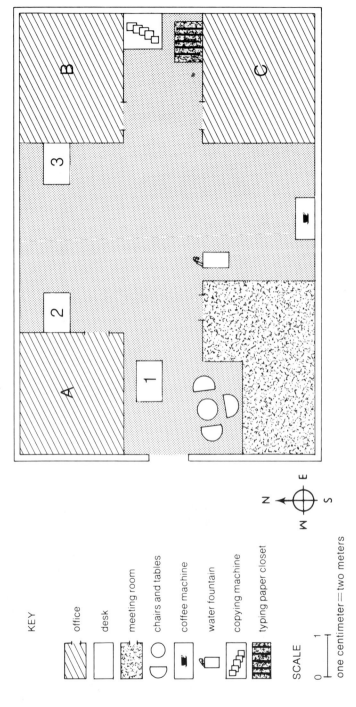

MAP A
AIRLINE OFFICE—MEXICO CITY

KEY

office

desk

meeting room

chairs and tables

coffee machine

water fountain

copying machine

typing paper closet

SCALE

0   1

one centimeter = two meters

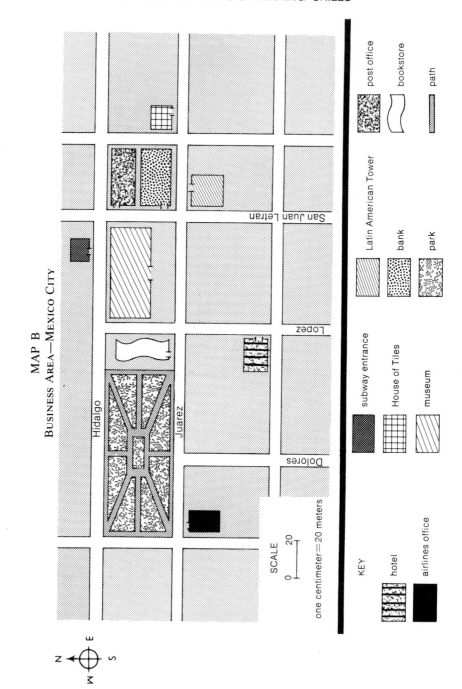

MAP B
BUSINESS AREA—MEXICO CITY

SCALE

0   20

one centimeter = 20 meters

KEY

hotel

airlines office

subway entrance

House of Tiles

museum

Latin American Tower

bank

park

post office

bookstore

path

| Questions | MAPS THAT GIVE US INFORMATION ABOUT MEXICO CITY | | |
	Map A	Map B	Other Maps
1. How many desks are in the airline office?	X		
2. Is Mexico City located on a plateau?			
3. Is Mexico City in the northern hemisphere?			
4. Is the House of Tiles west of the bookstore?			
5. What is the weather like in Mexico City?			
6. How many people live in Mexico City?			

IDENTIFYING YOUR MAP SKILLS
1. What does a map title tell you?
2. Where do you find out what map symbols stand for?
3. Where do you look to find which way is north on a map?
4. Where do you look to find how much Earth distance is shown on the map?

Analysis of Intended Affective Outcomes in This Lesson

The lesson was designed to promote *tolerance of ambiguity* in that it implied strengths in each of the maps, as well as limitations. Students learned that a given map was valuable for selected purposes. This was extended in the chart-making section. Through these and similar experiences, children will learn that information must be acquired from a variety of sources, selected intelligently, and used productively, to serve designated purposes.

The lesson was designed to *decrease ethnocentrism* and *promote world-mindedness* by focusing on a society outside the children's own. The exercise also avoids stereotyping Mexican people by suggesting that children may know adult office workers whose lives are similar in several ways to lives of adult office workers in Mexico City. Instructional experiences that draw exclusively on our own society may tend to reinforce ethnocentrism and stereotypic thinking.

Sequencing Considerations

What kinds of prior learning experiences should children have in order to do this exercise? What do teachers have to think about as they organize map skills experiences? Answers to these questions will help the teacher as the curriculum designer to meet an overriding affective objective—increasing students' self-respect. Knowledge of students' abilities and prior learning will help insure that they *can do* the things we expect of them. This, in turn, will foster their feelings of competence and a positive self-image.

It is our opinion that there are two essential dimensions to building map skills. One dimension includes experiences that are directly related to the child's immediate observable environment. Another is directly related to the use of maps.

Experiences Related
to the Child's Immediate Observable Environment

If children are to understand maps, they must be able to envision the realities represented on a map. For example, to use Map A, in the illustrative lesson, a child ought to be able to envision an office, a desk, a fountain, copying machine, etc. To use Map B with meaning, a child should be able to envision an urban business district. The implications here suggest that we must provide numerous experiences for children to observe and learn about objects and places in their own immediate environments—building an increasingly larger conceptual inventory of real phenomena. The real-life objects and places primary children should observe may be relatively simple and confined to concrete items (a house, a playground, a school, a table). Older children should have experiences observing more complex items (not just a store, but a shopping center; not just a distribution of classroom furniture, but the distribution of apartment buildings in a neighborhood).

Children should understand and have many opportunities to observe and describe their own locations as well as the locations of other real things on Earth. Very young children can talk about Susan being *in front of* Joe, the alley being *next to* the school yard, the book *on top of* the table, the door *to the left of* me. All these are observations about relative locations. Increasingly complex observations about locations of objects and areas will come with understanding of cardinal and intermediate directions (e.g., my house is west of your house) and with the use of grids.

Compass directions should be introduced to children in a familiar environment. They should have repeated opportunities to reinforce understanding of directions. An example of a useful reinforcing exercise would ask children to face or move toward selected cardinal or intermediate directions while they or others describe such movements. The main point is that children must understand the concept of direction on Earth in order to use the concept on a map.

Repeated opportunities to observe and measure concrete distances in a child's environment will help reinforce measurement skills and make mapped distances more meaningful. There is no way we can provide concrete measurement experiences with very large distances (as represented on maps of large areas). But we can develop familiar frames of reference relative to measureable distances in the child's environment. (For example, children can measure a length of 100 meters. When a task requires them to work with 1000 meters, they can envision what ten of the 100 meter measurements would look like.) Experiences of this type are essential to understanding the concepts of scale and distance on maps and globes.

Experiences Related Directly to Map Use

It appears to us that an ideal introduction to maps would include experiences in which children observe some reality, make a model of the reality, and then map it. For example, children can observe their classroom. Then they make a three-dimensional representation (the model) that can be viewed from head-on or from above. The view from above is the perspective of the map. In this way children are better prepared to make and understand the more abstract two-dimensional representation—the map. Detailed reality/model/map comparisons will help children conceptualize characteristics of models and maps, as well as evaluate relative strengths and weaknesses of each.

Suppose the teacher is satisfied that students have grasped the concepts and perspectives associated with maps. From that point, children must have repeated chances to work with maps in order to practice application of the concepts learned (e.g., symbol and direction) and the operations involved in using maps.

Introduction of new map-related concepts (direction, scale, etc.) should be systematic and compatible with a child's general development. There are some general guidelines we can offer related to increasing complexity in maps and tasks related to map-use.

1. Pictorial symbols are less complex than abstract symbols. For example, a school can be symbolized

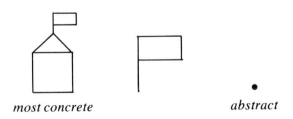

most concrete   *abstract*

Very young children should read and make maps with pictorial symbols, while older children can work with increasingly more abstract symbols.

Additionally, students can envision a real building on a real street that is symbolized on a map. There are no real, observable, concrete counterparts for symbols that stand for such things as the world-wide distributions of languages. Map work with such concepts must wait until children can comprehend the abstract realities.

2. Maps become increasingly more complex as the number of mapped details increase. A map that shows locations of three tables and three chairs is less complex than a map that shows store locations and public parking lots in a large shopping center.

3. Maps become increasingly complex as the mapped details become more difficult to observe in real life. Consider maps showing (a) use of rooms in my school (e.g., for classes, for gym, washrooms, offices, etc.); (b) use of buildings in a shopping center; (c) land-use in my community. Children can observe the school to find some rooms are used for regular classes, some for food preparation, some to store books, etc. A map of land-use in a given community will contain information the children cannot observe easily.

4. Map-related *tasks* can vary in complexity. For example, a simple task might require young children to count the buildings on a street. A much more complex task might require students to use several maps in order to test hypotheses about relationships between agricultural land-use and matters of temperature, rainfall, and elevation.

USING GRAPHS AND TABLES

We need only to skim daily newspapers or consumer magazines to be convinced that an ability to use tables and graphs has become an important kind of literacy. Tables and graphs are efficient ways to present information, particularly when information concerns matters of quantity (e.g., How many? How much? What percentage?). Look at Table A—Our Favorite Places To Play. Imagine the time and space it would take to communicate the same information in complete sentences.

Although graphs and tables are considered together in this section, they may not share exactly the same characteristics or advantages in their use. Graphs (including bar, line, pictorial and circle graphs) will

TABLE A
OUR FAVORITE PLACES TO PLAY

	Baseball field	My room at home	Park	School playground
Tony			✔	
Casey	✔			
Irene				✔
Elmira		✔		
Nilda		✔		
Miguel				✔
James			✔	
Bob	✔			
Hiram	✔			
Erika				✔
JoAnn	✔			
Mary		✔		
Jeff	✔			
Lauren				✔
Paul			✔	
Larry				✔
Donna			✔	
Margie	✔			
Lynn				✔
Steve			✔	
Alan			✔	
Lisa		✔		
Sammy		✔		
Juan	✔			
Linda	✔			
Total	8	5	6	6

GRAPH A
OUR FAVORITE PLACES TO PLAY

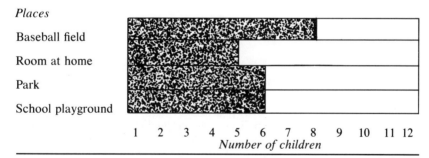

Places

Baseball field

Room at home

Park

School playground

1 2 3 4 5 6 7 8 9 10 11 12
Number of children

offer a distinctive *picture* of data presented. The same information can be shown in a table, but the table-user would have to create the picture in his or her own mind. Compare the examples in Table A and Graph A entitled Our Favorite Places To Play. The graph communicates a pictorial answer to the questions, "Where do most of the children like to play? Fewest?"

Basic and Transferable Operations in Using Graphs and Tables

Each of us has faced the frustration and sometimes despair associated with a task that seems overwhelming. A complex table, graph, map, narrative, or, in fact, any research problem may elicit the "Where do I begin? How am I ever going to do this?" feeling. We think that children can learn a step-by-step process that will lead to effective task management. The trick is to concentrate on one thing at a time, and momentarily ignore all other parts of the task. In the case of graphs and tables, the students should begin with the title. Secondly, they should study the categories listed on the horizontal and then vertical axis. (Order of consideration is not important, but slow and separate understanding of information on each axis is necessary.) Next, students will be able to extract *facts* from tables and graphs. Only then will they be ready to draw inferences and evaluate the data.

An Example of a Lesson on Graph and Table Use[5]

In reviewing the following example of a lesson on graphs and tables, it will be useful to think about these things:

1. Find the points in the lesson where the basic and transferable operations are utilized.
2. Identify the intended affective outcomes.

This lesson can be used by high school students. Instructions are addressed to students.

Using Graphs and Tables

READING THE FACTS IN GRAPH B
1. A good title will tell you the information you should be able to find in a table or a graph. What information do you expect to find in Graph B?
2. Look at the categories along the horizontal axis of Graph B. These categories focus on government spending for goods and services. What goods and services might be included in each category? For example, *military expenditures* includes money spent for helicopters and salaries for military people. What else?
3. The length of a bar and the number at the right tell how much money in billions of dollars was spent on goods and services for each category. How

GRAPH B
WORLD PUBLIC EXPENDITURES, 1972[6]

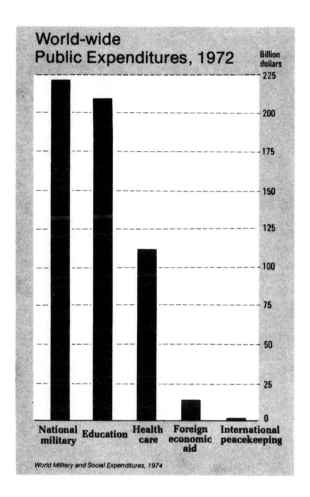

World-wide
Public Expenditures, 1972   Billion dollars

	225
	200
	175
	150
	125
	100
	75
	50
	25
	0

National military   Education   Health care   Foreign economic aid   International peacekeeping

World Military and Social Expenditures, 1974

much did governments spend on *military* in 1972? With a partner, record the amount of money spent in 1972 in each category. Compare your findings with other students.

MAKING INFERENCES FROM GRAPH B
1. According to Graph B, what was the world's highest priority in 1972? Second highest?
2. How many times greater were world expenditures for military purposes than for health care? Than for peacekeeping?

TABLE B
Major Military Powers*: Comparative Use of Resources—1973[7]

Countries	Military Expenditures Millions of US Dollars	International Peacekeeping Millions of US Dollars	Public Expenditures Education Millions of US Dollars	Health Millions of US Dollars	Foreign Economic Aid Millions of US Dollars
United States	78,462	23.664	73,300	35,902	2,968
USSR	67,000	.420**	43,000	20,600	750
Germany, West	12,029	1.915	15,714	16,063	1,102
China	12,000	.009	7,000	1,800	500
France	9,514	.688	14,929	10,872	1,488
United Kingdom	8,611	6.275	10,137	7,344	603
Italy	4,100	1.393	6,533	1,615	192
Israel	3,651	.015	352	51	+†
Japan	3,648	.894	18,000	14,137	011
Germany, East	2,540	.002	2,138	1,378	300
Canada	2,405	5.248	10,004	7,061	515
Iran	2,341	.051	904	269	−‡
India	2,261	.444	1,333	589	+
Netherlands	1,967	1.471	4,445	2,773	332
Poland	1,960	.034	2,784	2,058	300
Spain	1,870	.026	1,232	600	70
Australia	1,838	1.179	2,980	1,031	286
Sweden	1,729	2.519	3,980	3,234	275
Egypt	1,726	.093	393	199	+
Czechoslovakia	1,714	.023	1,615	1,436	300
Brazil	1,548	.872	2,017	189	+
Belgium	1,276	.596	3,148	1,868	235
Saudi Arabia	1,075	.073	435	115	192

*All countries with military expenditures above $1 billion in 1973.
**Because peacekeeping expenditures have been relatively small, they are listed in fractions of millions of dollars in order to show the maximum number of national contributors.
†Aid donor—amount not recorded.
‡None or negligible.

Reading the Facts in Table B
1. What information do you expect to find in Table B? Where did you look to make that decision?
2. Look at the list of countries on the vertical axis. Were they ranked by the amount of money spent for health? education? military? or what?
3. Look at the categories on the horizontal axis on Table B. How does the way information is given in each category here differ from Graph B?
4. Practice using the table. Use a sheet of paper as a guide, and note on scratch paper Australia's 1973 expenditures in each category listed across the top of the table (military, education, etc.).

GRAPHING DATA FROM TABLE B
Find a partner. Select one country to fill in the graph below. Give the graph a clear and complete title. Post your completed graph on the bulletin board.

```
┌─────────────────────────────────────────────────────────────┐
│        ─────────────────────────────────────────            │
│                        (title)                                │
│                                                               │
│                                                               │
│                                                               │
│                                                               │
│                                                               │
│                                                               │
│                                                               │
│                                                               │
│                                                               │
│                                                               │
│                                                               │
│                                                               │
│                                                               │
└─────────────────────────────────────────────────────────────┘
```

Military	Education	Health	Foreign economic aid	International peacekeeping

ANALYZING THE GRAPHED DATA
Use the posted graphs to describe the patterns you see. To describe exceptions to the patterns.

MAKING DECISIONS
1. With a group of four or five use your graphs to discuss the following:

Situation
   a. Imagine you lived in Iran. What would you think about government spending if you were the mother or father of four young children?
   b. Imagine you lived in Egypt. How would you feel about government spending if you and your family were in poor health and had little money for doctors or medicine?
   c. Imagine you lived in Sweden. How would you feel about government spending if your older brother was a soldier?

    d. Imagine you lived in Brazil. How would you feel if your government spent little money on military goods and services but the country that was your neighbor spent one billion dollars for military goods and services?

2. Did you react differently to each situation? Why?
3. You might enjoy finding more information and holding a debate or round-table discussion focusing on the following questions:
    a. Should nations buy or build the most up-to-date weapons to stay even or ahead of other countries?
    b. Should nations try to reach agreements with others to eliminate weapons?
    c. Does spending on military goods and services help or hurt a country's way of life?
    d. What are your recommendations for your government's spending policies?
    e. What would you recommend to other governments?

IDENTIFYING YOUR SKILLS
1. What information do titles of graphs and tables give you?
2. Where do you find the categories of information presented in a table or graph?

Analysis of Intended Affective Outcomes in this Lesson

The lesson was designed to *decrease egocentrism and increase empathy*. This was accomplished by asking students to imagine themselves in a variety of different roles and to tell how they might feel about the information if they were in very different shoes.

The lesson focused on several areas in addition to the United States or strictly western nations. This should suggest to students that the problems highlighted are of world concern. Thus, the lesson attempted to *decrease ethnocentrism and increase world-mindedness*.

Students would not be able to solve the problems reflected in the suggestions for debate and discussion. They would be required, however, to face basic questions that people around the world have to face. This entailed wrestling with some of the uncertainties inherent in thinking about how the world works. Thus, the lesson attempted to build *tolerance of uncertainty*.

Students learned the usefulness of focusing separately and slowly on only one small part of a larger task. When they mastered the first step, they moved to the second, and so on until, finally, they were able to put the pieces together. These experiences foster development of *tolerance of ambiguity*.

Sequencing Considerations

There are three reasons why this exercise was recommended for high school students: (a) the categories of information were complex (e.g., *military expenditures* stands for items that are numerous and far removed from most children's experiences); (b) the table (especially) and the graphs contained a large number of variables (e.g., Table A showed five categories of information pertaining to twenty-three different countries); (c) the tasks students were asked to perform were complex (e.g., they used the graphs showing data for each country to make complex judgments).

What are the implications for teachers of younger children? How do we bring students to the point of being able to do the example lesson? Again, attention to these questions and implications associated with answers will foster students' successful experiences and, thus, help to increase their self-respect.

First, consider work with graphs. Primary children can have repeated experiences with graph making/reading experiences. Visualize a set of pictures separated by perforated lines—an ice cream cone, a hot dog, a hamburger, and a dish of peas. Each child can be asked to select and cut out his or her favorite. On the chalkboard, the teacher can tape each of the pictures, one below the other. Students can take turns placing their favorite in the appropriate row of pictures, thus building a bona fide graph. Then students can agree on a suitable title for the graph. The completed product, constructed by the children, reflects their evaluation of four items with which they have had concrete and considerable personal experience. Graph-reading in this example can be used to suggest rather sophisticated, testable hypotheses (e.g., kindergarteners like ice cream cones best and peas the least).

From this introduction, the key is practice—practice with pictographs and bar graphs that focus on data compatible with children's interests, experiences, and vocabulary. In each experience children should analyze in a step-by-step fashion the information communicated in the graph title and along the vertical and horizontal axis.

Older children, given adequate early experience with simple pictographs and bars, will be able to use more complicated graphs showing more information, more abstract concepts, and demanding more complex tasks.

Line graphs may be used by many children in intermediate grades, providing they can mentally perform selected operations and are aware of the essential characteristics of line graphs. Look at Graph C on page 98.

GRAPH C
AVERAGE MONTHLY RAINFALL IN PLACE X

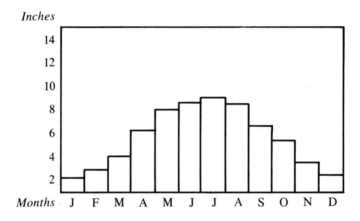

The bars on Graph C show rainfall for each of twelve months in Place X. Each bar communicates a fairly concrete picture of the average quantity of rain that falls on Place X. It is almost as if a bar could be seen as a vessel in which the inches of rain accumulated. Bars showing data other than rainfall convey similar concrete pictures. For example, think of bar graphs showing a given country's export data over ten years, or average income for selected groups, or voting results by state in a national election. If such information were shown in vertical bars, a bar would communicate a picture of "piled-up" exports, or income, or votes. If bars were horizontal, we would see a picture of quantities of exports, income, or votes "lined-up" in a row.

Now look at the line on Graph D and compare it to the bar graph. Both are alike in that they show the same data on rainfall in Place X. The graphs are different, however, in the following ways. Information is shown with a line drawn in a smooth curve. We have learned that the line actually connects points representing quantities that would correspond to the tops of the bars in the first graph. We are able to fill in this information with a glance at the line. Additionally, to the untrained observer, the line *appears* to enclose empty space. Our prior experiences have helped us to fill-in mentally that empty space with represented quantities. If children are to use line graphs with understanding, they will benefit from considerable prior experience with bar graphs.

GRAPH D
AVERAGE MONTHLY RAINFALL IN PLACE X

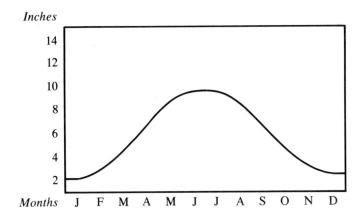

Circle graphs (or pie graphs) will be used with understanding only when students understand relatively abstract relationships involving fractions or percentages. It is acknowledged that very young children seem to use fractions with reference to "half a sandwich" or "half a piece of gum" or "half your marbles." Comprehension of these references is probably limited to the notion of an apparently "even split." Effective work with more refined fractions or percentages is possible some time during the intermediate grades. When the children are ready to use these abstract mathematical concepts, the use of circle graphs can help build and reinforce learnings about fractions and percentages.

Suggestions for developing skills in use of tables are similar to graphing (and mapping) suggestions. Experiences should move from simple to complex (in terms of amount of data to be processed, abstractness of data, and complexity of related tasks).

DIRECT OBSERVATION

Another way we learn about the world around us is by direct observation. The term "direct observation" suggests that we are obtaining unmediated information about the world around us. We are not learning about it from reading books, listening to a lecture, or watching a TV news report. We are using our own senses to gain the information directly from the environment.

It is essential to avoid being misled by the term "direct observation." Information can never be obtained "directly." It is always mediated—mediated by the peculiar biological or physical structure of the sensory organ—mediated by the human mind, which in turn is biologically and culturally shaped. Essentially this means that we cannot assume that all children will perceive the world exactly the same way. Nor can we assume that our perceptions are, or should be, theirs.

Western culture and western scientific tradition, in particular, have emphasized the eye and the ear beyond other receptors. Audio-visual equipment requiring the use of eyes and ears is now standard equipment along with the textbook in most classrooms. But, how many of us have used olfactory-tactile media requiring the nose, mouth, and skin as receptors, especially in the upper grades? "Show and tell" requires seeing and hearing. But is there any parallel information sharing event that requires touching, smelling, tasting, etc.?

We believe that the more tools our children learn to use skillfully now, the more effective adults they will be tomorrow. Sense receptors are tools that teachers can help children learn to use skillfully.

Basic and Transferable Operations in Direct Observation

Skill in using direct observation includes the ability to:

(1) use all sensory receptors
(2) recognize that all perceptions occur in a cultural context
(3) be conscious of the cues responded to
(4) recognize and compensate for the limitations of given receptors for given information
(5) make good and rational decisions about which receptors to use or trust in a given situation

All of us, unless physically impaired, *can* receive information from our environment through all our sensory receptors. However, as noted earlier, the degree of acuity with which individuals use these receptors varies greatly. The skillful observer should be able to recognize situations in which any of the above operations are called for and then select and apply the operation effectively.

Experiences in Direct Observation

The following is a brief description of a set of experiences focusing on the senses. Instructions are addressed to teachers. One primary objective of this lesson is to develop children's skills in increasing sensory awareness.

We invite the teacher to go with the children on their Sense Walks, return to the classroom with them, and talk about what everyone has experienced. Guiding the "Synthesizing Exercise," the teacher can sit back and reflect on what has happened. What learning was promoted? At the close of this section are questions to aid reflection on this learning experience.

Sense Walks

OPENING EXERCISE

Begin this set of experiences by taking the children to an area *without* telling them why they are going or what they are to concentrate on. Return to the classroom and have individuals record what they *saw*; what they *heard*; what they *smelled*; what they *felt* on their skins. Help them identify each receptor; i.e., eyes, ears, nose, mouth, skin. Have them share their observations and note similarities and differences in the things observed. Discuss possible reasons for differences. Do the children think they observed everything? Could they be better observers?

Tell the class that over the next few days they will be learning how to be better observers.

TAKING THE SENSE WALKS
1. Divide the class into groups of four or five. Assign each group one sense to use. The teacher may wish to increase their focus by decreasing the acuity of the other receptors in this way: Give those who are to "see" cotton for their ears and gloves for their hands. Give those who are to "hear" blindfolds and gloves. Give those who are to "feel" cotton for their ears and blindfolds. Give those who are to "smell and taste" blindfolds, gloves, and cotton for their ears. (Be certain to caution against indiscriminate tasting!)
2. Sense walks should be continued at least until all children have used all receptors. Be imaginative about places to take the children. These should include a range of places, such as: the gym while a class is in session or during a game; the auditorium stage with lights both on and off; the basement and/or custodian's workroom; the nurse's office; another classroom; hallways; lunch room and/or kitchen while meals are being prepared and/or served; the school yard when children are present and when they are not; sidewalk in a business district and in a residential district; forest preserve or park at different times of the day and/or seasons of year.
3. It is probably best to have each child concentrate on using only *one* receptor for each Sense Walk and to take only one walk a day or, at least, to space them several hours apart. The rationale for this is that after each experience the child will be reflecting on what was seen or smelled or heard or felt and, as it were, experiencing it again. In such retrospection, the child will not only build up a storehouse of "sensory memories" but is likely to bring to a

conscious level things that he/she was not consciously aware of during the actual experience.

4. Each Sense Walk will be more effective if the children do not go into the area until they are ready to rely on only one receptor. It would be especially effective to include among these walks an area none of the children are familiar with, and in which they are restricted to the one receptor until they leave.

In subsequent discussion, ask the children where they think they were. Begin with the touching, smelling-tasting people; then the hearing; and only at the last, the seeing. Such an experience will increase the children's awareness of the strengths and limitations of each receptor and our dependence on our eyes.

Debriefing After Each Walk

After each Sense Walk, debrief in the following manner:

1. Develop a retrieval chart[8] that has the names of the places visited across the horizontal axis and the senses used down the vertical axis. Title the chart something like: *Our Senses Tell Us About Different Environments* or *Our Senses Tell Us About the World Around Us*.

    (The teacher can get extra mileage out of this strategy by using the term "environment." The total experience then becomes a concept development strategy also. The teacher waits until several Sense Walks have been completed and the chart has data on several different environments; an understanding of environment will be easily arrived at inductively. As the teacher writes the title on the chart, he or she should suggest that the members of the class think about what the term "environment" means as they fill out the chart. Ask the children *not* to suggest any definitions now, but to wait. They should be encouraged, however, to discuss the term with friends in the ensuing days.)

2. Before filling in the chart, give individual children time to reflect on what they experienced in the Walk. Give explicit directions such as: "Describe what you *saw* in ___, what you heard here." Children can either write their responses, tape record them, or just spend time thinking about them.

3. After the children have had time to reflect individually, form groups for each sense. Give the children time to share and compare experiences.

Move from group to group. As the occasions occur, point out that although each person in the group was using the same sense, everyone did not report *exactly* the same things about the place. Pose the question: "Why?" But do not explore it now. Suggest that the children attempt to find out reasons for these differences as they experience more Sense Walks.

4. When the groups are ready, help them put their data in the proper places on the chart.

5. When data for all senses are recorded, have each group share its experiences with the rest of the class. Spend some time exploring these points:
    A. Are there any discrepancies in the information? That is, do the "see" and "feel" people report conflicting observations? If so, why? If there are any discrepancies here, spend time discussing the sources and how we can resolve the issue. (We can go back and each use all of our senses. We can cross-check with other people using other modalities.)

B. What information was obtained by all senses?

C. What information was obtained by only one sense?

D. What things would we really need only one sense to get the correct information about? What things would we need more than one? Which senses?

Repeat the above procedures for each Sense Walk.

Debriefing After a Set of Walks

After visiting several different kinds of environments, use the data for the following discussion:

1. Compare the information gained by the senses. Do we seem to be able to get a fairly equal amount of information from each sense? Or does one sense seem to dominate? (Note the amount and completeness or complexity of information gathered by each sense.)

2. Encourage the children to share their reactions and feelings in the different Sense Walks. Did they feel more "comfortable" when they were using any one sense? Did they feel particularly uncertain or uncomfortable relying on any sense? Which? Why?

3. Compare the data on the different places. Are there some places where we wouldn't want to leave our noses at home? That is, where we need to smell to get important information? Are there some places in which our ears were especially helpful? Where? Why?

4. Review the group-sharing experiences (see 5 above). Ask once again: "Did everyone in each group always report the same thing?" (Most probably, no.) Choose a specific instance and focus on one sense; e.g., "Did all of you hear the same sounds? Did you all think what you heard was the same thing?"

5. Guide reflection on these experiences to get children to see:

    A. What our senses "pick up" depends on:

        (1) our location (people on one side of room heard rustling—those on other side did not)

        (2) our concentration or attention (some may have been distracted and missed hearing the rustling)

        (3) the information and experiences we have had

    B. What we *believe* we are hearing, seeing, touching, etc. depends on the information and experience we have had (people who have heard a sound before are better able to identify that sound . . . etc.).

Synthesizing Exercise

Take class on another Sense Walk.

1. This time tell the children to use all their senses. Explain that this time we are all going to try to "experience" all the environment. We are each going to try to get as much information as possible. Suggest that we know some ways to do this. (The children should be able to identify at least the first of these themselves.)

    A. We can concentrate. Think about what we are seeing, hearing. . . .

    B. We can move around in the environment—not just stand in one place.

    C. We can find out as much as possible about the place before we go.

(Suggest that "experienced" travelers study about a place before they go there.)

2. Tell the class where they will be going. Describe what is there and prod the children with questions such as: "What sounds will you probably hear? What smells? What will you feel?" (Focus on each sense in turn.) Take the walk.

3. *Debrief.* Allow children time to write down or to think about what they heard, saw, etc. Then develop a class retrieval chart like the larger one done earlier.

4. Encourage revelations of differences in perception, and attempt to trace sources where possible. Generally, the children should be made aware that although we may have generally the same experience, each of us experiences the world in a unique way. Our sense organs are unique to us, as is the knowledge and past experience we bring to a situation.

5. Compare this experience with the Opening Exercise. This time the children had prior information on *where* they would be going. They have been *practicing* using their senses.

Analysis of Intended Affective Outcomes in the Experiences

Use these questions to guide your own analysis:

What affective outcomes were the authors striving to achieve? Identify specific points in the experiences where these were being sought.

Sequencing Considerations

What kinds of experiences might follow these early experiences in direct observation?

(1) What kinds of experiences would the teacher design for children to follow the Sense Walks? (Have they had enough opportunities to evaluate the reliability of given senses to acquire specific information? E.g., is *that* salt or sugar? How can I tell?) Sketch a lesson plan that would be useful.

(2) If children learn to use their sense receptors effectively in the early elementary grades, they should be better prepared to apply these skills in rather sophisticated social research in high school. If the reader is a high school teacher, what kinds of social research experiences using direct observation would you design to build on this firm base? Generate a quick list of five or so sketchy ideas. For example, students can suggest and evaluate alternative ways to use direct observation to find out which parking lot gets the most use.

SUMMARY

One step toward effective decision making is the ability to obtain pertinent information skillfully. In this chapter we focused on considerations related to helping children acquire such ability. We identified several elements that should be taken into consideration in designing and implementing strategies to develop information-acquisition skills. Basically these elements can be reduced to what amount to two overarching concerns.

First, children should be given learning tasks at which they can succeed while becoming ever more competent. Once we were able to identify the basic and transferable operations involved in acquiring information from a given type of source, we were able to structure more effective learning experiences for children at differing developmental and ability levels. But children will become competent and skillful in acquiring information only if they are given repeated opportunities to practice these skills.

Second, since all learning has affective outcomes, strategies should be consciously designed to insure that desired affective outcomes are fostered while negative ones are not promoted. In this chapter we identified and defined some affective outcomes we are committed to promoting. We illustrated how some of these could be incorporated in lessons on skills development. Decisions as to what affective outcomes should be fostered in a given situation are not easy decisions. But the more conscious we are of the affective dimensions which are part of any learning experience, the less likely we are to stumble inadvertently into fostering children with warped and damaging perspectives of themselves and others.

The instructional strategies presented here should be regarded as only one of several parts of a systematic plan to help children develop skills in acquiring information. From an even broader perspective, these strategies should be regarded as only one of several parts of a systematic plan to help children become enlightened, self-confident, and socially responsible decision makers.

FOOTNOTES

[1]We have deliberately borrowed the term "operations" from Piaget. One of the more useful explanations of the term, for our purposes, comes from Jerome Bruner's *The Process of Education* (New York: Vintage Books, 1963), p. 35. Bruner defines an operation as a type of action that "can be carried out rather directly by the manipulation of objects, or internally, as when one manipulates the symbols that represent things and relations in one's mind. Roughly, an operation is a means of getting data about the real world into the mind and there transferring them so they can be organized and used selectively in the solution of problems."

[2]For an expanded discussion of the conditions that influence learning and ways to design instruction to maximize learning, see Robert M. Gagné, *Essentials of Learning for Instruction* (Hinsdale, Illinois: the Dryden Press, 1974).

[3]*Ibid.*

[4]James M. Oswald, June R. Chapin, Roger La Raus, *Planet Earth* (Boston: Houghton Mifflin Company, 1976), pp. 330–331. Adapted with permission of the publisher. Maps on pages 85 and 86 are reproduced with permission of the publisher.

[5]William A. Nesbitt and Andrea B. Karls, "World Military Interdependence," *Intercom* #78, Center for War/Peace Studies (June, 1975), pp. 11–13. Adapted with permission.

[6]Ruth Ledger Sivard, *World Military and Social Expenditures, 1974* (Leesburg, Virginia 22075: WMSE Publications, 1974). Used with permission.

[7]*Ibid.*

[8]The term "chart" is used in a variety of ways. *A Chart of My Progress in Spelling* might actually be a graph. The charts that list the "top forty" recordings are actually tables or data expressed in tabular form. Sometimes even diagrams or stylized maps are referred to as charts. We are using the term to mean the recorded arrangement of information in a windowpane form.

"If decision making is to be more than a laudable but remote goal, teachers and teacher educators must recognize that skills in reading are an integral part of the decision-making process."

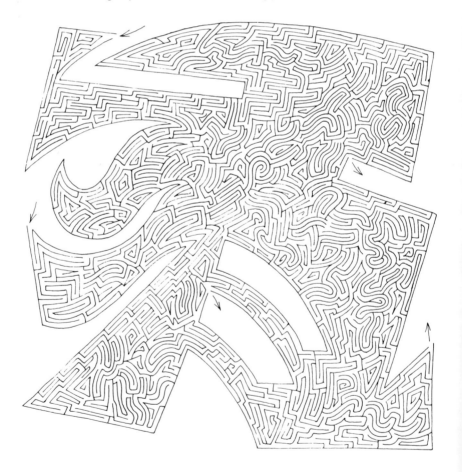

.4.

John P. Lunstrum

Reading
in the Social Studies

READING AS A PRIORITY IN THE SOCIAL STUDIES

For at least a decade, a rising tide of public concern has been forcing a reassessment of the teaching of reading in the public schools of America. More recently an increased emphasis on reading skills in content areas has been reflected in the trend to require more preparation in reading for those seeking certification to teach in secondary schools. In the last three years (1973–1976), one report shows an increase of over 100% in requirements in secondary reading established by state education authorities for either temporary or permanent certification.[1] Emphasis on content area reading skills seems to be based in part on the realization that the responsibility for developing reading proficiency cannot be delegated solely to the elementary language arts teacher, and that skill in reading and comprehending the content of various disciplines can be better taught by properly trained instructors in those fields. For the social studies, this realization is long overdue. Teachers in that field (both elementary and secondary) are not reluctant to express their frustrations with the inability of large numbers of their students to read even basic materials.

In the process of teaching and learning in the social studies, the development of competence in reading is clearly a compelling priority. The significant curricular reforms of the past decade have contributed to a new social studies with a more sophisticated conceptual structure and an emphasis on modes of inquiry, as distinguished from the more narrative or expository forms of the traditional social studies. Moreover, the infusion of new knowledge from anthropology, sociology, and other behavioral disciplines has enlarged substantially the technical vocabulary required to comprehend many of the new programs. A further challenge stems from the practice (a probable legacy of early Brunerian psychology) of introducing in lower grades concepts and methodologies formerly reserved for upper grade levels.

At the same time, the social studies must continue to struggle with a persistent problem: how to encourage students to make informed decisions in areas that affect their lives as citizens and private individuals. If decision making is to be more than a laudable but remote goal, teachers and teacher educators must recognize that skills in reading are an integral part of the decision-making process. Sound decisions in areas of social controversy, for example, clearly require an ability to locate and read objectively significant, alternative views or proposals, notwithstanding the fact that some views may clash with deeply cherished personal or community values. Other reading skills may play a vital role at various stages in decision making, including, for example, the ability to perceive the meaning of complex terms through the use of context and the capacity to draw valid inferences from what is read.

The task undertaken in this chapter is to present a succinct and candid appraisal of the problems which have adversely affected the reading performance of elementary and secondary students in the social studies, and to describe strategies and resources which may be used to improve reading skills. No assumption is made that this can be accomplished by adding new content to an already crowded curriculum. Instead, a proposal will be made to utilize procedures and materials which can be integrated with the teaching and learning of the content of social studies courses. Before consideration is given to the development and use of materials in the classroom, it seems appropriate first to note briefly certain conditions which have contributed to the present problem in reading in the social studies.

CONDITIONS AFFECTING THE STATUS OF READING
IN THE SOCIAL STUDIES

Reflecting the current apprehension, two social studies educators, Chapin and Gross,[2] have concluded on the basis of the testimony of the late James E. Allen, former U.S. Commissioner of Education, that there is a "crisis in reading in the social studies." Studies in three states appear to support this view.[3] In fact, one reading researcher has declared that 25% of the high school population lacks the reading skill required to read materials with the comprehension expected of them.[4] On the other hand, after an examination of standardized test data over several decades, other investigators[5] reported they could find no evidence of deterioration in reading achievement up to 1965, and they reported only a slight decline after that date. (However, the investigators describe their findings as tentative in view of the difficulties encountered in developing a firm data base.)

While there is disagreement concerning the thesis of widespread decline in reading,[6] there still appears to be sufficient reason to warrant concern about the state of reading performance in the social studies.[7] This is underscored in a recent study in a representative school system in which the researcher found that one fifth of the pupils (grades 4–6) failed to comprehend their social studies texts, which were at or below grade level in terms of readability.[8] (It should also be noted that the school system had been embarked on a reading improvement program for two years.)

Inadequate Attention to Reading/Study Skills

It appears that social studies teachers and most content teachers have not demonstrated much knowledge about the reading process. Nor have they been actively engaged, as various studies have indicated, in assisting students with reading problems. This is not to suggest that teachers are deliberately negligent; in fact, until recently few secondary teachers received any training in reading. In the long run, the trend to increase certification in reading requirements may have a favorable impact; but for the foreseeable future, any improvement will be largely dependent upon the willingness of teachers to engage in inservice programs or to undertake their own independent study programs.

In the meantime, students continue to pay the price for the lack of preparation of their teachers in reading. A case in point is the seeming inability of some teachers to grasp the significance of readability. In one study (which included a sample of social studies teachers) over 80% said they "almost always" or "most of the time" knew the reading levels of the texts being used.[9] When queried later on how they derived this information, they indicated dependence on a source by no means disinterested or altogether reliable—the publishers. In another study[10] of disabled readers (3rd–5th grades) who were judged to have the potential to improve reading performance, it was found that their social studies and English teachers were assigning them texts to read which were at their frustration levels in terms of readability. In the words of the researchers this was simply an "indefensible practice."[11] (And one might add it is a practice which could have been avoided if the teachers had acquired some insight into the procedures for the assessment of readability.)

Those involved in both the pre-service and in-service preparation of social studies teachers cannot escape responsibility for the present problem. Even a cursory examination of the widely used methods texts will reveal little constructive treatment of the topic of reading skills. (As one social studies educator remarked to this writer in a spirit of candor, "lacking any knowledge of reading, what we tend to do is to try to show our students how to teach social studies concepts without reading printed materials.") Regrettably, it must be conceded, as one recognized scholar in reading in content areas puts it, "The paucity of research on methods of teaching reading as an integral part of the teaching of the social studies is almost appalling."[12]

Readability Levels of Social Studies Texts and Materials

The evidence has been unmistakable for at least a decade that the readability levels of elementary social studies texts have been unrealistically high. Herman[13] reviewed the evidence in 1969 and concluded that the publishers were largely indifferent to the problem. In 1973, after an analysis of some sixty-eight social studies texts, Johnson and Vardian[14] found that the tendency still persisted to publish texts at readability levels above grade levels. In addition, as Dohrman[15] discovered, encyclopedias (on which teachers and students depend for reference aids) are also likely to contain a substantial number of topics written on a level above the intended grade level.

Secondary social studies texts and materials have not escaped the problem of unrealistic readability levels. One study by Janz and Smith[16] compared the readability levels of social studies (established through the Flesch formula) with the reading ability of a sample of 590 students in grades 8–10. Their findings revealed: (1) all social studies texts ranged from readability levels of grade nine through college, (2) for the eighth grade the texts were too difficult for more than 60% of the students, (3) for the ninth grade the texts were too difficult for more than 75% of the students, and (4) for the tenth grade the texts were too difficult for from 36% to 93% of the students. Hash's study[17] (although preliminary in nature) raises some questions about readability of new social studies materials, particularly with reference to the wide range of readability within a given set of materials or a text—a condition which some reading specialists view as more critical than high levels of readability.

Some publishers have recently begun to report on the assessment of readability and the revision of materials according to certain formulas (e.g., Dale-Chall, Fry graph, etc.). While this is an encouraging development, some cautionary notes are in order with reference to the uses and limitations of readability formulas. Application of formulas, which utilize two variables of word length and sentence length, may be useful in obtaining estimates or predictions of levels of difficulty of printed materials. However, the formulas are not sensitive to concept load or idea complexity; hence, they cannot be used alone as guidelines for preparing or revising instructional materials.

Still another problem plagues the reader of social studies texts. There is a tendency for social studies texts to present concepts in a cursory manner. "The reader," one investigator[18] reports, "is not provided with sufficient information and in many cases he is required to infer definitions." Another investigator, Martorella,[19] believes that some authors of social studies materials tend to employ a narrative style including extraneous material which diverts the reader from the task of attaining the given concept. Still the problem is not insurmountable; it is possible for a teacher to improve comprehension significantly by restructuring social studies materials (according to a concept attainment strategy, as Peters[20] has shown in a recent experiment).

Limitations on the Performance
of Culturally and Linguistically Different Students

Much concern has been expressed regarding the conditions which limit the performance of some culturally and linguistically different students on standardized tests of verbal skills. Some linguists have advanced a thesis of dialectical interference with the development of reading skill, but more recently this view has not been supported by research.[21] This persistent problem bears directly on reading performance in the social studies, since that field has been vulnerable in the past to charges of neglecting the role of minorities in portraying the nature of human history and culture. It follows, therefore, that a good case can be made that until the recent appearance of ethnic studies materials, there has been little content in the social studies to address the concerns and needs of culturally different students. Accordingly, it is logical to assume that it is difficult for these students to establish a purpose in reading materials which deal with a society which seems alien or remote.

Admittedly, this view or explanation of lack of motivation of some minority children to read the content of the social studies is not grounded on hard empirical evidence. Still, it merits serious attention since there is substantial evidence that affective conditions or factors can influence the reading process. For example, the self-concept of pupils, the teacher's expectation of student performance, and the attitude of pupils toward the content have all been linked in research literature to variations in reading performance.[22] Some specialists in psycholinguistic research believe that negative attitudes of some teachers toward children's use of a non-standard dialect may adversely affect the development of reading skill.[23] Summing up the research in this basic area, Ruddell concluded, "the affective development of students thus deserves careful consideration in reading-language instruction."[24]

PSYCHOLINGUISTIC ORIENTATION

The position taken in this chapter will be to present examples of varied reading strategies and resources applicable to the social studies. Still this should not be construed as simply a non-theoretical, grab-bag approach of developing reading skills in the social studies. Proposals, suggested applications, and techniques and strategies will be grounded on a sound psycholinguistic orientation. Based on recent research of both cognitive psychologists and linguists, this field offers a perspective on reading which is consistent with many assumptions about the nature of the learner and the role of the teacher implicit in the new social studies. What is meant by a psycholinguistic orientation in this chapter can be summarized in the following principles:

(1) Reading is viewed as "an active process in reconstructing language represented by graphic symbols."[25] It is not a passive act of simply assimilating the words on a printed page; it involves interaction between the thoughts of the reader and the author.
(2) Effective reading is dependent upon the legitimation of risk-taking in predicting and testing meanings.[26] Essentially the pursuit of inquiry into basic issues and the clarification and testing of values flow logically from this proposition.
(3) Three language systems interact in reading materials, including: (a) graphophonic (patterns of letters and sounds), (b) syntactic (grammatical relationships), and (c) semantic (relationship of words and phrases to objects and ideas).[27] Efficient language processing, however, is more significantly related to the application of semantic and syntactic skills.[28] Moreover, all of the language systems are influenced by the reader's experiential background (including motivation, attitude, and other affective conditions), conceptual ability, and language facility.

The following section addresses the question: "What are the basic reading skills in the social studies?" It contains descriptions of categories of skills and brief commentaries on their application to social studies instruction. This is then followed by a third section (Diagnostic and Instructional Strategies), which explains how elementary and secondary teachers of social studies can assess both strengths and weaknesses in skills through individual and group procedures. Instructional and remedial measures appropriate to the development or strengthening of these skills in the social studies are then presented.

READING SKILLS ESSENTIAL
FOR LEARNING IN THE SOCIAL STUDIES

Until recently it was generally assumed that reading skills could be assigned to two major categories: (a) those considered generic—common to all disciplines and fields, and (b) those viewed as unique to a given field of study. Thus, writers proceeded to compile lists of reading skills considered unique to mathematics, science, social studies, etc. Unfortunately, upon closer scrutiny it appears that virtually all of these so-called unique skills (e.g., "comparison and contrast," "distinguishing between fact and opinion," etc.) can apply equally well to most fields. Uniqueness then does not seem to reside in the skills themselves, but in their adaptation to the particular needs of each discipline. Concluded Herber,[29] after weighing the evidence, "current thinking related to comprehension and research into its application in content classes suggests that emphasis on broader process rather than specific skills is more profitable."

While an examination of a sample of current literature treating reading in the social studies indicates that some authors are still prone to associate skills with specific disciplines, the emphasis in this chapter is on the development of broad process or skill categories. These categories are derived from an analysis of the skills most frequently linked to the social studies by recognized specialists in the field. The categories seem to be logically related to and sufficiently inclusive of most of the specific reading skills proposed as requisite to effective learning in the social studies.

Reading Readiness

This term has at least two distinct meanings. In the primary grades it refers to the level of maturation required before the child can begin to read effectively (e.g., left to right orientation, visual acuity, etc.). Ordinarily, except for instruction in social studies in the primary grades and in the case of some severely disabled readers in advanced grades, this meaning is not particularly relevant to the concerns of this chapter. In yet another sense, the broad process of reading readiness is associated with the principle that *effective reading is purposeful reading* which is influenced by: (1) experiential background of pupils—interests, attitudes, socio-cultural milieu, etc., (2) affective conditions—attitudes, self concept, and (3) general language facility.

Interest in and attitude toward content are related to achievement in the social studies, as the evidence suggests. Yet all too often in the past the studies of pupil attitudes toward school subjects have disclosed a notable lack of enthusiasm for the social studies. This points to a need for the teacher of social studies to be sensitive to the affective influences on reading. Some researchers[30] believe that personality traits and value structures may account for the role of what they term "affective mobilizers" (or the "initial kick," in simpler parlance) in providing a stimulus toward effective reading performance. Also, other researchers[31] report that the use of value clarifying strategies has had a significant effect on self-concept and reading achievement.

Vocabulary Building and Concept Learning

It should come as no great surprise that vocabulary development, particularly the acquisition of a specialized vocabulary, has been recognized for some time as a basic reading skill or process in the teaching of the social studies. However, the infusion of new social science content into the traditional social studies has done little to alleviate the problem. The specialized vocabulary of the social studies now seems to include four basic categories:

(1) Common words such as "wing," "class," "power," which take on unique or special meaning according to context.
(2) Names of places and names of (or titles assigned to) historical personages remote from the pupil's experiences. Examples here include: "Pharaoh," "tsar," "Hwang Ho," "almami," and "Habib Bourguiba." Notwithstanding the usually ineffective efforts of authors to provide pronunciation guides, words in these categories pose serious problems in phonic analysis; many of the familiar rules do not apply. Some authors even choose to disrupt the continuity of a passage by placing a phonetic spelling after these words.
(3) Terms assigned to abstract social science concepts. Terms that come to mind here are: "ethnocentrism," "political socialization," and "gross national product." However, concepts that are "conjunctive"—i.e., defined by the joint presence of several attributes, such as "social class"—are easier to learn than "disjunctive" concepts, where such cues are not available.[32]

(4) Figurative expressions—terms which require an understanding of the connotations of words. Here one may point to such examples as "fertile crescent," "iron curtain," "paper tiger," "straw man," "dark horse candidate," "waving the bloody flag," and "twisting the lion's tail."

While the emphasis has been placed on problems associated with a technical or specialized vocabulary peculiar to the social studies, the pupil's general vocabulary development cannot be neglected. (By "general vocabulary," reference is made to the store of words associated with daily activities or routine.) Hopefully, as pupils mature, their vocabularies reflect greater breadth of word knowledge and depth of meaning. As Simmons[33] puts it, "Teachers in all content areas, through direction of both written and oral activities, must help students become more at ease with the word stock of serious adult discourse."

Comprehension

Comprehension refers to the complex process of obtaining meaning from printed or spoken language. It is a broad term which includes specific processes for deriving meaning and identifying levels of meanings. With reference to levels of comprehension, there seems to be a tendency to make a distinction on the basis of logical analysis between literal comprehension (or simple recall of what is explicitly stated) and inferential or interpretive levels which reflect what some call "reading between the lines." On the other hand, one must concede that research[34] to date has not provided much support in the clear delineation of subskills. Even though the existence of clearly distinguishable levels and subskills of comprehension is not presently supported by a firm data base, there is still value in providing opportunities for pupils to respond to different types of comprehension questions. "When this is done," observe two authorities,[35] "students can improve their ability to reason while reading many kinds of materials with a variety of specific purposes."

Notwithstanding the present unresolved questions, a case can be made for a logical analysis of comprehension in the interest of instruction. Such an analytical scheme is essential in (1) determining what are essential reading (comprehension) behaviors in achieving the objectives of a particular course, (2) developing an appropriate oral and silent pupil response sampling system (techniques for diagnosis or assessment), and (3) developing and applying strategies to improve comprehension. For social studies teachers, a valuable logical analysis may be found in Thomas Barrett's "Taxonomy of the Cognitive and Affective Dimensions of Reading Comprehension."[36]

In an unpublished paper, Barrett proposed a classification system characterized by five major levels: (1) Literal Comprehension, (2) Reorganization, (3) Inferential Comprehension, (4) Evaluation, and (5) Appreciation. The summary which follows suggests by brief comments, examples of questions, or exercises how the taxonomy is applicable to the assessment and improvement of comprehension in the social studies.

1. *Literal Reading Comprehension.* Literal comprehension emphasizes "ideas or information which are explicitly stated in the selection."[37] It involves the recall or recognition of a single fact, series of facts, or main idea. Typically, this type of comprehension is stressed in the teacher's question: "Will you list the major events which led up to the American Revolution?"

2. *Reorganization.* This stage involves the synthesis or organization of main ideas *explicitly* stated in a selection. This is usually exemplified by the directions: "Summarize what is said in your book about the myths of the Netselik Eskimo."

3. *Inferential Comprehension.* At this level the student demonstrates his ability to synthesize the literal content, using his intuition, personal knowledge, and imagination as a basis for conjectures or hypotheses. To facilitate the development of this level of comprehension, the student might be directed in an exercise to study selected folktales of the Hausa of West Africa and infer what values they stressed.

4. *Evaluation.* On this level the student is encouraged to engage in critical reading; i.e., to make judgments concerning what has been read with reference to accuracy, worth, truthfulness, and quality. Judgments may be grounded on criteria provided by the teacher, expert authories, or the assumptions of students. Usually provided here are exercises which direct the student to appraise advertisements or political speeches, with particular attention to the presence of propaganda devices. More recent schema for assessing the effort to manipulate human behavior by language (for example, "Public Doublespeak") focus on the processes of intensification and downplaying of rhetoric.[38]

5. *Appreciation.* This final level calls for a student to "react in an emotional and aesthetic way to a work and to judge its worth as well as its psychological and aesthetic elements."[39] Such skills as "emotional response to content" and "identification with characters and incidents" have not typically been seen as relevant to social studies. However, with the emergence of values education and increasing emphasis on affective development of children, it seems highly appropriate to sensitize pupils to the power of words to create images and arouse deep feelings. As an example of one approach, a reading of the

Diary of Anne Frank might be legitimately followed by an examination of the emotions aroused.

Study Skills

Reading skills traditionally have been closely related to study skills in the literature. This is not to assert that there can be no study without reading, but there seems little doubt that effective reading performance in the new social studies requires the application of a wide range of investigative and reference skills in the use of varied printed media. A representative sampling of study skills applicable to the social studies would include:

1. *Dictionary skills.* A sense of alphabetical order is a prerequisite to effective dictionary use by younger children and is also an important tool in general and specialized vocabulary building in terms of selecting the correct word according to context.

2. *Library Skills.* This familiar category of skills is frequently applauded but often overlooked by teachers. It refers to the knowledge and use of the card catalog, the library arrangement system, and the *Readers' Guide to Periodical Literature*. In addition, the transition of some school libraries to media centers emphasizes the application of locational and related skills involved in use of microfilm and microfiche.

3. *Textbook Utilization.* Textbooks still have a major responsibility for transmitting the content of the new social studies, and all too often students make inefficient use of the aids provided by texts. Some of the specific skills associated with this topic include use of the table of contents, glossary, index, graphic aids, etc. Related to this category are other familiar skills, including the organization and presentation of information (note-taking, outlining, etc.) and following directions.

Rate of Reading

One characteristic of the poor reader is a relatively slow speed for all types of materials. Clinical experience indicates that one particular pattern of reading which impairs comprehension and adversely affects motivation is a labored "word by word" style in which the reader focuses on each word as an independent unit. This results in a neglect of context and a loss of continuity. Since some studies[40] have pointed to a wide range of readability levels within social studies texts, it is important that pupils learn to adapt their reading rates to their purposes and type of material. Reading specialists refer to this skill as "reading flexibility." The following outline identifies various reading rates in descriptive terms and suggests how the principle of flexibility may be applied to the reading of social studies content.

Rate of Reading	Purpose	Material
1. Intensive (very slow and precise)	analytical and synthesizing	demographic data: *Statistical Abstract of United States*
2. Average	reading assigned material at instructional level	descriptive accounts in regional geography
3. Casual (unhurried)	reading for pleasure and enrichment.	the novel, *Johnny Tremaine*, American Revolution
4. Selective Reading: Skimming (fast)	swift coverage to obtain gist of page.	overview of next chapter in text or front page news
5. Selective Reading: Scanning (fast)	rapid search for particular topic, name or occurrence	looking in *Reader's Guide* for articles on Watergate

The rates indicated in the preceding outline are not intended to indicate precise lines of demarcation but to suggest a range of variations. No standards or norms for speed of reading expressed in words per minute (wpm) are provided since they can be misleading; rates will vary widely according to the content used and the comprehension checks employed. However, Harris and Sipay[41] offer, as a "rough estimate," the rate of 250 words per minute for high school students, reading material of average difficulty (level two in the outline). As another rough gauge, these authors[42] have presented median rates (wpm) for reading for varying grade levels as established by selected standardized tests. Ranges of medians from lowest to highest tests in words per minute may be summarized as follow:

Grade	Median Range	Lowest	Middle	Highest
IV	120–170	120	155	170
VI	171–230	171	206	230
VIII	188–267	188	237	267
IX	199–260	199	252	260

In dealing with the topic of rate of reading, a note of caution is in order. Increasing rate or speed of reading is not a blanket remedy to be employed whenever a student appears to be reading social studies material too slowly. A slow rate may be a symptom of a number of basic skill deficiencies (e.g., vocabulary, concept formation, etc.) which require corrective measures before speed of reading is accelerated. However, slowness in word recognition may also be a contributing factor, and speed may be increased by direct practice in viewing words exposed briefly.

DIAGNOSTIC AND INSTRUCTIONAL STRATEGIES

The purpose of this section is to describe and illustrate those strategies, techniques, and resources which may be used to ascertain strengths and weaknesses with reference to certain dimensions of the reading process applicable to social studies instruction. Following the discussion of assessment or diagnostic procedures, instructional strategies appropriate to the problem will be treated. The breadth of this approach regrettably precludes much treatment in depth of issues or the inclusion of detailed sample exercises, outlines, etc. However, references will be made to useful resources or publications which include exemplary materials or offer detailed directions to teachers on how to prepare and use instructional aids.

Assessing Reading Readiness—Pupil Interests, Attitudes and Preferences

In dealing with the problem of motivation, there is no substitute for firsthand knowledge about students' interests, attitudes, and aspirations obtained from informal observation and personal interaction. At the same time, valuable and essential insights can be derived from interest inventories, structured interviews, attitude scales, questionnaires, and circulation records of school libraries. Typical of the kinds of questions contained in interest inventories are: "Do you read a newspaper regularly? If so, what sections do you read? (Please indicate news stories, sports page, editorials, etc.)" Other questions may be asked about preferences for school subjects, television programs, hobbies, etc. Some writers advocate the use of a projective technique involving the use of incomplete sentences, illustrated as follows: "When I read history, (or geography, government) I _____." "If I could read what I want, I would _____." These instruments (most of which can be administered on an individual or group basis) are designed to provide the teacher with information to be used in individualizing assignments, suggesting possible book reports, or planning projects appropriate to the interests of the pupil which will also be relevant to the instructional program. The information may also be used to effect *flexible* grouping of students, according to interests or needs, to carry on a project, or present a role-playing situation. Since the incomplete sentences technique may disclose symptoms of serious emotional problems, the social studies teacher is probably well advised to use this technique carefully, avoiding any embarrassment to the student. However, the teacher should be prepared to make referrals to a counselor if he or she does not feel competent to deal with the problem.

For further exploration of this area and examples of interest inventories and incomplete sentences tests at various grade levels, reference may be made to Wilma Miller's *Reading Diagnosis Kit*.[43] (Miller has given permission for sample forms to be duplicated and used by teachers, or the forms may be adapted to content areas and reproduced.) In addition, Estes[44] has made available for use by teachers an interesting reading attitude scale which is designed to measure objectively how pupils feel about reading. (It can also be used on a pre- and posttest basis.)

Structured interviews are very useful diagnostic tools which can be used by both elementary and secondary teachers. They are probably little used on the mistaken assumption that they are too time-consuming; however, interviews can be held after school or while other pupils are in the library, working on assignments, or at Learning Centers. They are particularly recommended in the cases of poor readers who are consistently unresponsive and withdrawn in class.

To point up the uses of the structured interview, excerpts are reproduced below of an actual interview conducted with a tenth-grade social studies student who will be assigned the fictitious name of "Tim Enfield." Tim, the social studies teacher learned from colleagues, had a long history of reading and discipline problems. Little was expected from Tim by most teachers, although a few thought he had potential. He had asked in his social studies class to have his chair moved away from the other students. He was a tenth grader, but his reading level had been estimated as grade two; his previous efforts to read aloud a passage of material at the fifth-grade level had been disastrous, characterized by frequent omissions, substitutions, and distortions.

Teacher: One of the things I wanted to ask you about in terms of your reading problem is how you managed to obtain all this information about guns. You probably didn't get it through a lot of reading?

Tim: No.

Teacher: Did you talk to a lot of people about it?

Tim: Yeah, I talked to a lot of people and jes' herded it up . . . picked it up here and there and that's the way I got it.

Teacher: Would you tell me, what are some of the guns that you have in your collection?

Tim: I got Brownings, Remingtons, Mossburgs, Winchesters, Colts and a Kentucky muzzle loader pistol, and, uh, a little Russian-made Derringer . . . both with black powder.

Teacher: You told me earlier you were interested in the uses of black powder and you were talking about the Kentucky rifle. You mentioned that in addition to the Kentucky rifle there was another rifle used on the Frontier . . .

Tim: Yeah, the Hawkins.

Teacher: The Hawkins? O.K. And what was the difference between the musket and these Frontier rifles?

Tim: Well, the Hawkins had a heavy barrel on it. Really, what that was good for was the Mountain Men . . . always kept getting knocked off their horses by trees 'n stuff and the stocks kept breaking off or they'd break a barrel or somethin'. And they had to have a gun heavy enough and sturdy enough to go out and knock down some of this North American Big Game like Grizzly and Moose 'n stuff. And the little forty-five caliber Kentucky flintlock wasn't heavy enough. And it was too long to nav . . . navigate through brush and that undergrowth so they had to have a gun heavy enough and short enough to get the job done.

Teacher: O.K. Very interesting.

Teacher: Let's come back to your reading for a minute. What do you do when you come to words you don't know?

Tim: Try to figger it out, but mostly ask somebody.

Teacher: O.K., Tim, what do you think reading is?

Tim: Hunh? Well, I guess jes' readin' words.

The preceding interview contained several surprises for his teacher. First, Tim's speaking vocabulary was more extensive than his reading vocabulary. His use of the words, "navigate," "Derringer," "undergrowth," etc., underscores a verbal facility not previously observed in class. Secondly, a surprising factor was the depth of his knowledge about firearms acquired through listening skill (later verified by a listening comprehension test which placed him at grade eleven).

Questions similar to those relating to Tim's perception of reading are helpful in structured interviews, since research[45] has disclosed a relationship between pupil perceptions of reading and reading success. Far too many poor readers such as Tim have seemingly learned in school to view reading as simply a word recognition (or word calling) process.[46] Later in the interview other questions threw light on Tim's language-processing skill. He was asked what he did when he came to a word he didn't know, and he replied that most of the time he would ask somebody; clearly he did not know how to use context to obtain meanings. This was further confirmed by his response to the question, "Do you look at every word when you read?" Tim replied, "Yes." (This question has reference to an "average rate of reading"—not an intensive, precise speed.) When asked about his reading, Tim said despondently, "I got to more or less struggle. Most of my teachers think I'm dumb." He traced his problems in reading back to second grade when, in Tim's words, "the teacher kept drillin' on all those rules about what sounds those letters make."

Tim's case reflects the classic problem of negative self-concept in reading. He had consistently experienced failure in reading; most teachers expected him to fail; and, finally, his basic reading strategies were inefficient. The implications for his teacher were to find opportunities for Tim to use his interests and strengths to experience success. Specifically (with some help from a reading specialist), his teacher developed the following activities with Tim:

a. Tim began to use his skill in drawing to create cartoons of historical events or persons and to provide captions for those cartoons, which were then displayed in class.
b. A modified "language experience" activity was created in which Tim dictated his interpretation of one of the historical cartoons. The interpretation was transcribed and presented to Tim in typewritten form as a reading activity. (This approach is treated in more detail in the topic on vocabulary.)
c. Arrangements were made for a volunteer tutor to assist Tim with improvement of basic reading skills (e.g., expanding his sight vocabulary, learning to use semantic and structural cues in reading, etc.). The content chosen initially was on firearms and their relationship with history (based on Tim's interests).

Improving Reading Readiness (Motivation) in the Classroom

In addition to the motivational aids described briefly, and with specific reference to the preceding case study, there are other varied strategies and resources which can be used to develop a social studies classroom climate more supportive of reading. For the purposes of this discussion these are treated under two broad categories: (a) instructional strategies and techniques, and (b) resources or activities having intrinsic interest or broad appeal.

Among the instructional strategies which may have motivational impact are inquiry into controversial issues, value clarification, and the building of interpersonal communication skills. Shaver[47] has stressed the role of controversy in demonstrating the relevance of the reading task. A bored, apathetic student can often be aroused when confronted with data contradicting his own cherished (and usually unexamined) beliefs. Needless to say, the emphasis is on a disciplined, constructive approach to the examination of controversy, reflected, for example, in the case studies and issues contained in *American Political Behavior* by Howard Mehlinger and John Patrick.[48] For students with severe reading handicaps it might be well to introduce visual evidence in the form of still photos or cartoons symbolizing conflict. (Photo-study card discussion kits on controversial topics, based on the work of Kohlberg and Simon, are available from Greenhaven Press.[49])

As noted earlier, value clarification procedures have been linked to the improvement of self-concept and reading comprehension according to recent studies. Value clarifying activities particularly useful in the elementary school have been developed by Simon and his associates.[50] Some examples include the "Coat of Arms" exercise, "Baker's Dozen," and "Alligator River" (the "G" rated version). Related to value clarification procedures are interpersonal communication skill-building activities[51] such as "Listening Triads" (to develop skill in active listening and note barriers to effective listening), and "Brainstorming" (suspending criticism in order to create a large number of possible solutions to a problem).

Supportive of this thrust is Moffet,[52] who believes that language use in a broad sense contributes to reading comprehension; he explains, "The only way to provide students with enough language experience and feedback is to develop small group interaction into a sensitive learning method."

Activities and resources which draw on a wide range of interests include music, art, the mass media, and tradebooks. The possible applications or contributions of resources in these fields are summarized briefly in the following paragraphs.

Music has been found effective in the early elementary years in developing an oral vocabulary and in providing experience with a common phrase structure and syntax pattern. In upper elementary grades and in junior high school, folksongs with historical settings or themes have been used to generate interest. Ritt[53] has provided a description of the application of folksongs to the development of reading skills at these grade levels. In the high school, teachers have used popular music in social studies to stimulate discussion and reading about contemporary problems.

Art and art-related activities have also been applied to the improvement of motivation to read in the social studies. Massialas and Zevin[54] have used visual evidence in the form of slides of paintings and other art objects to encourage students to hypothesize about differing conceptions of warfare and to contrast two societies (Britain and China). Creating color/line representations of concepts is recommended by Simon, Hawley, and Britton,[55] who feel that the selection of colors and manipulation of materials "may deepen one's self-understanding as well as one's understanding of the concept." After providing explanations on how to create color/line representations, these authors propose an exercise in which students depict "Mother," "Love," "Sex," and "War." More appropriate to lower grades, however, may be the depiction of "Ideal Home"; but teachers may choose to portray other words or concepts appropriate to the content of their courses.

With reference to the use of mass media, Berryman[56] has reported that systematic use of newspapers (a popular source of information on numerous topics) has produced gains in reading skill in upper elementary and secondary grades. Berryman has developed modules[57] (published by the Atlanta, Georgia, *Journal-Constitution*) which provide the social studies teachers with options ranging from the analysis of comic strips (values, system of classification, etc.) to critical assessment of editorials. From another perspective on the uses of media, several writers contend that student film-making activities contribute to both motivation and reading. However, since many schools lack the resources to engage students in the production of their own documentaries, they might consider the use of the "write-on" blank 35 millimeter filmstrips and slides which allow pupils from elementary through high school to create their own audiovisual productions and to augment them with sound effects or with musical background on audio tape if they choose.

For some students, trade books, biography, and historical fiction can translate what is dull, sterile, and factual into compelling, lively accounts of human drama and courage. A versatile writer, Stephen Meader, for example, has written interesting junior novels which span two centuries of American history. Laura Ingalls Wilder is another author whose books are noted for realism. One of them has provided the background for a popular television series. Another rich resource is science fiction, with its vivid portrayals of future worlds. Ray Bradbury's *Fahrenheit 451*, about a society which has banned all books, is a compelling, provocative interpretation that will raise questions about the expansion of governmental controls. Finally, a useful source of information for the teacher who wishes to interest the "reluctant," handicapped reader in fiction and biography is George Spache's *Good Reading for the Disadvantaged Reader*.[58]

Assessing Vocabulary and Concept Learning

An assessment of a student's general vocabulary can be obtained from standardized tests. While such test data may be useful to a social studies teacher for broad screening purposes (assuming the tests meet basic criteria of validity, reliability, and representative norms), it is still important to appraise pupil knowledge of the specialized social studies vocabulary and ability to employ certain skills essential in expanding word meanings and facilitating word recognition, particularly through the use of context aids.

One way of assessing level of vocabulary in the social studies is to employ a sight word test to be administered on an individual basis or adapted to group administration. Proponents of this technique recommend that the sight words for a given test (numbering at least 25) be selected randomly from glossaries of graded social studies texts. The student is required to "recognize" words in the sense of correctly pronouncing them. According to one set of criteria,[59] instructional reading level may be defined as 90% accuracy; hence a student who misses more than 10% of the words in a list for given grade level would be assumed deficient in essential specialized vocabulary. Following are examples from two lists prepared for the social studies at different grade levels by two different authors.[60]

Fifth Grade Sight Words (Miller)		*Secondary School Words* (Aukerman)	
abolitionist	climate	monarchy	technological
cultural pluralism	strike	diplomacy	postglacial
pollution	technology	colonization	fertile

There are certain limitations in the utilization of sight word tests (as suggested in a close scrutiny of the examples from both lists). First, one must assume that the author of the "graded" lists did in fact adjust his writing style and his choice of words to the appropriate grade level. (All too often, as previously noted, this has not been the case.) Secondly, the student using the lists must identify the words only by sounding them correctly, and it is quite likely that some students skilled in phonic analysis may pronounce the word correctly but have no idea of its meaning. Conversely, a student may know the meaning of the word but be unable to reproduce the correct sounds. Still, a sight word list can be useful in obtaining a quick, tentative gauge of specialized vocabulary, provided further data are sought. Also the graded word list can be converted into a group vocabulary survey instrument through the construction of a matching exercise.

Informal inventories of context clue usage in social studies materials can be developed by teachers. Usually a key word is deleted and the student must draw upon both grammatical and semantic clues to find the correct word or synonym. In the examples which follow (using a procedure called "cloze"*), pupils are asked to predict the meaning of the missing word. All that is required is a reasonable substitute which does not change the author's meaning and is grammatically correct.

"New people live in this neighborhood now. There are new stores and tall office _____." (third grade[61])

"In the Mayflower Compact the Pilgrims agreed to be _____ by law." (ninth grade[62])

Other versions of context clue inventories use a multiple-choice format (i.e., providing alternative responses from which to choose). There are no firm, agreed-upon criteria for assessing the results of such inventories. Yet it would appear reasonable to assume that a student consistently unable to complete at least 50% of the blanks (or select 75% of the answers in a multiple-choice format) is deficient in the use of context.

A brief explanation is in order concerning context clues. Various schema have been proposed to classify such clues.[63] However, most clues appear to fall into three main categories: (1) meaning-bearing clues (drawing on the "sense of the sentence," synonyms, etc.), (2) language-bearing clues (structural or grammatical elements), and (3) organization clues (relationship of main idea, etc.).[64] Following are examples of different types of context clues applied to social studies content. The word underlined is assumed to be the unfamiliar word, the meaning of which may be obtained from a careful scrutiny of available clues.

Synonym Clue: The homesteader, or settler, paid only $10.00 for all this land.

Definition or description: The Congressman's conduct was inexplicable. No one could tell why he was late.

Main idea and supporting details: Slowly the first glacier built itself up from billions of tons of Canadian snow. The snow became packed into heavy ice by its great weight.

Informal inventories may also be devised if teachers wish to assess the students' ability to use structural analysis. This term refers to the use of

---

*This term is derived from the concept of "closure" and is used here for instructional purposes; it has also been used extensively for another purpose—the assessment of the ability of students to comprehend a given set of materials (as noted later).

parts of words to ascertain meaning and pronunciation of unfamiliar terms. This form of analysis usually draws on the uses of prefixes, roots, suffixes, and syllabication. Normally, social studies teachers lack both the time and the knowledge for any intensive work in this area. However, for those who are interested, Miller[65] provides clear, helpful explanations on how these skills can be assessed and taught.

A basic element in concept formation is the ability to categorize words according to some meaningful relationships. In assessing this skill among elementary children, one may ask them to study a series of slides or photographs carefully and to enumerate or list what they see. The listing on the board of various objects may be followed by the question, "What connection do you see between any of these words?" As children point out relationships, they are asked why the words are related, and then finally what terms they would give to the clusters or groups of words they perceived as connected. This approach is based on Taba's concept learning strategy.[66]

Improving Vocabulary Development and Concept Learning

Before assignments are made to students, teachers should take time to identify technical terms or abstract terms likely to cause difficulty and to provide clarification of these words. Students need to be encouraged to use the glossary, and exercises should be developed to facilitate that use. Instructional media, including overhead projector and filmstrip projector, should be used to illuminate new ideas or words. (Some schools have even set objectives for teachers in content areas to introduce a given number of new words each week.) These techniques are generally well-known, even though they are not regularly applied by some teachers who are unaware of the heavy vocabulary and concept load of their texts.

In developing skill in using context, two approaches are recommended. First, the cloze instructional procedure may be used to induce a student to try to predict the meaning of words deleted from passages of material to be assigned. The emphasis again is on providing reasonable substitutes. An oral version of cloze may be utilized, in which the teacher records newscasts, commercials, and even sports commentaries on audio tapes. During the playback, the teacher will stop at various intervals and ask how the sentence can be completed. Comparisons can then be made with the actual syntax on tape, and the class can determine if the prediction was appropriate syntactically and semantically. This activity can be developed into a game in which groups of students compete.

For students with serious vocabulary deficiencies, it is helpful to employ the language experience activity in conjunction with Visual, Auditory, Kinesthetic Tactile (VAKT) tracing technique developed by Fernald.[67] In this approach, which requires some individual assistance from a volunteer tutor, an aide, or perhaps an older student, the pupil develops an interpretation of an event or problem related to the content of the course. The interpretation, given orally, is then taped and transcribed to be used as a reading activity. The words in the account which the pupil is unable to read are identified, and one is selected for tracing according to the Fernald technique. The teacher first writes or prints the word and then traces it, pronouncing it and maintaining contact between finger and paper. The student then follows the example of the teacher, tracing and pronouncing the word several times. Then the student is given blank paper and asked to write the word from memory and to use it in a sentence (orally).

If the student responds to this approach (called "multisensory" by some) and begins to build a sight vocabulary, he should in time be able to use context aids and structural clues in word recognition and discontinue the tracing procedure. It is, of course, possible to use this procedure to assist groups of disabled or slow readers to learn specialized vocabulary words, although it is not likely to be as productive as when used with a language experience approach. Complete directions on how to use this tested clinical tool in the classroom are provided by Gentry.[68]

An interesting and promising procedure to improve vocabulary and concept development through the use of morphemes has been proposed by Burmeister.[69] This author explains that a morpheme is the "smallest unit of meaning in the English language" and morphemes may be "free" (capable of standing alone) or "bound"; i.e., prefixes, suffixes, and some roots which must be attached to another morpheme to complete a word. While students may have encountered bound morphemes in reading, it may not have been apparent to them that these meaningful units may be combined with others to compose new terms.

The social studies teacher may employ morphemic analysis inductively by listing on the board "automobile," "automat," "autobiography," and asking what morpheme the terms have in common. Students then may be asked to define "auto" (done for or by oneself) and apply it to other known elements to obtain meaning (e.g., "autosuggestion"). Other bound morphemes frequently found in social studies materials may be used in context and then studied as in the example above (e.g., "cracy," meaning power and might) and combinations explored.

Two additional resources to facilitate this use of morphology in vocabulary and concept building are provided by Burmeister.[70] A list of "morpheme families" derived from social studies content is made available.

Also, directions for playing two interesting games, called "Morpheme Concentration" and "Morpheme Wordo," are included in the article.

Assessing Comprehension

One of the most important tasks a social studies teacher must undertake at any grade level is the determination of the ability of her or his students to comprehend the materials to be assigned. At the same time, the teacher must effect the best possible match between the comprehension level of pupils and the readability of the materials. (To check readability of materials, instructors may now use formulas such as the Fry Graph,[71] which will yield a quick and fairly accurate indication of grade level.)

Readability formulas, however, suffer from certain limitations; they do not measure concept load or complexity, nor do they provide for other factors, such as interest of the reader. Nevertheless, there are two procedures available to teachers which provide a helpful prediction of the ability of a given class or groups of students to comprehend specific content. One of these procedures, cloze, is also sensitive to concept loading; but the other procedure, called "maze," has some advantages over cloze. Both are described in the following paragraphs, and examples of their application are provided.

Widely used by a number of researchers in the last two decades, cloze presents the student with a passage of material, previously not seen, in which there are systematic deletions of words. The student must then attempt to replace the words deleted, usually every fifth word in a 250-word passage, according to Bormuth's technique.[72] The first sentence and last sentence contain no deletions. The number or percentage of words correctly replaced indicates the extent of the match between the student's comprehension and the material.

One advantage of cloze is its ease of preparation and administration. Students can simply write the words in the blanks (which are all of equal size) of the cloze inventory based on representative passages of a book, magazine or article.

Following is an example of a cloze inventory in an abbreviated form from an eleventh-grade United States history text.[73]

These provisions made amendment difficult but not impossible. They gave the minority _____ power to block change, _____ they placed virtually no __1__ on what an amendment __2__ do.
          3   4

In the interpretation of scores, the teacher should exercise a measure of professional judgment. As a case in point, if there are fifty blanks and the student correctly replaces the words in twenty, his score is 40%. According to the Bormuth readability technique, he would have scored slightly below the instructional level. Bormuth's[74] criteria are summarized as follows:

58–100%   correct replacements—independent level
44–57%   correct replacements—instructional level
0–43%   correct replacements—frustrational level

However, it should be noted, as Feely[75] has pointed out, that cloze interpretations in several different studies have varied somewhat. He has analyzed the studies and identified the mean scores which he treats as guidelines or "central points"; the instructional level mean score is 39% and the independent level mean is 54%. In any event, these guidelines should be used cautiously. Since most of the previous research testing, the use of cloze has drawn largely on narrative basal reading materials.

Another useful tool which can be used to predict and monitor comprehension of social studies materials at both elementary and secondary levels is a deletion technique called "maze." To prepare and administer maze passages, these procedures should be followed:[76]

1. Select several representative passages from the materials to be taught. (The material should be new to the student.)
2. Delete every fifth word and replace with three alternatives: (1) the correct word; (2) an incorrect response of the same part of speech, e.g., noun, verb, preposition, etc.; and (3) an incorrect word of a different part of speech. Provide beginning and ending sentences from which no deletions have been made.
3. Passages should be approximately 120 words in length.
4. The student is asked to circle or check the correct answer.

In an abbreviated form, a maze technique applied to a third-grade social studies text[77] might look like the following:

It is election time in Danbury. The people of the
town   by
boat are going to elect then new city government.
sang   a

While research does support the use of maze, clearly formulated standards for the interpretation of scores are not yet available. Guthrie, a proponent of maze, views 60–70% accuracy as "optimal" for instructional purposes.[78] On the other hand, Feely argues that for social studies content, the cutting points should be higher. However, the teacher may elect to utilize either of the guidelines and determine which is more reliable. (It should be noted that Guthrie does not use the terms instructional level, independent level, etc., in explaining scores.) Feely estimates the following cutting points: independent level—92% or higher, instructional level—80–91%, and frustrational level—75% or less.[79]

In comparing maze and cloze, several points should be noted. Cloze is well-grounded on research; but it appears, at least to younger children (so some have observed), more threatening. In contrast, maze is sometimes seen as a puzzle or game. On the other hand, cloze is less difficult to construct. Under these conditions, it might be desirable to administer a maze exercise prior to the cloze inventory in order to orient students to the task and reduce apprehension. The content in both cases should be different and not previously seen by students.

Improving Comprehension in the Social Studies

Much could be written on this topic. However, in view of space limitations, emphasis will be placed primarily on developing comprehension at two levels of the Barrett taxonomy: inferential and evaluative (or critical) reading. These areas are essential in the effective teaching and learning of new social studies materials; moreover, there are indications that, despite much rhetoric, these areas suffer from neglect in an instructional program which still places much value on the recall and recognition of details at the literal level of comprehension. Accordingly, the following paragraphs include strategies or ideas suitable to both elementary and secondary grades for developing reading skills at inferential and critical levels utilizing social studies content. (For teachers who seek more information and assistance on the improvement of specific comprehension skills [comparison and contrast, sequence, etc.], references are made to several appropriate resource kits and media packages available from publishers.)[80]

At the inferential level of comprehension, one approach which has appeal in the elementary grades, and possibly early junior high, is the use of folk tales, or "prose narratives," as anthropologists call them. Folk tales are clearly within the realm of the social studies since they deal with the transmission of cultural values and sometimes serve as a medium of political persuasion. "People's folk tales," observed anthropologist Ruth Benedict, "are in this sense their autobiography and clearest mirror of their life."[81] Folk tales also have the power to stimulate the imagination, and they have long held a fascination for adult and child.

One procedure, proposed here as an example, is the study of a West African folk tale, "The Man and the Mango Tree."[82] Written at a fifth-grade readability level, the story still communicates indirectly a significant lesson about the penalties of being unable to make up one's mind. The teacher might read the story while the children follow by viewing a transparency of the tale. At the end, they might draw pictures depicting what happened (the man could not decide which fruit to pick) and then explore the meaning of the narrative. Similar strategies may be followed in using folk tales from Appalachia, New England, the Southwest, and other regions of the United States.[83] In addition, a rich resource may be found in the folk tales of other cultures.[84] Some stories may be recorded by children and played back to the class, the teacher stopping in several places to ask, "How is this tale from Greece similar to the one we heard from Mexico?," or "What do you think will happen next?"

To challenge more mature readers, the teacher may develop "discovery episodes," at various readability levels, which draw on interesting historical documents, letters to Presidents, eyewitness accounts of major events, etc. Students may be placed in groups of three or five, given the episodes, in which explicit references to the identity of the author or the event have been removed, and asked to determine from the available clues what was happening, who was involved, etc. (Students with reading difficulties may be given episodes which contain more clues and are less complex.) One episode which the author has used with secondary students successfully is based on a Kikuyu story related by Jomo Kenyatta in *Facing Mount Kenya*.[85] The story is presented in the form of a fable involving animals and a man; in reality, it served as a political indictment of the British colonial policy in East Africa which preceded the Mau Mau rebellion.

At the level of critical reading, one activity which may be used in upper elementary and secondary social studies classes focuses on a case study of the memorable, well-publicized "War of the Worlds" radio broadcast, which induced widespread panic in 1938.[86] The basic steps in introducing this activity to the class are: (1) listen to selected parts of the broadcast while the actual script[87] is shown on a screen by an overhead projector; (2) identify the panic-inducing elements of the broadcast (e.g., selection of words, simulation of eyewitness news reporting, appeals to scientific authority, etc.); (3) study the defense or explanation offered by Orson Welles, by the producer, and by the Columbia Broadcasting System; and (4) examine the reaction of people of the period as expressed in letters to the editors of major newspapers. In addition, a role-playing activity may be created in which an imaginary hearing by the Federal Communications Commission is undertaken. (This is not entirely imaginary, for the FCC was urged to take vigorous action, and information concerning this may be derived from accounts in the *New York Times* shortly after the broadcast on October 30, 1938.)[88]

Other possible activities focusing on aspects of critical comprehension may be suggested in the following:

(1) If the teacher or students have access to a shortwave receiver (or perhaps to a member of a short wave listening club—a "DXer,"[89] to use their parlance), recordings may be made and played back in class of English language news broadcasts and commentaries from Radio Moscow, the British Broadcasting Corporation, Radio Havana, and Radio Nederland—to suggest only a few of the more active governmental short wave stations. Students can be asked to note differences and similarities in coverage of controversial news events, types of programs, appeals to listeners, etc. It would also prove interesting to pick up and record for playback and study in class some of the clandestine, exile, liberation, or revolutionary broadcasts in different parts of the world. Some possibilities would include Freedom Radio (Irish Nationalist, Provisional IRA), Voice of Ulster (Orange, pro-British Northern Ireland), and Radio Euzkadi (Basque nationalist government in exile). Valuable resources for this activity are *How To Listen to the World*[90] and the current *World Radio TV Handbook*.[91]

(2) Analyze contemporary and historic political speeches in terms of Hugh Rank's "Doublespeak" schema of intensification and downplaying of language. Rank contends that the traditional propaganda analysis techniques ("testimonial," "bandwagon," etc.) are outmoded. Information is provided in an NCTE publication, *Teaching About Doublespeak*.[92]

Finally, it should be noted that the strategies and resources for improving reading skills in the social studies, as suggested in this chapter, are many and varied. Social studies teachers are not expected to assume the role of reading teachers or specialists. Nevertheless, there are many opportunities for the social studies teacher, without an extensive investment of time and effort, to make a difference in the ability of students to read about and comprehend the persistent vital issues which affect human destiny. If students are to participate effectively in decision making about such issues, there is no substitute for reading skills.

FOOTNOTES

[1]Lois A. Bader, "Certification Requirements in Reading," *Journal of Reading* 19:237–240, December, 1975.

[2]June R. Chapin and Richard Gross, *Teaching Social Studies Skills* (Boston: Little, Brown and Co., 1973), p. 20.

[3]Robert Karlin, "What Does Educational Research Reveal About Reading and the High School Student?", *The English Journal*, 58:386–395, March, 1969. See also A. Sterl Artley, *Trends and Practices in Secondary Reading* (Newark: International Reading Association, 1968), pp. 4–5.

[4]Karlin, *op. cit.*, pp. 586–595.

[5]Roger Farr, Jaan Tuiman, and Michael Rowls, *Reading Achievement in the United States: Then and Now* (Bloomington: Indiana University Reading Program Center and the Institute for Child Study, 1974), p. 1.

[6]Compare, for example, the conclusions in Chapin and Gross, *op. cit.*, p. 25, with those in Farr, Tuiman, and Rowls, *op. cit.*, p. 1.

[7]Reports from the National Assessment for Educational Progress to the mass media on so-called "dramatic gains" in the 1974–75 reading now appear unduly optimistic as the result of a more objective scrutiny. See George McNeill, "Washington Report," *Phi Delta Kappan* 58:291–292, November, 1976.

[8]Billy R. Campbell, "A Study of the Relationship of Reading Ability of Students in Grades 4, 5, and 6 and Comprehension of Social Studies and Science Textbook Selections" (unpublished doctoral dissertation, The Florida State University, Tallahassee, 1972).

[9]Arthur V. Olson, "Attitudes of High School Area Content Teachers Toward the Teaching of Reading," *Teaching Reading Skills in Secondary Schools*, eds. Arthur V. Olson and Wilbur Ames (Scranton: International Textbook Co., 1970), pp. 235–241.

[10]Richard E. Arnold and Natalie Sherry, "A Comparison of the Reading Levels of Disabled Readers with Assigned Textbooks," *Reading Improvement* 12:207–211, Winter, 1975.

[11]*Ibid.*, p. 207.

[12]Harold L. Herber, "Reading in the Social Studies: Implications for Teaching and Research," *Reading in the Content Areas*, ed. James L. Laffey (Newark: International Reading Association, 1972) p. 2.

[13]Wayne L. Herman, "Reading and Other Language Arts in Social Studies Instruction: Persistent Problems," *A New Look at Reading in the Social Studies*, ed. Ralph C. Preston (Newark: International Reading Association, 1969), p. 6.

[14]Roger Johnson and Ellen B. Vardian, "Reading, Readability and the Social Studies," *The Reading Teacher* 26:483–488, February, 1973.

[15]Mary H. Dohrman, "The Suitability of Encyclopedias for Reference Use in the Intermediate Grades," *Journal of Education Research*, 68:149–152, December 1974.

[16]Margaret Janz and Edwin Smith, "The Students' Reading Ability and the Readability of Secondary School Subjects," *Elementary English*, XLIX:622–624, April, 1972.

[17]Ronald J. Hash, "The Effects of a Strategy of Structural Overviews, Levels Guides, and Vocabulary Exercises on Student Achievement, Reading Comprehension, Critical Thinking and Attitudes of Junior High Classes in Social Studies" (unpublished doctoral dissertation, State University of New York at Buffalo, 1971), pp. 20–25.

[18]Charles W. Peters, "The Effect of Systematic Restructuring of Material upon the Comprehension Process," *Reading Research Quarterly* XL:94, 1975–76.

[19]Peter H. Martorella, *Concept Learning in the Social Studies: Models for Structuring Curriculum* (Scranton: International Textbooks, 1971), p. 67.

[20]Peters, *op. cit.*, pp. 87–113.

[21]Vernon C. Hall and Ralph L. Turner, "The Validity of the Different Language Explanation for Poor Scholastic Performance by Black Students," *Review of Educational Research* 44:69–81, Winter, 1974.

[22]See, for example, Irene J. Athey and Jack A. Holmes, "Reading Success and Personality Characteristics in Junior High School Students," ed. C. W. Gordon, Vol. 18, *University of California Publications in Education* (Berkeley: University of California Press, 1969), pp. 1–80; Samuel Weintraub, "Teacher Expectation and Reading Performance," *The Reading Teacher* 22:555–559, March, 1969; and Ahmed Fareed, "Interpretive Response in Reading History and Biology: An Exploratory Study," *Reading Research Quarterly* 6:493–531, Summer, 1971.

[23]Kenneth Goodman and Catherine Buck, "Dialect Barriers to Reading Comprehension," *The Reading Teacher* 27:7–12, October, 1973.

[24]Robert Ruddell, *Reading-Language Instruction: Innovative Practices* (Englewood Cliffs: Prentice-Hall, Inc., 1974), p. 37.

[25]E. Brooks Smith, Kenneth Goodman, and Robert Meredith, *Language and Thinking in the Elementary School* (New York: Holt, Rinehart and Winston, 1970), p. 247.

[26]John P. Lunstrum, "Reading in the Social Studies: A Preliminary Analysis of Recent Research," *Social Education* 40:17, January, 1976.

[27]Yetta Goodman and Carolyn Burke, "Reading: Language and Psycholinguistic Bases," *Reading: Foundations and Instructional Strategies*, eds. Pose Lamb and Richard Arnold (Belmont: Wadsworth Publishing Co., 1976), pp. 94–98.

[28]Goodman and Burke note: "Proficient readers resort to an intensive graphic/sound analysis of an entire word only when other cues have been used unsuccessfully." See Yetta M. Goodman and Carolyn Burke, *Reading Miscue Inventory Manual: Procedure for Diagnosis and Evaluation* (New York: Macmillan Publishing Co., 1971), p. 15.

[29]Herber, *op. cit.*, pp. 198–199.

[30]Jack A. Holmes, "The Substrata Theory of Reading: Some Experimental Evidence," *Theoretical Models and Processes in Reading*, eds. Harry Singer and Robert Ruddell (Newark: International Reading Association, 1970), pp. 187–197.

[31]Karen Fitzpatrick, "An Experimental Study to Investigate the Effects of Selected Value Clarifying Strategies on the Self Concept and Reading Achievement of Seventh Grade Students in Nonpublic Schools of a Large Roman Catholic Diocese" (unpublished doctoral dissertation, The Catholic University of America, Washington, D.C., 1975).

[32]Maurice P. Hunt and Lawrence Metcalf, *Teaching High School Social Studies* (New York: Harper and Row Publishers, 1968), pp. 84–88.

[33]John S. Simmons, "Word Study Skills," *Developing Study Skills in Secondary Schools*, ed. Harold L. Herber (Newark: International Reading Association, 1969), p. 17.

[34]Albert Harris and Edward Sipay, *How to Increase Reading Ability*, sixth edition (New York: David McKay Company, Inc., 1975), pp. 472–473.

[35]*Ibid.*, p. 474.

[36]Barrett's taxonomy was reportedly not published by the author; it is set forth, however, in Theodore Clymer, "What Is 'Reading'?: Some Current Concepts," *Innovation and Change in Reading Instruction*, Sixty-seventh Yearbook of the National Society for the Study of Education, Part II, ed. Helen M. Robinson (Chicago: University of Chicago Press, 1968), pp. 19–23.

[37]Clymer, *op. cit.*, p. 19.

[38]Hugh Rank, "Teaching about Public Persuasion: Rationale and a Schema," *Teaching About Doublespeak*, ed. Daniel Dieterich (Urbana: National Council of Teachers of English, 1975), pp. 3–19.

[39]Clymer, *op. cit.*, p. 22.

[40]Johnson and Vardian, *op cit.*, pp. 483–488.

[41]Harris and Sipay, *op. cit.*, p. 549.

[42]*Ibid.*, pp. 549–550.

[43]Wilma H. Miller, *Reading Diagnosis Kit* (New York: Center for Applied Research in Education, 1974), pp. 245–256.

[44]Thomas Estes, "A Scale to Measure Attitudes Toward Reading," *Journal of Reading* 15:135–138, November, 1971.

[45]Duane R. Tovey, "Children's Perceptions of Reading," *The Reading Teacher* 29:536–540, March, 1976. See also Jerry L. Johns, "Concepts of Reading Among Good and Poor Readers," *Education* 95:58–60, Fall, 1974.

[46]Tovey, *op. cit.*, p. 536–540.

[47]James R. Shaver, "Reading and Controversial Issues," *A New Look at Reading in the Social Studies*, ed. Ralph Preston (Newark: International Reading Association, 1969), p. 36.

[48]Howard Mehlinger and John J. Patrick, *American Political Behavior*, Book I (Lexington: Ginn and Company, 1974).

[49]"Photo Study Card Discussion Kits on Meaning and Values," (Minneapolis: Greenhaven Press Inc., 1976).

[50]Sidney B. Simon, Leland Howe, and Howard Kirschenbaum, *Values Clarification* (New York: Hart Publishing Company, Inc., 1972).

[51]J. William Pfeiffer and John E. Jones, *A Handbook of Structured Experiences for Human Relations Training* (La Jolla: University Associates Publishers, Inc., 1974).

[52]James Moffett, *A Student-Centered Language Arts Curriculum, Grades K–13: A Handbook for Teachers* (Boston: Houghton Mifflin Co., 1968), pp. 12–13.

[53]S. I. Ritt, "Using Music to Teach Reading in the Social Studies," *The Reading Teacher* 27:594–601, March, 1974.

[54]B. G. Massialas and J. Zevin, *Two Societies in Perspective, World History Through Inquiry* (Chicago: Rand McNally and Co., 1970).

[55]Sidney B. Simon, Robert Hawley, and David Britton, *Values Clarification Through Writing* (New York: Hart Publishing Co. Inc., 1973).

[56]Charles Berryman, "The Athens Model: Results of a High Saturation Program in Newspaper Reading Skill," paper presented at the International Reading Association National Convention, New York City, 1975.

[57]Charles Berryman, *Improving Reading Skills* (Atlanta: The Atlanta-Journal Constitution, 1973).

[58]George D. Spache, *Good Reading for the Disadvantaged Reader* (Champaign: Garrard Publishing Co., 1970).

[59]Miller, *op. cit.*, p. 132.

[60]Derived from Miller, *op. cit.*, p. 197, and Robert Aukerman, *Reading in the Secondary School Classroom* (New York: McGraw-Hill Book Company, 1972), p. 112.

[61]Lawrence Senesh, *Our Working World: Neighborhoods* (Chicago: Science Research Associates, Inc., 1973), p. 25.

[62]From an unpublished set of materials by the author.

[63]Roger J. Quealy, "Senior High School Student Use of Contextual Aids in Reading," *Reading Research Quarterly*, 4:512–533, Summer, 1969.

[64]Robert Emans, "Use of Context Clues: Reading and Realism," *International Reading Association Proceedings*, Vol. 13, Part I (Newark: International Reading Association, 1969), pp. 76–82.

[65]Wilma Miller, *Reading Correction Kit* (The Center for Applied Research in Education, Inc., 1975), pp. 67–92.

[66]Hilda Taba, "Implementing Thinking as an Objective in Social Studies," *Effective Thinking in the Social Studies*, 37th Yearbook, eds. Jean Fair and Fannie Shaftel (Washington, D.C.: National Council for the Social Studies, 1967), pp. 34–36.

[67]Grace Fernald, *Remedial Techniques in Basic School Subjects* (New York: McGraw-Hill Book Co., 1943).

[68]Larry A. Gentry, "A Clinical Method in Classroom Success—Kinesthetic Teaching," *Journal of Reading*, 18:298–301, December, 1974.

[69]Lou E. Burmeister, "Vocabulary Development in Content Areas Through the Use of Morphemes," *Journal of Reading* 19:481–487, March, 1976.

[70]*Ibid.*

[71]Edward Fry, "A Readability Formula That Saves Time," *Journal of Reading* 11:513–516, 575–578, April, 1948. (The Fry Graph is not copyrighted and accordingly may be used without permission; it is found in the article cited.)

[72]John Bormuth, "The Cloze Readability Procedure," *Elementary English* 45:429–436, April, 1968.

[73]R. N. Current, A. DeConde, and H. L. Dante, *United States History* (Glenview: Scott, Foresman and Company, 1967), p. 116.

[74]Bormuth, *op. cit.*, pp. 429–436.

[75]Theodore M. Feely, "The Cloze and the Maze," *The Social Studies* LXVI:252–257, November-December, 1975.

[76]John T. Guthrie et al., "The Maze to Assess and Monitor Reading Comprehension," *The Reading Teacher* 28:161–168, November, 1974.

[77]Lawrence Senesh, *op. cit.*, p. 92.

[78]Guthrie, *op. cit.*, pp. 161–168.

[79]Feely, *op. cit.*, pp. 252–257.

[80]Particularly worth mentioning are: Grace A. Ransom, *Reading, Researching and Reporting in Social Studies* (upper elementary grades) (Santa Monica: BFA Educational Media, 1975); Harold L. Herber, *Go: Reading in Content Areas* (grades 4–8) (New York: Scholastic Book Services, 1973); and Theodore Clymer and others, *Read Better-Learn More: A Reading Skills Program in the Content Fields* (Books A–C for secondary grades) (Lexington: Ginn and Company Inc., 1973).

[81]Ruth Benedict, "Folklore," *Encyclopedia of Social Sciences*, ed. E. A. Seligman, (New York: Macmillan Publishing Company, 1931) pp. 288–293.

[82]Virginia Holladay, *Bantu Tales* (New York: The Viking Press, 1970), pp. 30–31.

[83]Richard Chase, ed. *American Folktales and Songs* (New York: New American Library, 1956).

[84]Ruth Carlson, *Folklore and Folktales Around the World* (Perspectives in Reading No. 16, Newark: International Reading Association, 1972).

[85]Jomo Kenyatta, *Facing Mount Kenya* (New York: Vintage Books, 1962), pp. 47–51.

[86]Hadley Cantril, *The Invasion from Mars* (Princeton: Princeton University Press, 1952).

[87]Howard Koch, *Panic Broadcast* (Boston: Little Brown and Co., 1969).

[88]"Letters to the Editor," *New York Times*, November 2, 1938, p. 27.

[89]Ed. C. Shaw, *DXing According to NASWA* (Liberty, Ind.: North American Short Wave Association, 1975).

[90]J. M. Frost, *How to Listen to the World*, Seventh Edition, (Hvidore, Denmark: World Radio-TV Handbook, 1972).

[91]J. M. Frost, *World Radio TV Handbook* (New York: Billboard Publications, 1976).

[92]Hugh Rank, *op. cit.*

"Every problem is affected by those forces which are at counterbalance with one another. By listing those forces which are impelling changes in the present condition as well as those forces which are holding back the changes, the group will more effectively focus on the difficulties to be overcome. . . ."

.5.

Murry R. Nelson and H. Wells Singleton

Small Group Decision Making
for Social Action

DEVELOPING EFFECTIVE SMALL GROUPS

Introduction

Scarcely a day goes by that we are not involved in groups of some form. From family groups to work groups we are becoming increasingly involved in developing relationships with others. With our socially complex and interdependent world, the ability to be an effective member in a variety of social groups is of basic importance for the survival and growth of the individual.

Our lives are filled with ambiguity and rapid change, requiring us to make decisions based on immediately available information. Those who recognize the need for healthy group settings are able to help steer groups toward positive productivity, while at the same time individuals become more effective in their abilities to work with one another. In this time of rapid social change, new organizational patterns are emerging, requiring us to know more about the process of social and organizational development, the need for social action, and the skills of bringing about change. Decision making is an integral part of the small group process.

The schools have long expressed an interest in small groups and social action but have struggled with the idea of identifying the skills to be used in such activities. Beginning with John Dewey, grouping has been advocated as an essential part of any school curriculum. Dewey, who believed that the child's mind grew through meanings acquired in social interchange, asserted that methods of scientific investigation and social cooperation were the constants of curriculum; subject matter was the variable.[1]

141

In the absence of a clear understanding of the parameters of cooperation in group endeavors, attempts at establishing small groups in the classroom have met with a less than adequate record of success. Despite the large body of literature presently available which has increased our understanding of the task and reward structure in small groups and has pointed to the beneficial outcomes of intergroup cooperation, many educators are still frustrated at having experienced at best limited successes at both the elementary and secondary levels.

The authors count themselves among those who have said in effect, "Well, I tried the small group thing for awhile, but it just did not work out."

In examining classroom experiences with small groups, it can be seen that the problems encountered are common at all levels. The groups may be unable to focus on the topic or task. Without care, the small group can degenerate into a session of argumentation, debate, and a general sharing of ignorance, with little relevant or factual data exhibited. In many instances, the small groups tend to be dominated by either the most vocal or the most physically powerful individuals. Students with limited communication skills may remain that way and can, in fact, be negatively reinforced through small group experiences. The good student often continues to do well, while poor students continue to do poorly in spite of (or perhaps because of!) small group experiences.

Both the values and the pitfalls of small group work are easily recognizable. It is our intent in this chapter to examine the rationale for small groups, particularly equal status interaction groups in which cooperation is stressed, and to present some strategies for success. Our desire is to provide a beginning point for what we believe is a necessary function of social studies; namely, the development of a curriculum aimed at practicing decision making and social action through small groups.

Definitions

This discussion of decision making will refer to several terms which require definition. *Small groups* are defined as a number of individuals (3–7) in interdependent role relations employing a set of values that regulate the actions of members in matters of concern to the group, matters in which a stated goal has been identified. There is a close relationship between the feelings of individuals and the successful pursuit of a goal-oriented task. Therefore, recognition of personal, individual feelings is seen as an integral part of the decision-making process in small groups. *Consensus* in small group decision making refers to the point at which general agreement has been reached. This is not to be confused with majority rule in the decision-making process. Rather, consensus in the small group requires a greater understanding of the various feelings within the group and a need to develop a high degree of cooperative effort among the participants.

Equal status means the idea that all members of the small group have equal power in determining the group's destiny. Equal status is a means through which cooperation can be achieved in the small group by each member recognizing the worth and uniqueness of every other member.

Cohesiveness in the small group setting refers to the overall attraction of group members to each other. Cohesiveness is evident when group members have a sense of belonging and are dedicated to the well-being of the group. Such factors as morale, team effort, and group spirit all affect the cohesiveness of the small group.

A *platform* provides a foundation and a point from which to develop an idea or structure. A platform provides the beginning framework and the link to a known entity. In our discussions, platform indicates the basis of our ideas related to small groups and decision making.

Group size has been a subject of interest to researchers. Both participation and the quality of interaction are affected by the size of the group. Studies have shown that groups of three or four provided the optimum conditions for equal status. As group size is increased to more than eight members, the groups tend to be dominated by the more aggressive participants.[2] An earlier study has shown that smaller groups are better at dealing with concrete problems, while larger groups are more effective in dealing with abstract issues.[3] From our point of view, small groups ought to consist of from three to seven members. It is recommended that dyads or pairs be used as a beginning approach to enable students to get to know one another. After a reasonable period of time two or three dyads could be combined.

Preparing for Small Groups

There are three major sets of variables at work in classrooms which affect group functions: teachers' perceptions and expectations of students; students' perceptions and expectations of teachers; and students' perceptions and expectations of each other. When the three variables are in harmony—that is, when all perceptions and expectations are realistic—then the class has become a cohesive group.

Teachers are faced with many anxieties and emotions as they first come in contact with a new class. They have certain expectations of students which are based partly on past experiences, partly on the training received in teacher preparation programs, and partly on societal norms. For example, expectations of third graders are somewhat different from expectations held for fourth graders, and markedly different than those held for eleventh graders. The actions of the members of a group are perceived and interpreted in the light of teacher expectations.

Students in the class have a more difficult adjustment problem than do teachers, since they are constantly adjusting and readjusting their perceptions and expectations not only of the teacher but of their peers as well. (While teachers must adjust perceptions and expectations of peers just as students do, much of their adjustment takes place outside the classroom.) Students have certain expectations of teachers which have been ingrained over the years. Their expectations often include the idea that the teacher is an imparter of knowledge; that the teacher will subscribe to a rather standardized procedure for conducting lessons; and that the teacher represents some form of authority. Any action on the part of the teacher which deviates from the expected mode will cause a readjustment in the expectations of students. In addition, students spend much time and concern in developing relationships with peers. Their relationships are based on expectations and perceptions, both of which are undergoing constant adjustment.

A high level of cohesiveness in a class will provide the teacher with a platform from which to begin the development of small group activities. For, once there is a feeling of "togetherness" in the large sense, the orientation required for small groups becomes a manageable task.

The establishment of functioning small groups is not an easy task. It is not something to be done once or twice during the term. Nor is it an endeavor from which immediate success can be expected. However, studies have shown a high correlation between frequency of small group activities and cohesiveness within groups.[4] The evidence, then, indicates that cohesiveness is more likely to be maintained in the classroom when small groups are formed frequently. However, simply forming small groups three or four times a week will not necessarily produce cohesiveness. Other factors must be considered.

One such factor is the liking/disliking attitude expressed by students. Four main types of students tend to be rejected by peers:[5] (1) those who are limited in physical ability, (2) those who have difficulty in developing meaningful social relations with others, (3) those who have intellectual limitations, and (4) those who have mental health difficulties. Recognition of the like/dislike factors is an initial step in developing cohesion within groups.

It must be stressed that small groups will only be as effective as are the group building and maintenance efforts on the part of the teacher and students. Some major requirements for building and maintenance can be listed as a check sheet in assisting in the development of an atmosphere conducive to group work:

1. Shared decision making about group goals and behavior whenever possible.
2. Shared diagnosis of group difficulties and shared analysis of group successes.
3. Shared analysis of required teacher and student roles and functions.
4. Acceptance of all individuals as members of the group.
5. An accepted standard of working on individual and group problems which hold up the group task of developing a learning group.
6. An accepted standard of willingness to be experimental in procedures, clarifying or changing goals, and modifying group behavior.
7. Efforts to utilize member resources.[6]

In essence, then, varying backgrounds, attitudes, and emotional responses are brought into the group by each participant, which can either enhance or inhibit the group decision making. The teacher must take the time to determine the composition of each student's personality as it may relate to each task embarked upon. Students need to be able to listen to each other carefully, and they must also be aware of the many value preferences inherent in their own assertions and those of others.

In one simple and easy exercise, students list fifteen things that they like to do. (Fifteen is not a magic number—it may be reduced or enlarged depending on time and group. Third graders might list ten; high schoolers might list twenty.) Since these lists are not to be shown to anyone else, students should be encouraged to be as honest as possible. Items may be as simple as sleeping or as complex as back-packing in the High Sierra in May. After students list the things they like to do, have them make six columns next to the list. Above the six columns, put signs to indicate what the significance of that column is. The following are examples of possible column headings.

$$\$ \mid A \mid F \mid L \mid \odot \mid 6$$

For the $, have students put a check next to activities requiring a direct cash outlay to do them; e.g., swimming does not usually require that direct outlay, but a student might *always* choose to swim in a pool that has an entrance fee. Going to the movies always requires cash; showering does not. A is for alone, and students should check those activities that they prefer to do alone. Some may be done with others, like fishing, but the concern is with value preferences. F is for family, and those activities which they like to do with their family should be checked. If a student has had formal lessons in an activity, he should check it in the L column. For example, a student choosing piano playing who had taken piano lessons would mark the L column. However, if a student played on his own with some encouragement from family members, L would *not* be checked. The smiling face is used to symbolize the amusement a close friend or relative might display at seeing particular activities. A student who lists "watching the sun rise" but hates to get up in the morning can recognize that his family would hoot at this choice. Another source of humor might be reinforcement; e.g., a student lists reading and the student's brother is constantly commenting on how the student always has a book in his/her hand. Thus, the brother might chuckle knowingly at the activity listed. Finally, the 6 column should be checked for any activity which has not been engaged in during the past six months.

Following this, students should be asked if they see patterns that surprise, please, or disappoint them. For example, one student noted that fourteen things that she liked to do involved *no* cash outlay; yet she was always without money. She concluded that she must be spending quite a lot of money on things she possibly neither wants nor needs. Students should be encouraged to verbalize any patterns that they see. This will aid others in being aware of diverse values; e.g. I had only two things that I like to do with my family; he had nine. Additionally, students have the opportunity to look at themselves from this value perspective. Seeing a pattern of preferences juxtaposed against their actions (or lack thereof) should help them in clarifying and understanding that we all have our own values, if we just take the time to think about that fact. In addition, our personal actions are based on those very values. Being cognizant of that will enable students to accept various courses of action put forth by others, since it should be clear that individual courses of action are at least partially determined by personal values.

This activity can be used by teachers from third grade to adult learners. The column headings and symbols can, and should, be altered to fit the goals or objectives of an individual teacher or class. For example, the "6" is less applicable to younger groups than to older groups that have more responsibility and demands on their time. To initiate discussion of physical behavior and indoor and outdoor activities, sedentary and active ones might be given a column heading.

Listening

After students have been given the opportunity to become aware of their own values, through some such value clarification exercise, the teacher must be sure students can, and do, listen to other students. Listening is an important skill in social education, and the cultivation of careful listening habits will be a determining factor in whether a group accomplishes its task successfully or not. Chapin and Gross[7] suggest thirteen hints for teaching listening skills (see Figure 1), along with some short exercises to develop student ability to listen to one another. One idea is to assign student partners and have them discuss an issue. After the first student has spoken, the second student must summarize his partner's views before putting forth his own, with this pattern continuing until a solution of sorts is reached.

FIGURE 1

HINTS FOR TEACHING LISTENING SKILLS

1. Check the amount of speaking that you do during a class. Are you talking too much? Requiring too much listening?
2. Have students record the amount of time they listen both in class and outside of class.
3. Give oral directions or announcements only once. Have other students repeat instructions if necessary.
4. Give listening tests; occasionally give oral quizzes.
5. Be a good model yourself in listening.
6. Tell your students what to listen for. With practice they can learn to listen for the main ideas without the assistance of lists of questions or written scripts.
7. Have students outline and compare their views of the major points of a speech the class has heard.
8. Have students look for speakers' different frames of reference.
9. Occasionally ask your students to rate their own listening skills.
10. Be sure that you as well as the students speak clearly enough to be easily heard.
11. Most important, have something for students that is worth listening to. Part of this job is for the teacher to arrange an interesting class.
12. Allow the student (initially) to communicate in a language he already knows. This is especially important for the culturally different. Utilize what happens in his outside environment to generate his willingness to listen in class.
13. As the student's language power increases with more adult contacts, bring more adult volunteers into the classroom.

One extremely rewarding activity is the Magic Circle. This exercise was developed by, and is part of, the Human Development Program under the direction of Uvaldo Palomares and Geraldine Ball.[8] The Magic Circle is elegant in its simplicity of form and magnificent in its possibilities for growth. A circle session has only four basic rules:

1. Each person may have a turn to speak, if he/she wishes to, taking only his/her fair share of the time.
2. Everyone will listen to the person who is speaking, without any interruptions, and will accept the speaker's feelings by not confronting him/her in any way.
3. Each person will stay in his/her own space.

4. Destructive behavior, such as coercing someone to speak, probing, interrupting, or making "put down" remarks, will not be accepted or allowed to continue.

In order to make these rules truly operational, the teacher as well as the students must follow them closely. Thus, if a student speaks in a grammatically incorrect manner, it is to be accepted as such. An interruption by the teacher, even in the interest of good grammar, is likely to inhibit the responses, not only of the particular child, but of other children. The teacher must model the behaviors expected of the students in abiding by the rules of this exercise.

The teacher-leader must set a positive atmosphere by drawing everyone into the circle. A concerned yet enthusiastic attitude will reinforce the feeling that this is an important part of the day's learning; yet it can be approached with warmth and fervor. Eye contact and personal address are important in capturing each student for this exercise. The teacher should go over the rules and make clear to the students that if they do not wish to speak today, they may still exercise that option tomorrow or whenever the circle session is held again. The opportunity to speak can be likened to a piece of pie—all students get one, but they may wish to consume it later that day or even the next day.

Emphasis on the essential nature of listening is vital to the circle session. Remind students that when they talk, they wish to have people listen. Similarly, they must listen to others. Following the ground rules, the leader explains that the question is one that demands an individual answer. They might then be asked to elaborate on one topic chosen from the following list (referred to as "Warm Fuzzy Awareness Topics"):

"On a Warm Summer Day I Feel . . ."
"Something That Delighted Me . . ."
"In the Rain I Feel . . ."
"At Sunset I Feel . . ."
"Little Puppies Make Me Feel . . ."
"A Time I Was Laughing and Couldn't Stop . . ."
"If I Were on the Beach Right Now . . ."
"My Favorite Song Is . . ."
"The Smell of Fresh Baked Bread Makes Me Feel . . ."
"A Thrilling Moment in My Life . . ."
"Gift I Enjoyed Giving . . ."
"The Funniest Movie I've Ever Seen . . ."
"When I Look at Trees I Feel . . ."

Each student who wishes to speak should get a turn. Once or twice during the session, a review of what has been shared thus far by each child should be made by asking the children, "Who can tell (Andy) the main part of what he said and what his feelings were?" Ask the children to address each other directly, and reward good listening with positive comments of approval. This may be a good way to draw reluctant speakers into the circle. Reviewing may be held off altogether until the end of the session, when all students who wished to speak have done so; but it is vital to promoting listening and to the ultimate success of subsequent circle sessions.

The Magic Circle does not require reading or writing ability and is ideal for primary grades. It is not limited to younger children, however. The activity has been tried successfully with high school and adult learner groups working on listening skills and personal respect.

DECISION MAKING
AS A PROCESS SKILL IN SMALL GROUPS

Rationale

As Fantini and Weinstein have indicated, "Learning to learn skills refers to those processes, ways of thinking, examining, or behaving which help the child become more adept at learning. . . ."[9] Such skills as critical thinking, analytic procedures, discussion techniques, inquiry, evaluating, problem solving, hypothesizing, planning, analogy and inductive and deductive reasoning all fall in the category of process skills, and all are utilized to varying degrees in small groups. Decision making provides an umbrella for many of the process skills as each skill is utilized in developing an idea to fruition.

Small groups can be established to focus primarily on developing the decision-making skills. The teacher who is interested in the functioning of small groups may want to concentrate the group's efforts on decision making in order to improve the overall group ability to work toward a goal. There are two formats which lend themselves to developing the decision-making skills.

Routine Decision Making

Routine decision making exists in situations where the means for reaching a goal or completing a task are pre-existent. Once the group recognizes the goal, its task becomes one of selecting the best means, from a series of options, of achieving it. A classroom activity which fits this mode would be one in which the group goal consists of identifying three causes of the Revolutionary War. The task becomes one of establishing what sources should be consulted to determine the causes. The decision-making process would involve determining the best sources of information.

A more abstract form of routine decision making provides a forum for the exchange of value ideas. It might involve the goal of establishing a form of punishment for untoward classroom behavior. In this instance, the group task would consist of deciding which punishment would best suit the act. The student who feels strict punishment should be employed as a deterrent has equal opportunity to debate with an opponent who advocates a more lenient approach.

The key to the routine decision-making approach is in the number of options available to complete the task. The more limited the number of available options the more routine the decision becomes. The value of such an approach lies in the decision-making process itself, rather than in the actual choice. The routine decision-making mode in small groups permits participants to get to know one another and provides a means for each to examine his or her, as well as others', perspectives in a controlled setting.

Creative Decision Making

The creative decision-making mode is characterized by a general lack of an agreed-upon method for reaching the goal. The options available for reaching the goal vary widely. This form of decision making includes a mandate that every idea be explored fully and completely regardless of ''credibility'' at the time.

An example of the creative decision mode in social studies classrooms is one in which the group goal is to establish a location for a new highway. The task of the group is to decide which plan would be best according to the criteria the group establishes to define the best route.

Another example, and one which we refer to later in this chapter, concerns the group goal of establishing a new community on earth. The group task is to decide, from a list of varied community resources, which ones the group will take to the new community.

In creative decision making, the process provides for a greater diversity of explanatory hypotheses and a wider range of opinions and ideas. The key to creative decision making lies in the group's ability to develop a high degree of cohesion and consensus.

Both the routine decision making characterized by limited choice and the creative decision making characterized by a wide range of choices provide a means for developing the decision-making skills. The advantage to developing decision-making skill in a small group setting is that opportunity is provided for a collective effort without excluding any participant. This is particularly true in an equal status cooperative group setting in which every contribution is weighed in equal terms based on group criteria.

Group Process Activities

What types of activities enhance cooperation and equal status interaction decision making in any classroom? A number of easily obtainable exercises illustrates the steps of making group decisions while promoting equal status interaction.

Jay Hall has devised two useful activities which promote group cooperation in decision making.[10] They are "Twelve Angry Men" and the "Moon Survival Game." The former is used with a clip from the movie of the same name. Students view the clip from the film, which stars Henry Fonda, Lee J. Cobb, and other well known Hollywood stars. In the film, a teenaged male is being tried for murder of his father. The opening sequences of the movie focus on each juror as arguments are made in preliminary discussion; then on a vote which finds eleven jurors voting "guilty" and one, Fonda, voting "not guilty." There is interaction among the jurors, revealing different aspects of their backgrounds. Cobb, for example, had a teenaged son who left home after one of the frequent arguments father and son had. Another juror's prime concern is alacrity in voting—he wishes to be finished in time to attend a baseball game on the other side of the city. Fonda makes a skillful and impassioned plea for the defendant, focusing on the dubious nature of the evidence. The jurors vote again, and the vote is now ten to two.

The film is then stopped. The task of each small classroom group is to determine in which order the jurors will change their votes as they reverse themselves to find the youth ultimately "not guilty." Fonda is given number one, and the group proceeds from there. Before group discussion and interaction, individual group members must make their choices, following the stages of decision making similar to those presented in Chapter One.

After each group reaches consensus, the remainder of the film may be shown or, if time is short, the right answers, with rationale, given. Students then subtract their score on each juror from the correct answer and total that up. For example, if student A thought Cobb would change tenth and he changed fourth, the difference is six. Negative numbers are not a factor since the difference between the two numbers will always be positive. This is done for both individuals and the group. The group total will almost always be lower and more close to "perfection" than the average of the individuals' totals, and usually the group total will be lower than any group member's individual total. Hall calls this phenomenon synergy—that is, where the output of the group is greater than the input of any individuals.

From this base came the most well known and widely used of synergistic experiments—the "Lost on the Moon" game. In that game, the group is faced with a dilemma as they play members of a moon landing team that has crash-landed 200 miles from its destination. Fifteen items are salvageable, and group members must decide which should be taken on their journey to base camp and in what order. Scoring, process, and rules are similar to those used in the previous exercise, with each "crew member" rating the fifteen items on the basis of most to least important. After this "game" was created by Hall, he went to NASA officials, who established a correct order; so there are right answers complete with rationale for this activity.

Because of the more complex nature of these activities, they are more useful at the junior or senior high level. In the latter game, "Lost on the Moon," intermediate-grade students may have enough scientific background to weigh the alternatives involved. The format of the game could be used as a model by a teacher to emphasize a different content and the same process. For example, the question of nutrition and health could be explored by listing ten foods and deciding which is most important for prolonged survival. A nutritionist might be used as a resource for the right answers.

Both of the previous activities serve to reiterate the most important "message" of this chapter; viz., a small group will be more efficient if it cooperates, and cooperation is enhanced by equal status recognition and interaction in the small group.

A teacher may determine that students are not adequately prepared for social action after this phase of "training." Small groups might be given the opportunity to practice decision making in a less structured setting, but still within an artificially based framework. Activities may be inserted that do not "require" consensus, but are enhanced through its use. Students can then demonstrate their ability to function as equal status interaction groups in a less rigid format. This type of format will be a useful stepping stone in the realities of social action.

Jeffrey Schrank in *Teaching Human Beings—101 Subversive Activities for the Classroom*[11] provides a number of activities that accentuate small group processes, particularly small group decision making. One of the most useful is the "World-Championship Paper Airplane Contest." This may be used, with various modifications, at one of a number of places in small group development. One possibility is after listening and values clarification experiences, as an introduction to group processes. Similarly, it can be used after introduction of the process but before social action group process experiences. The following is from Schrank's book.

First, divide the class into two equal groups. One group acts as observers, and the other as participants. Then divide the participants and observers into separate groups of four or five persons each. Each group of observers should, if possible, sit in a circle outside the circle formed by the plane makers.

Once this is done, give out the instruction sheets.

Participants' Instruction Sheet for Airplane Contest

Your group is to compete with the other groups to produce the world's best paper airplane. You must use the paper provided but can add any of your own material. Your group must produce *one* plane. Final planes are given points for airworthiness, accuracy when thrown, and artistic design.

Observers' Instruction Sheet for Airplane Contest

You are to select one participant in the group to observe. You are to watch him during the entire contest and notice how he contributes to the group or keeps his talents from the group. Decide what role he plays in the group's attempt to design and build the paper plane. The group's task is to design and build a paper plane that will stay in the air the longest, will fly most accurately, and will look best.

Here are the common roles that people play in groups:

1. Take-charge Guy	He thinks he's the only one in the group with any ability.
2. The Do-nothing	This person sits off to the side and makes no contribution to the group.
3. The Dart Thrower	This person throws darts at almost any idea suggested by anyone else but rarely, if ever, offers a better idea.
4. The Soapbox	This person talks and talks and talks.
5. The Clique	This is part of the entire group that actually does the work. They make the others feel unwanted and do the work themselves.
6. The Coordinator	This person takes charge but accepts the ideas of others. He does feel that others in the group can help.

7. The Mediator   This person helps keep peace in the group. He acts as a go-between for people and thereby helps the smooth flow of ideas.

8. The Follower   This is the "yes" man. He or she simply says "yes" whenever a strong person makes a suggestion.

9. The Traveler   This person seems more interested in the activities of the other groups than in his own.

The plane makers should not be told what the observers' directions say. The activity should be carried out according to the rules outlined on the Participants' Instruction Sheet, and one group's design should be selected as the winner.

After fifteen minutes of building and the judging, observers and participants in each group should discuss how each of the participant builders took part in the group process. Each builder should reflect back on his/her behavior and see clearly how he/she operated and why.

The process should then be repeated with the roles reversed. The builders' behavior might be different because they know they are being observed. Discuss the differences between the two sessions and the reasons for them. Did the second session produce a better plane with less effort?

The nine roles might be observed in other group tasks as well as in this exercise. This particular exercise, as we have said, may be most useful to give students additional preparation for social action, but it need not be limited to that function. The Paper Airplane Contest would be useful in seeing just how thoroughly students have grasped the notion of equal status interaction.

Equal Status Cooperation

The key to group processes is equal status interaction in the small group setting. Equal status means that each member of the group recognizes the need for contributions from each other member. As such, an equal status group will recognize the worth and uniqueness of each member and will endeavor to develop the cohesiveness and cooperation necessary to achieve a group goal. Moreover, equal status in a cooperative small group setting provides a viable means of making legitimate decisions through the equal distribution of power.

In many instances small group experiences reflect the power structure evident in the larger classroom setting. The use of power in the classroom setting will directly influence the degree of open cooperation small groups are able to achieve. By virtue of position, societal mores, and school rules, the teacher is perceived by students as a source of power. The teacher's attitude toward the use of power is an important aspect of trust development in small groups.

Students also wield power in the classroom.[12] Their power is operationalized through the use of peer influence. Often, with a smile or other form of encouragement and reward, students can influence peers. It is also true that peer influence can be exerted through the use of coercion and threats. Influences on student leadership include his/her ability to lead, the attractiveness of the leader, and the perceived expertness of a leader. Studies have shown that students who are regarded as leaders, and thus powerful, usually possess attributes that are valued by classroom peers and are able to accomplish things. Those students perceived as being powerful usually are more closely watched and followed by peers than are other members of the group.[13, 14] It seems reasonable, then, to assume the teacher who conscientiously shares power with student leaders will have an easier time influencing the entire class than the teacher who does not.

Cooperative group structure seems to provide a viable means of making legitimate decisions through the equal distribution of power. However, there are some erroneous assumptions that are often made concerning cooperation.[15] It is sometimes thought that: students in groups involved in cooperative effects will not be able to pursue individual interest; some students involved in the cooperative efforts will be "carried" by others; students with less ability will be punished by their peers; the noncontributing, lazy student will receive all the benefits and rewards of the group; cooperative group efforts will provide students with continued opportunities to do those things they are good at without an opportunity to explore new areas. Such erroneous assumptions can be, and are, overcome in small groups which are established to (a) serve as a forum for the open exchange of ideas; (b) provide a means for the development of social skills and democratic values, regardless of participants' abilities; and (c) support and help maximize the opportunities for every child to experience psychological self-worth.

Small groups, particularly ones in which cooperation is the major emphasis, can be seen as more beneficial to almost all forms of desired learning outcomes. A chart on page 156 indicates competition and individualization ought to play a minor role in the formation of learning experiences.[16] It would be remiss, however, not to mention that competitive and individualized approaches have a place in the social studies

APPROPRIATE CONDITIONS CHART

	Cooperative	Individualized	Competitive
Type of Instructional Activity	Problem solving; divergent thinking or creative tasks; assignments can be more ambiguous with students doing the clarifying, decision making, and inquiring.	Specific skill or knowledge acquisition; assignment is clear and behavior specified to avoid confusion and need for extra help.	Skill practice, knowledge recall and review; assignment is clear with rules for competing specified.
Perception of Goal Importance	Goal is perceived as important for each student, and students expect group to achieve the goal.	Goal is perceived as important for each student, and each student expects eventually to achieve his goal.	Goal is *not* perceived to be of large importance to the students, and they can accept either winning or losing.
Student Expectations	Each student expects positive interaction with other students; sharing of ideas and materials; support for risk taking; making contributions to the group effort; dividing the task among group members; to capitalize on diversity among group members.	Each student expects to be left alone by other students; to take a major part of the responsibility for completing the task; to take a major part in evaluating his progress toward task completion and the quality of his effort.	Each student expects to have an equal chance of winning; to enjoy the activity (win or lose); to monitor the progress of his competitors; to compare ability, skills, or knowledge with peers'.
Expected Source of Support	Other students are perceived to be the major resource for assistance, support, and reinforcement.	Teacher is perceived to be the major resource for assistance, support, and reinforcement.	Teacher is perceived to be the major resource for assistance, support, and reinforcement.

From David W. Johnson and Roger T. Johnson, *Learning Together and Alone* (Englewood Cliffs, New Jersey: Prentice-Hall, 1975), p. 62. Used with permission.

curriculum. Whenever competition is used, it should be used in an intergroup setting, as opposed to interpersonal competitive activities. The social studies teacher who establishes small groups and then has them compete with one another in investigating the same dilemma is doing more to protect student feelings than one who pits individual students against each other. Losses are easier to handle when cushioned by a group effort. Moreover, there appears to be more protection for easily bruised egos in groups working on a common task.

Individualized approaches might be best used in social studies when students are working on a specific skill and there is room available for such activity. After such activities, students can be brought together in groups to work jointly on a project in which their individual expertise can be utilized.

There are four essential ingredients in the establishment of cooperative groups based on trust. First, each individual in the group must be strongly committed to reaching the goal. Second, the individual must realize that he/she cannot reach the goal without the help of other persons and that they are able to be helpful. Third, the individual must realize that the other members are dependent on him/her in order to reach the goal. Fourth, each individual must realize that all members are mutually dependent on each other in order to achieve the goal.[17] The last ingredient leads to an equal status interaction setting and will be extremely useful in promoting task completion through group cooperation.

Most teachers practicing small group processes find certain difficulties in establishing and maintaining group focus on the four essential ingredients. The intergroup conflicts that develop often serve to disorient the members to such an extent as to subvert the focus on the goal at hand. Teachers can become victims of "group paralysis" wherein the communication within the group centers on personality differences and the process degenerates to a point of seething hostility.

To avoid such hostility and assure open and free expression within groups imposes major responsibilities on the teacher. In the first instance, the teacher has an obligation to train students in, and then maintain, the idea of respect for the worth of each person's statements and ideas. This is admittedly a difficult task as it entails conducting group sessions which deal primarily with group communication skills. Secondly, the goal established for the group must be strong enough to be maintained despite conflicts. Such a goal must be clearly stated and understood by all group members and then reëmphasized periodically. The goal should be specific enough so that the group members will recognize when it has been achieved. Specificity of goals is important in small groups for three reasons: "First, the members must be able to know what type of proposal will take them to their target. Second, they must be able to tell when, if ever, a specific problem has been solved. Third, an effectively high commitment and concerted group effort cannot be maintained forever."[18] The group will at some time need to recognize some specific accomplishment.

Need for Checkpoints and Checklists

In light of the importance of clear goals and the ever-present threat of group conflict, it will be helpful for the teacher to establish checkpoints along the way. Such checkpoints help to monitor group progress, but, more to the point, the teacher can use them to provide the group with reinforcement for the progress that is made. In planning for small group experiences, the teacher needs to estimate the sorts of reinforcement which encourage continuation toward the ultimate goal, completion of the task, and/or solving the problem. An example of using the checkpoint idea would be an exercise in which the participants are asked to prioritize a list which they have individually ranked prior to the small group session. As agreement is reached on each of the priorities, the group collectively feels rewarded and is prepared to attempt the next priority and so on until the task has been completed. With no opportunity for continued success, the chances of reaching an ultimate goal are greatly diminished.

In offering the checkpoint idea, the assumption is that the teacher probably has several small groups in operation at the same time and spends much time rotating from group to group, observing and monitoring. Too often the monitoring aspect becomes unmanageable simply because there is not enough time to spend with each small group. By utilizing a checkpoint system the teacher can monitor each group while permitting other groups the freedom to explore uninterrupted. It must be stressed that the idea of a checkpoint system does not necessarily mean a physical interruption of a group's progress. Rather, it is a mental process whereby the teacher responds to a group at particular intervals, both encouraging and monitoring progress through the use of a mental checklist. Items on the checklist would include an awareness of problems: lack of progress, off-task behaviors, and group anxieties.

The teacher's mental checklist could also include the following skills exhibited by students: (a) ability to evaluate hypotheses; (b) ability to recognize a problem; (c) speaking skills; and (d) listening skills. The more aware of and involved in the group process experiences the teacher is, the easier it will be to recognize approaching decision points.

In addition to the mental checklist, a paper/pencil checklist of cooperative experiences is provided for teacher use in developing and monitoring small groups. If after completing the checklist the teacher determines that small group cooperation is not achieving the goal, there remain the options of either changing to a competitive or individualized form of instruction or rethinking the goal in order to present it in a form more conducive to cooperative group efforts.

TEACHER CHECKLIST FOR COOPERATIVE SMALL GROUP EXPERIENCES[19]

1. What are the desired outcomes for the experience?
   A. Cognitive

   B. Affective

2. What is the identified task goal of the small group?
   ____ A. Are the students aware of the group goal?
   ____ B. Are the students aware that the group reward will be based on quality according to announced, fixed criteria?
3. Does the classroom arrangement provide a means of:
   ____ A. Open communication for students, clustered in small groups?
   ____ B. Freedom to move about in the quest of information?
   ____ C. Sharing of both verbal and written information within small groups with relative ease?
4. Are students aware that they should:
   ____ A. Interact with each other within the small group?
   ____ B. Share ideas and experiences as well as materials and information in a helping fashion?
   ____ C. Divide tasks as well as integrate individual findings into a group product?
   ____ D. Demonstrate an acceptancy attitude, limited or mutual respect for the status of each member of the group, and provide encouragement for further contribution in an atmosphere of genuine friendliness and warmth?
   ____ E. Speak and think in terms of the cooperative group, rather than the individual sense?
   ____ F. Explore various avenues in an attempt to classify or expand particular contributions while continuing to maintain an awareness of the task as the major focus?
5. Do students know and understand the teacher's role:
   ____ A. As facilitator, observer, and supporter of the group?
   ____ B. As a strong supporter of group cooperative effort in which the capabilities of each member are utilized to the greatest degree possible?

DECISION MAKING FOR SOCIAL ACTION

Rationale

Society confronts the citizen with a confusing complexity of interacting organizations. Both public organizations and private social conversations influence legislation. Whenever a group of people come together for whatever reasons, there exists a potential for action. Many people are not able to participate in decision making in our society because they do not understand their appropriate role in a small group. They fail to grasp the significance of utilizing the small group decision-making process to exert influence in community issues. Suppose a city council received a request to construct a new factory in a residential area. The final step in the decision-making process would be a vote of the members to accept or reject the request. Prior to that final decision, however, the city council would have received input from various solicited and unsolicited sources:

a. A group of concerned citizens might have expressed alarm at the change in the neighborhoods brought about by any new industry.
b. A group of environmentalists might express concern for the effect a new industry would have on the environment of the community.
c. A group of businessmen and merchants might express a favorable opinion since a new industry would provide additional economic benefits.
d. A group of local politicians might express an interest in seeing the new industry located in their district for potential votes.
e. A group representing the schools might express concern about possible overcrowding due to the influx of families.

The commonality here is that groups exerted influence on the decision-making process, and individuals made decisions to join groups. Decision making is at the heart of groups which play an important part in community programs.

As Engle and Longstreet point out, "The heart of citizenship is decision-making. Whatever his state of preparation, the citizen is called upon to make a myriad of decisions. These decisions may concern societal goals and the means of their attainment or they may concern his own personal behavior regarding these goals."[20] Therefore, if citizenship is to be an integral part of the social studies, decision making for social action must be dealt with realistically.

We agree with Dewey in the efficacy of the "organic" approach as the most realistic option for the individual in his relation to society.[21] In the organic approach, the individual is both subservient to and in control of society. If managed correctly, the balance struck will prove profitable for both the individual and society. In order to prepare students to maintain this balance, schools need to embark on social action programs designed to provide students with the tools necessary to participate in social change. In addition, social action programs would provide a forum for young and old alike to combine idealism with experience to form a realistic approach to democratic living. What, then, constitutes a social action program? In this regard, Newmann has offered a comprehensive definition:

> It (social action) should be construed . . . generally to include any behavior directed toward exerting influence in public affairs. As such, it can include telephone conversations, letter writing, participation in meetings, research and study, testifying before public bodies, door-to-door canvassing, fund raising, media production, bargaining and negotiation, and also publicly visible activity associated with the more militant forms. Social action can take place in or out of school and, if out of school, not necessarily in the streets, but in the homes, offices, and work places. It might involve movement among several locations or concentration at one.[22]

This is not to imply a condoning of radical social involvement. Nor is it to convey the idea that all social action will automatically guarantee students' ability to exert influence in public affairs. We are more concerned that students of all ages develop the abilities needed to understand and influence public affairs. Such a program should be the focus of an entire curriculum in which every student would participate in a laboratory setting. The social studies provide a logical beginning point for a social action laboratory, since much of what we teach in social studies is directly associated with society and its dilemmas, issues, and problems.

Newmann suggests that before a person attempts to exert influence or implements a position, the individual "should clarify and justify particular policies, candidates and actions that he or she supports or opposes."[23] The result of such clarification becomes one's goals or desired outcomes in public affairs. As soon as the individual's goals have been formulated, the citizen works to gather support from within the community (once it is determined whose support is necessary to achieve the goal). A number of skills are required in developing the competence needed to exert influence in public affairs. Skills in communication, such as writing, speaking, and listening, would be essential in developing the means to justify the goal in attempting to influence others. Knowledge of group behavior and skills in group dynamics would also be essential in developing a strong influential approach.

Policy Goals and Social Action

A crucial element in the development of influence lies in the individual's ability to make decisions on policy goals. For, without a well thought-out goal, an individual would rightfully stand a small chance of success in exerting any degree of influence. Through the use of small groups, such policy goals can become more sharply defined and recognized. Small groups working cooperatively on a policy framework in an effort to develop goals will have the advantage of providing not only a collective effort but a sounding board as well. In a well functioning social studies laboratory, such policy research as advocated by Newmann would be brought to fruition through a series of trial efforts using the resources of the cooperative group. In addition, the group effort would provide the individual student with the skills necessary to function in the larger community setting and in dealing with and persuading other citizens. An examination of the relevant procedures to be utilized in a social action program should prove helpful at this point.

Once a group has identified a common concern, the members must determine and examine what are known as impelling and constraining forces.[24]

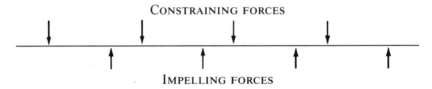

CONSTRAINING FORCES

IMPELLING FORCES

Every problem is affected by those forces which are at counterbalance with one another. By listing those forces which are impelling changes in the present condition as well as those forces which are holding back the changes, the group will more effectively focus on the difficulties to be overcome as they develop support for their goal. It is important to note how individual and societal value systems influence the impelling and constraining forces. Once the impelling and constraining forces have been identified, the group is ready to gather relevant information and test various suggested solutions. It is at this point that community involvement becomes a necessity. The group search for solutions must involve a segment of the community that is both interested in and affected by the goal. One approach to use is to think as if you were they and examine the problem and proposed solutions from the eyes of those most affected by the problem.

In the final analysis, the group must become an advocate of the point of view to which its members feel committed. The advocacy role is an individual one, as the advocate who once worked closely with others in analyzing the problem must take a stand in favor of his own reasoning in an effort to prove his solution as the best one. If the groundwork for the group interaction and investigation has been carefully laid, the advocacy portion of social action becomes an increasingly meaningful one to which students eagerly look forward.

One of the authors recalls vividly a social action program in which his students became involved. The decision occasion for the students was prompted by concern about dumping of waste from a meat packing house directly into a nearby river. The dumping of waste became the focal point of concern within the small group. Working cooperatively, they set about to gather evidence by taking pictures, reviewing laws, and interviewing the city attorney and mayor, as well as the owner of the packing house. The cooperative group then decided that there was a need for a change of policy toward the dumping of waste in the river. In order to effect that change they would have to mobilize some support. Before mobilizing the support, the group drew up a list of those forces which would not want to see any changes made and a list of those which would like to see a change. From the impelling and constraining lists the students were able to key in on the groups most in need of convincing. They demonstrated their concern to various citizen groups, including the city council, through the use of slides and results of interviews and polls conducted. As support mounted, the group was expanded to include concerned citizens and representatives of local agencies. While the group was hypothesizing solutions, the owner of the meat packing house was again interviewed and he indicated his concern about the cost of any changes.

Eventually, after many meetings over a period of several months, a solution was agreed upon by the group, and the owner made the necessary changes. It is important to note that the course of action finally agreed upon was one offered by the students who, through their skills of communication and group processes, were able to advocate and convince others of the desirability of their well-researched decision. That is not to say the deliberations were not at times heated, emotional, or without the application of pressure in the form of implied threats to force a particular view. However, because the small group originally had some idea of what to expect and more importantly because they were adept at dealing with decision-making skills in small groups, the experience was well worth the effort.

Banks and Clegg present social action as the heart of a social studies design and discuss social action projects that students might undertake in the areas of automobile safety, political affairs, consumerism, hospital or prison conditions, and drug abuse, among others.[25]

Moving Toward Social Action with a Decision Grid Game

The most useful example that we have found of a small group activity which embodies all the characteristics necessary to foster cooperation and enhance decision-making skills is the Decision Grid.

This is a game which emphasizes group decision making while focusing on a specific cognitive area, the most successful of which has been community services. The game is designed for four participants in a group and may be most appropriate for junior high students and above, although some fifth- and sixth-grade classes might be able to use it profitably.

The initial motivation is provided by telling participants that they are going to an unpopulated part of the earth, similar in climate to their own (done to reduce the number of extraneous factors to be considered), to establish a new community. They must decide which community services they hope to retain there. Thus, they must examine the status of their present community and extrapolate from those findings.

Before deciding on group ratings, students are given individual rating sheets where they determine their own answers. Students are usually given about twenty minutes to complete their own small grid. In other words each student decides his degree of agreement—from "strongly agree" to "strongly disagree"—about including a particular community service (e.g., libraries) in the community. The need for these individual rankings was explained earlier; but unlike the moon game, there is no one right answer, and students will be much more opinionated in this real-life situation.

Motivation is maintained continuously through the next stage by the control and decision-making elements of the game. Each of the participants in the group of four has control of one horizontal row of the grid. Which one is immaterial, since row one is no more powerful than row four. Such individual control, however, provides each participant with the power to accept or reject the use of any compartment in any of his/ her five value sections across the grid. In the time allotted (which really is determined by outside constraints—length of class period, teacher's lesson plan), students must assign each of twenty cards to various spaces on the grid. Each card depicts different community services or functions similar to those services students personally ranked. Through the use of a forced choice format, each card must be placed in a different category and all the spaces must be filled by group consensus in order to achieve successful completion of the task.

As each picture is disclosed, participants decide collectively where to place it on the grid, depending on the group consensus of strong positive feelings or strong negative feelings for the depicted community item.

The cards are disclosed in a random order. Each picture is disclosed separately and placed on the grid before the next depiction is seen by the participants.

DECISION GRID

Partic-ipant	Strongly agree	Somewhat agree	Neutral	Somewhat disagree	Strongly disagree
#1					
#2					
#3					
#4					

The key here is that all the depictions must be placed on the board and that each participant has absolute control over his/her horizontal element. Therefore, a highly competitive participant may opt to "hold out" and not permit any depiction to be placed on his/her row. However, as the game progresses, that individual is forced to compromise his/her degree of control in order to complete the task successfully. Three basic rules govern the progress of the activity: (1) Each depiction must be placed before the next one is revealed; (2) No depiction may be placed in any category without the permission of the individual who controls that category; (3) No depiction may be moved laterally in any row without consensus. Despite the "simplicity" of these rules, severe constraints are placed on a group in which individuals refuse to cooperate with one another.

It becomes obvious at some point during the activity that some depictions have universal appeal, while other community services have little or no universal appeal. Therefore, participants are confronted with the problem of first deciding which depictions are not appealing, and, second, how best to accommodate the desires of the other group members. The successful completion of the task depends on the amicable resolution of the various feelings. A great deal of compromise generally ensues. For example, an adult (x-rated) theater might have negative appeal for most, but the two categories in which that depiction would normally be placed are filled. Therefore, a decision must be made in order to reach consensus. If the group attitude is strong enough, one of the depictions in the "somewhat disagree" and "strongly disagree" columns will be moved to another category. The degree of compromise will depend on the persuasive abilities of the group as a whole.

Equal status, or power control, it can again be emphasized, directly influences the successful completion of the task. In some group activities which do not rely on cooperative decision-making skills, a high degree of competition may prevail to the consternation of group members and the teacher. Since a competitive spirit often fosters forcefulness, it is usually the most vocal or physically strongest who perform and reinforce their own decision-making skills in a negative mode. In such competitive group endeavors, the shy, non-verbal participant is often easily maneuvered to a position of quiet passivity and is completely dominated by the aggressive participant. In the forced equal status group situation of this game, power is distributed equally and each participant shares equally in the group effort. Thus, the passive youngster may choose to "hold out," as described above, simply to "flex his muscles," to really experience the thrill of having others recognize his parity and appreciate his unique contributions to group decision making. The reinforcement of acceptable decision-making skills requires a group effort, then, in which equal status is maintained and ultimately respected.

The game does not end when all the cards have been placed. As in most simulation games, the debriefing is probably the most important part of the gaming situation. Students should be encouraged to view the finished grid as a framework for, in this case, community development. The group should try to focus on inherent inconsistencies and decide if they can/should be altered to achieve a more viable community. For example, a group may decide it is committed to public transportation and an elaborate highway system. Is this consistent? Where do parking facilities fit in such a scheme? Can you be strongly for higher education and strongly against a public school system? If students can reconcile these apparent inconsistencies, then another area must be considered— that of consequences of their choices. While this is an integral part of the decision-making model presented in Chapter One, future consequences must be considered too.

Following the completion of the game and the search for inconsistencies, students should consider the overall consequences of their choices. For example, a group might rate police service low as a community value, but they should understand what consequences might arise if there were no police. Is the new community to be an idealistic utopia with few or no rules? Can such a community exist? If rules are needed, who will enforce them? Who will protect individuals from the encroachment of others upon their individual rights? A group might also decide apartment housing is undesirable, but is it realistic not to have such housing in a community? Can we reasonably assume all people can afford to buy a home and, if they can, will not the population of the community be quite uniform economically? Of course, students may decide that the "state" will provide all individuals with adequate housing. This might provide stimulus for research or unit work on various socioeconomic systems and their consequences.

The Decision Grid really takes students to the shoreline of social action. With a little prodding, they will be in the water attempting to implement some of their ideas or preferences. For example, substandard housing is always going to be looked upon with strong negative feelings. If that is the case, why does it exist? When a group is a cohesive, cooperative, trusting organism, it is ready to solve, or try to solve, social problems. Students can now share opinions and solutions on an equal status basis as they wrestle with real social problems. Questions on community life and problems which were considered too dull for discussion now leap into positions of unavoidable reality. Students are now confronted with how best to deal with such problems.

When this activity is followed and supported by parallel activities embodying the same criteria—namely, equal status among participants, cooperation in the final outcome, and a definable, accessible goal—attention is then concentrated on decision-making skills, while permitting the teacher to shift the cognitive emphasis to any particular subject deemed important in the overall curriculum design of that particular course.

GENERAL MAINTENANCE

Do's and Don't's

At this point it may be useful to review the preparation for small group decision making and offer some do's and don't's in forming groups and completing the tasks at hand. The thirteen points listed below are not given in a sequential order. That, indeed, may vary according to the classroom climate and situation at hand. Since some of these points may seem unimportant, a rationale based on research findings is provided.

1. Brainstorm when time is limited and the problem or task is simple.
2. Continue to use task groups in later activities, such as simulation games.
3. Determine (examine) roles in the group by keeping an anecdotal record of group interaction, member roles, and task orientation.
4. Foster a social climate helpful to group work.
5. Try to break up previously established patterns of familiarity: friendship groups, bus groups, ethnic groups, sociocultural groups should be discouraged.

6. Use established student leaders to aid in group formation and development.
7. Shift group members after a series of tasks.
8. Clarify the task explicitly.
9. Try to discourage autocracy and encourage status interaction.
10. Aim towards consensus without unjustified acquiescence.
11. Discourage conflict among *ad hoc* groups.
12. Be a silent non-obtrusive listener.
13. Encourage conflict among established groups.

Brainstorming is commonly used to get as many solutions to a problem aired in as short a time as possible. However, brainstorming, for the most part, limits the quality of solutions. It is good for solving simple problems, but not as good for solving complex ones. In some cases a teacher may wish to "structure" brainstorming through cued recall, rather than just calling for free recall situations. Essentially, most researchers have found that group participation in brainstorming may indeed inhibit creative thinking because it is hard not to conform to group "boundaries," and divergent thinking may be suppressed.

Groups seem to lend themselves to simulation and gaming with high motivational gains. If one accepts the premise that the use of small groups enhances successful decision making, then the successful completion of other tasks should also be enhanced through the use of groups. Discover other tasks that a group may solve, and use previously formed small groups to develop solutions.

The determination or examination of student roles in the group is of prime import. It may be that a leader develops naturally. The teacher may be quite surprised at who the leader (or facilitator) turns out to be. Note the leadership choices and role developments that occur, as well as the form and evolution of a group. Not only will this aid the teacher in understanding a bit more of the complexities of group process, but it may also aid in classroom management. Seeing the potential a student exercises in an equal status confrontation may aid in planning a student's tasks and program in other areas of the curriculum. It should be noted, however, that working in groups will not *necessarily* aid later individual abilities. In our experiences a big talker may be "shut out" in an equal status situation, unless the other group members feel that his contributions are aiding the group's task. Even then, if group members have not begun to appreciate the contributions of the talker in class, his contributions in the group may be ignored. In one small group experience, just such a situation was observed. It was the initial exercise, and preconceived patterns of distrust and disrespect were evident. When one student of obvious low group status suggested a solution to their problem, two group members rejected it because (Bill) "was always babbling." When the group later discovered that other groups had used "his" solution to solve the same problem, his status was enhanced, and in later exercises more parity was perceived.

Some studies have shown that using student groups resulted in greater student peer tutoring and greater perceived mutual concern in the classroom. Keeping an anecdotal record of group interaction, member roles, and task orientation permits a teacher to keep track of such changes and make use of them in class procedures and management.

Decisions on the social climate may be vital to task completion. In a group problem-solving situation a permissive social climate will often prove superior to a traditional climate for students with high levels of intelligence, while students with only average intelligence may be considerably handicapped. In an equal status situation, most groups are of a mixed intellectual character. A permissive social climate with relatively visible parameters has proved to be most successful in group decision making and task completion.

Breaking up previously established patterns of familiarity is a necessity if equal status interaction is to be achieved. To enhance cooperation, random assignment usually assures a good mixture of boys and girls, highly verbal and passive students, leaders and followers, and enthusiastic and reluctant learners. We have used random grouping to break down these barriers and to dispel the student suspicions of "sabotage." In some cases, however, it may be necessary to manipulate classroom groups. In one of our classrooms, certain leaders were apparent and certain students were almost never listened to. We made sure the leaders were split from their faction of followers and made great allowances for equal status. The results certainly justified our manipulation. Scientific? Not really. Humanly valuable? We believe so.

In some classrooms, "capturing" the school leaders may, indeed, aid in small group formation and development. What we just said about breaking up patterns and encouraging equal status interaction does not preclude using respected class members to enhance the development of the initial stages of small-group decision making.

After a series of tasks a group may become so stable as to lose its creativity. Shifting group members will break up stultifying cliques or embattled rivalries and minimize possibly erosive effects of social "classness." After a time students seem to enjoy a new group also. Do not rush to break up small groups, however, until you perceive their creativity and efficiency diminishing.

Clarifying the task may seem patently obvious, but it is important. A group that feels confused over its task assignment can devote its time to destroying its task, rather than doing it. Thus, it is imperative to clarify the task to the satisfaction of the small group. Do not be adverse to repeating the "instructions" later, if asked, but *do not* direct group progress.

Discouraging autocracy means, obviously, fewer autocratic decisions. Autocratic decisions, almost always, will not lead to informed and insightful decision makers. This means that using a rational group model may complete the task but not allow for real decision making in the group. A consensus model is then imperative. Note that the discouragement of autocrats must be done in more than a verbal way. Leadership role models are far stronger than words. A teacher who espouses consensus decision making must take every opportunity to practice it.

Just because consensus is the goal does not necessarily mean it will be achieved. Often students will acquiesce merely to get the task completed, or they will "trade" one idea for another. This should be discouraged. Despite the demand for cooperation, students should not give in unless they are convinced they are wrong. To reillustrate this, view Henry Fonda in "Twelve Angry Men."

Much of this Yearbook has examples based on conflict decisions. Conflict is disruptive generally in *ad hoc* groups and should be discouraged. However, a wide variety of opinions is usually beneficial to established groups, and thus conflict should be encouraged among such groups. The rationale for this appears to be that when group members know each other well, they do not take attacks on ideas personally. *Ad hoc* group members often feel threatened and possibly embarrassed by disagreeing with persons they know casually, at best.

Being a patient listener really sums up the teacher's role throughout the process of small-group decision making. In order to follow some of the suggested hints, a teacher must be as unobtrusive as possible. Float from group to group. Sit and listen for a time. Answer questions but discourage students from appealing to you. Do not volunteer information unless there has been some obvious discrepancy in your task assignment. In such a case, get the entire class's attention, give it the correct information, and fade again into the woodwork. If you wish to make anecdotal observations, do that between group "sittings" so as not to distract the group from its task unduly. This may seem surprising, but if the teacher does not interject his/her opinion, the students will still solve their task quite adequately. This may leave a teacher with a question about his/her utility. But in order to give students the power to make decisions, teachers must share their power.

The last point is really reinforced throughout. Without calling equal status interaction by such an appellation, encourage students to listen and evaluate all points of view before making a decision in their group.

CHECKLIST

Here is a summary of the teacher steps to promote the process of small-group decision making.

1. Determine the degree of development of listening skills.	Teacher can do a number of listening skills "tests."
2. Promote and develop listening skills.	Allow students to fully express their thoughts and encourage the class to react to them in a positive way.
3. Provide a climate for expression of thought.	Be a listener, not a talker; a model, not a modeler.
4. Allow and encourage individual values clarification.	Any number of exercises can be useful here.
5. Determine task.	Teacher must make task clear or the the group may act against task. Student skill in problem recognition is necessary.
6. Allow individuals to "solve" task.	This gives students a base from which to work.
7. Set up groups.	Seek to split class friendship or leadership patterns.
8. Observe role development.	Are all participating? What roles have developed—e.g., leader, facilitator, cynic, "yes-man," etc.?
9. Analyze task completion.	What model (is/was) used for task completion? If not consensus and equal status interaction, return group to another exercise, such as the Paper Airplane Contest.
10. Promote social action.	Group discusses problem(s) of society. Steps are taken or proposed to remedy social problem.

Before we close this chapter we should make some *caveats*. Groups are not necessarily better than individuals in problem solving. They *may* not be better in all aspects of decision making. Yet, given the nature of the tasks that we have discussed, small groups are a superior way of making certain decisions, particularly those of a social action nature. Most decisions in our society are either discussed in a small group or decided there. If a social studies goal is better prepared citizens, then small-group decision making is a necessary skill to develop and encourage, in and out of the classroom.

FOOTNOTES

[1]John Dewey, *The School and Society* (Chicago: University of Chicago Press, 1899).

[2]Robert F. Bales, "Channels of Communication in Small Groups," *American Sociological Review*, 16 (1951), pp. 461–468.

[3]E. B. South, "Some Psychological Aspects of Committee Work," *Journal of Applied Psychology*, 11 (1927), pp. 437–464.

[4]J. Calonico and B. Calonico, "Classroom Interaction: A Sociological Approach," *Journal of Educational Research*, 66 (1972), pp. 165–169.

[5]Richard A. Schmuck and Patricia A. Schmuck, *Group Processes in the Classroom* (Dubuque, Iowa: Wm. C. Brown Co., 1975), p. 94.

[6]Leland P. Bradford, "Developing Potentialities Through Class Groups," in *Forces in Learning*, Selected Readings, Series Three (Washington, D.C.: National Training Laboratories and National Education Association, 1961), p. 45.

[7]June Chapin and Richard Gross, *Teaching Social Studies Skills* (Boston: Little Brown and Co., 1973), pp. 53–58.

[8]Geraldine Ball, "Level VI Activity Guide," *Human Development Program* by Uvaldo Palomares and Geraldine Ball (LaMesa, California: Human Development Training Institute, Inc., 1974).

[9]Mario Fantini and Gerald Weinstein, *Making Urban Schools Work* (New York: Holt, Rinehart and Winston, 1968), p. 30.

[10]Jay Hall, "Decisions, Decisions, Decisions," *Psychology Today*, Vol. 5, No. 6 (November, 1971), pp. 51–54, 86, 88.

[11]Jeffrey Schrank, *Teaching Human Beings—101 Subversive Activities for the Classroom* (Boston: Beacon Press, 1972). Copyright © 1972 by Jeffrey Schrank. Reprinted by permission of Beacon Press.

[12]R. A. Schmuck and P. A. Schmuck, *op. cit.*, p. 69.

[13]N. Polonsky, R. Lippitt and F. Redl, "An Investigation of Behavioral Categories in Groups," *Human Relations*, 3 (1950): pp. 319–348.

[14]M. Gold, "Power in the Classroom," *Sociometry*, 21 (1958), pp. 50–60.

[15]David W. Johnson and Roger T. Johnson, *Learning Together and Alone* (Englewood Cliffs, New Jersey: Prentice-Hall, 1975), pp. 54–56. Adapted by permission of Prentice-Hall, Inc.

[16]*Ibid.*, p. 62.

[17]James L. Loomis, "Communication, the Development of Trust and Cooperative Behavior," *Human Relations*, 12 (1959) pp. 305–315.

[18]Bobby R. Patton and Kim Giffin, *Problem-Solving Group Interaction* (New York: Harper & Row, 1973), p. 147.

[19]Adapted from David W. Johnson and Roger T. Johnson, *Learning Together and Alone*, (Englewood Cliffs, New Jersey: Prentice-Hall, 1975), pp. 54–56.

[20]Shirley H. Engle and Wilma S. Longstreet, *A Design for Social Education in the Open Curriculum* (New York: Harper & Row, 1972), p. 14.

[21]John Dewey, *Reconstruction in Philosophy* (New York: Henry Holt, 1920), p. 87.

[22]Fred M. Newmann, *Education for Citizen Action* (Berkeley, California: McCutchan, 1975), pp. 54–55.

[23]*Ibid.*, p. 76.

[24]B. R. Patton and K. Giffin, *op. cit.*, p. 144.

[25]James E. Banks and Ambrose Clegg, *Teaching Strategies for the Social Studies* (Reading, Massachusetts: Addison-Wesley, 1973).

"Effective visual material (graphs, charts, maps, mounted pictures, slides, time lines, cards, models) should be prepared on every important point."

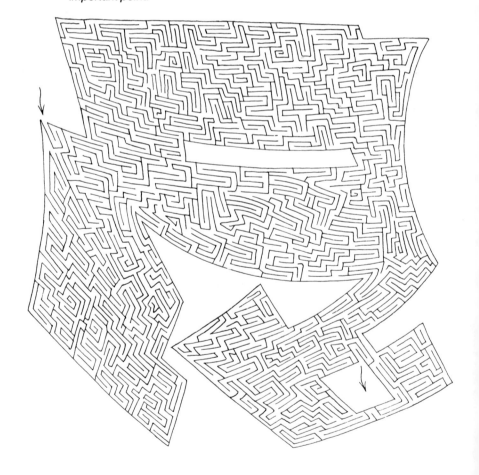

.6.

Barbara J. Capron

Developing Decision-Making Skills in Elementary Schools

The preceding Yearbook chapters have defined the decision-making skills, suggested sequential patterns, and identified a number of teaching strategies. Chapter Six will present teaching strategies particularly useful for elementary grades. The emphasis of these strategies is on developing thinking, information gathering, and group process skills. The models used in this chapter are selected to illustrate the decision-making skills and to reflect the current emphases in elementary social studies. The programs are easy for teachers to adapt and have proved successful with elementary children. Primary and intermediate lessons are included.

SEPARATE SKILLS UNITS
OR THE INTEGRATION OF SKILLS IN CONCEPTUAL UNITS

To avoid a haphazard and ineffectual treatment of skills, a flow chart[1] is needed in every elementary school. This then becomes the basis for a systematic development of student skills. Teachers can use the school's skills flow chart as a checklist for student attainment. The most useful flow charts show the best age placement for each skill and indicate which skills are the primary (and which are the shared) responsibility of the social studies program. However, learning rates differ so much that exact grade placement must be kept flexible and instruction individualized to provide optimal learning for each student.

Throughout the 1963 Yearbook of the National Council for the Social Studies, *Skill Development in Social Studies,*[2] it was emphasized that students develop skills most effectively when there is both planned instruction and continued practice and application of the skills. Knowing which skills need separate skills units and which are best integrated into

175

conceptual units saves time for teachers and improves interest for learners. Geography provides an example of this distinction.

According to Hanna and his associates in *Geography in the Teaching of Social Studies Concepts and Skills*,[3] geographic skills can be identified with the levels where students can learn and use them. Units can be planned and direct instruction can be provided for such geographic skills as scale, geographic terms, directions, symbols, latitude, longitude, and projection. Many teacher units in grades two-four testify to the popularity of separate and direct instruction in geographic skills. Though such geographic skills are most efficiently taught in directed lessons, practice should also be related to the conceptual units being considered at the time.[4] Opportunities to practice these skills should be included in incidental teaching, such as current events, which calls for map reading and interpretation.

Reading, interviewing, observing, thinking, and social process skills are best realized in elementary programs when they are part of conceptual units and the total learning experience. Even with these skills, however, at times it will be appropriate to include directed lessons. When students are unable to interpret a bar graph or have difficulty in classifying information, separate lessons, mini-units, or learning stations will be a necessary precondition to further progress in learning about the American Frontier or Nigerian ways of living. Developmental procedures for many of these skills are presented in Chapters Two, Three, Four, and Five of the Yearbook.

To individualize and manage these skills within the total elementary social studies program needs continual attention. No administrative design nor set ability groups can care for all learning styles or individual differences. Each teacher must analyze the differences in the development and ability of the group involved. Some ways to deal with individual differences and other procedures for developing decision-making skills are suggested in the sections which follow.

PUPIL-TEAM LEARNING

Pupil-team learning consists of dividing the class into groups of two to five students. Tasks are defined for students to work on together—to plan activities, and to correct and evaluate findings. Paired practice works especially well in intermediate grades. Teams can be organized for working on topics of mutual interest, according to skill attainment level or along sociometric lines. For long-range projects, students work best when they have a chance to choose their working partners. Tasks of short duration can be handled by randomly numbering the students or "pulling numbers out of a hat" type of selection.

Pupil-teams gather information through group and individual processes (i.e., instructional media, interviews, field trips). Team discussion techniques such as those which follow can be applied to answering workbook questions, using learning centers, and planning projects, oral talks, field trips, and dramatic presentations:

1. Teams are presented with topics or questions, and they discuss the questions or problems and dictate answers to a student recorder. With experience, pupil-teams formulate their own topics for study;
2. A recorder from one team presents a group's findings, and other teams check their answers or opinions, reporting only on additions and corrections;
3. Team discussions, followed by class discussion, summarize the findings of the whole class; and
4. A class chart is made for summary of the information.

The design of questions for the teams influences the level of thinking skills. Questions which ask *who, what, where,* and *when* will elicit simple recall. Questions which ask students to *compare, relate, infer,* and *judge,* or *apply* will call for more critical thinking, which is elaborated on in Chapter Two.

What each team produces in information can be efficiently shared. Reports by group chairpersons certainly offer more channels for information than a teacher could in direct teaching; and time is saved, since each individual does not report. Three possible ways in which team-learning could be used follow:

1. Children are given study guide questions and work in pairs or in teams of three. Students read paragraphs assigned, consult on and write their answers. Team discussion, then whole class discussion follow. When the student recorders report, other teams check their answers. This particular method is a good one to start pupil-teams, since it is directed and involves a short assignment.
2. As a review at the end of a unit, student teams work with problems in which there are many parallels but also important differences. This type of problem can be an effective discussion technique: "Canada and the United States were both explored and settled by Europeans at about the same time in history. Natural regions (the Rockies, the Great Plains, the Appalachian Mountains, the Great Lakes) are shared by both countries. They have many common resources and industries (farm products, fishing, coal, iron ore, oil, etc.). Why did the United States grow to be a nation with over two hundred million people, while Canada has about one-tenth that number of people?''

3. On a field trip to a historical village, students formulate or are given questions to answer, places to find, pictures to take, word meanings to check on, routes to follow, and activities to do. Teams report on their findings when they return to class. This is an especially rich experience if teams are assigned or choose different routes, houses, and activities.

Pupil-teams can work on long-range projects when they have had experience with shorter tasks. Study guides can cover several weeks of work, with problems to be solved, materials to be used, and a variety of activities to be done.

The "Pupil Specialty," which follows, is a long-range project on which pupil teams can work.

THE PUPIL SPECIALTY

"The Pupil Specialty" offers experience in using information gathering and group process skills on a long-range project. "The Pupil Specialty" is adapted from unpublished materials first developed by George Moore of the Wellesley, Massachusetts, Public Schools. The model presented here, *A Handbook for Preparing a Pupil Specialty on Europe*,"[5] is one adapted by the Chelmsford, Massachusetts, Public Schools. This research model is appropriate for use in intermediate grades.

A PUPIL SPECIALTY ON EUROPE

INTRODUCTION

Congratulations: You have selected a subject to study which is closely associated with your work in social studies. You have discovered, in working with other subjects, that no one book can possibly give you all the information you need on a particular topic. By looking through different books, films, filmstrips, magazines, encyclopedias, and other media, you can find many different things about interesting subjects. When you have finished doing your research, you will probably know more about that subject than anyone else in your class, and probably more than anyone in the whole school. You will then become a specialist in that subject, and will have something to tell the rest of the class.

Most students enjoy doing this type of work. You have chosen this subject because you selected it, are able to do it, and feel you can do it well. This guidebook is to help you in working out your specialty. Read it carefully and follow the directions. It will make your work much easier. This is not a project on which you must work all alone. Ask your parents, your teacher, and your librarian for help if you need it. Remember the whole world is full of materials and people from whom you can learn a great deal. Seek out valuable sources of information. *Good Luck!*

Now that you have chosen your subject and have had your completion date assigned, you will want to get right down to work. Plan to use as much free time as you can in the classroom. Plan also to spend some time each school evening on your special project.

1. Have at home each evening the materials you will need.
2. Have a place at home where you can work.
3. Plan to visit the library frequently.

As you proceed through your specialty you will complete each of the following stages:

Stage One—Note-taking
Stage Two—Outlining
Stage Three—Preparation of the Display
Stage Four—Oral-Visual Reporting

When you have completed your oral-visual report you:

1. May wish to ask the class several questions that deal with what you have reported on, or you may wish to give them a test.
2. Will be closely questioned on your subject by your classmates.
3. Will arrange your specialty for display in an assigned place in the classroom.

Each day should see a little more of your specialty completed. When you have an assignment that covers a long period of time it is surprising how quickly time passes.

1. As you complete each section of your pupil specialty, check it off on your "Pupil Specialty Check List." (See page 180.)
2. Consult with your teacher whenever you run into trouble.
3. Assemble at each stage the material you will need to complete successfully that stage.
4. Refer frequently to your copy of this book.

Maintain high standards of workmanship, and your pupil specialty will be a success.

STAGE ONE—NOTE-TAKING

1. Make up a series of general questions that you will answer about your subject. Questions such as:

    a. Where is it located, and what is its size?
    b. How does the physical environment affect the lives of the people?
    c. How does family life in the city differ from family life in the village?
    d. What are the resources of the country and how well are they developed?
    e. How well developed is the technology in this country?

(Continued on page 181)

PUPIL SPECIALTY CHECK LIST

	Pupil Check	Teacher Check
Note-taking		
a. Questions completed		
b. Changed to statements or phrases		
c. Placed each statement or phrase at the top line of a white sheet of paper		
d. Read widely on topic		
e. Identified the source for each note		
f. Completed note-taking		
Limiting the Topic		
a. Decided what part of the general topic to write about		
b. Established a point of view about topic		
Outlining		
a. Used each statement or phrase as a main division . .		
b. Used the next most important ideas under each statement or phrase as main ideas		
c. Used the facts that tell about the main ideas as details		
d. Completed outline		
The Display		
a. Selected all possible display material related to specialty		
b. Made display material covering important points . .		
c. Printed important ideas and words on cards		
d. Printed on back of display material information needed in talking about it		
e. Completed display material		
Oral-Visual Report		
a. Selected information from outline needed to tell about the subject		
b. Jotted notes on 3 by 5 index cards		
c. Selected visual material from display to go along with oral report		
d. Worked visual material into the oral report		
e. Completed a summary		
f. Practiced giving the report		

   f. What effect does the economic system have on the way people live?

   g. What effect does the government have on the daily lives of the people?

   h. How dependent are people in this country on one another and on other European nations?

   i. What are the problems faced by this country today?

2. Change each of these questions into statements or phrases. Such statements or phrases as:

   a. Location and Size.
   b. Physical Environment and Its Effect on the Lives of the People.
   c. Family Life in the City and Village.
   d. Use of Natural Resources.
   e. Technology and Its Development.
   f. Economic System and Its Effect on People.
   g. Government and Its Effect on Daily Lives of People.
   h. Interdependence.
   i. Problems Faced by This Region Today.

3. For each statement or phrase above use a separate sheet of paper.
4. Write the statement or phrase on the top line as the heading.
5. Gather information widely on your subject.
6. As you find information that goes with one of the headings, write this information, in your own words, under the heading where it belongs.
7. Add new headings as new questions on your subject come up.
8. Take your notes in phrases or short sentences.
9. Number or put a dash before each new note.
10. Skip a line between each new note.
11. Take your notes neatly. It will do you no good now to take notes you can't read later.
12. On a separate sheet of paper keep the information on each source used. See "Procedure for Making a Bibliography."

STAGE TWO—OUTLINING

1. Use each main heading that you placed on the top line of the sheet of lined paper as the main division. Sample main divisions:

   I. Location and Size
   II. Physical Environment and Its Effect on the Lives of the People
   III. Family Life in the City and Village

2. Read through the notes you have taken under each heading. You might cut these rough notes apart to arrange them more easily. Select the most important items. These will become main ideas.

   I. Location and Size (first main division)
     A. Where it is in the world (main idea)
     B. Bordered by (main idea)

    C. Points of reference (main idea)
    D. Size (main idea)

3. The items or facts that tell about the main ideas appear under them as details. Sample details with main ideas and with a main division:

    I. Location and Size
        A. Where it is in Europe
            1. Region (detail)
            2. Latitude and longitude (detail)
        B. Bordered by
            1. Other countries (detail)
            2. Bodies of water (detail)
        C. Points of reference
            1. To United States (detail)
            2. To Africa (detail)
            3. To Asia (detail)
        D. Size
            1. In square miles (detail)
            2. Compared with other countries (detail)
                a. Compared with China (detail)
                b. Compared with Middle East (detail)
                c. Compared with Africa (detail)
                d. Compared with United States (detail)

4. Check with your teacher and language book if you have difficulty constructing your outline.

STAGE THREE—THE DISPLAY
AND ITS IMPORTANCE IN ORAL–VISUAL REPORTS

1. The display is an important part of the specialty.
2. Effective visual material (graphs, charts, maps, mounted pictures, slides, time lines, cards, models) should be prepared on every important point.
3. Visual material should be selected from the display material for use in the report.
4. Without the use of good visual material it is difficult to hold an audience for more than five minutes.
5. Effective use of visual material can assist you in holding an audience for as long as fifteen minutes.
6. Visual material selected to be part of your oral-visual report should be of a size that is meant to be viewed at a distance.
7. Visual material should be selected on the basis that it highlights and makes important points clearer.
8. Important or unusual names, places, or ideas can be placed on cards and shown to your audience as you refer to them.
9. Many times in talking about something, such as a product or a custom, it is wise to show a picture or model and a card giving its name.

10. Maps of places in the world should be kept simple, illustrating only those ideas you want to get across.
11. In using maps, show not only the place in Europe that you are discussing, but also the relationship of that place to where we live and to other places in the world.
12. A good use of graphs and charts can keep your report clear and effective. Do not copy graphs and charts from textbooks or encyclopedias. Make your own.
13. Nothing is so dull as that type of visual material that has been copied from textbooks that you only half understand yourself.
14. Large pictures, maps, and other illustrative material can be sent for from sources of free and inexpensive materials.
15. Old magazines such as the *National Geographic* and *Holiday* offer a wealth of visual material. Pictures cut from magazines should be well mounted.
16. If you are in doubt as to what your material should be, ask yourself the question, "Will words alone put across the idea, or will I need some display materials to make my thoughts clear?"

STAGE FOUR—ORAL–VISUAL REPORTING

1. Much of the success of your report will be decided before you say your first word to the audience. How thorough was your research? How well are you at home with your subject?
2. If you are still at the "I will have to read every word when I report" stage, your knowledge of your subject is rather slight.
3. Equally bad is memorizing your report. This is, in a way, the same as reading from your mind. It is important that you know your subject so well that you feel at home with it.
4. You will know much more about your subject than you will have time to report, so your report needs to be carefully organized. Select the items that seem most interesting and relate most clearly to your main idea to include in the oral-visual report. Don't try to tell everything you know. Allow your display to tell about the rest of your specialty. During the question period you will have plenty of opportunity to show how well informed you are on your subject.
5. From your outline select those items your report is going to deal with. Jot these items on three by five index cards. This will allow you some notes to refer to as you present your oral-visual report.
6. Select from your display materials (graphs, charts, maps, mounted pictures, models) those items that best go with your report.
7. Practice giving your oral-visual report. Add and subtract items from your outline and display materials as they seem to fit or not to fit. As you practice giving your report, work in your visual material. Try to tape record one of your practice reports, and then listen critically to your presentation.
8. Select only visual material that will help you illustrate important points or highlight your report. Use visual materials when words do not seem to make clear what you are saying.

PUPIL CHECK LIST
FOR JUDGING A SPECIALTY REPORT

	E Excellent	G Good	F Fair	P Poor or None
Name of Pupil Making Report_____ Title of Report_____				
1. Showed he was well acquainted with this subject				
2. Spoke in a clear voice				
3. Presented his report in an organized way				
4. Brought out important points				
5. Looked at his audience while speaking				
6. Made sense in the things he said				
7. Used visual material to clarify his report				
8. Visual material was easily seen				
9. Visual material was used to illustrate important points				
10. Visual material was not just used at start or finish of report but used throughout report				
11. Visual material was well labeled				
12. Visual material was held so all could see				
13. Spoke from notes				
14. Summarized important points				
15. Answered correctly most of the questions asked				
16. Held the interest of his audience				

9. Do not put all your visual material either at the beginning or the end of your report. Locate the visual material in your report so that these illustrations are used with the words or ideas they are meant to clarify. Have the words and pictures go together.

10. In giving your oral-visual report you will be either sitting or standing, facing your audience. You will undoubtedly be nervous. Do not allow this nervousness to upset you. Nervousness is normal. It means you are excited. Take a deep breath and begin.

11. In order to attract the audience's interest, have a well prepared and colorful first sentence. This will get you off to a good start. For example: "Have you ever thought what it might be like living on a mountain?" "Although most

kids don't know it, there's more to France than French bread, French toast, and French fries.''

12. Look at your audience as you report. Talk directly to it. Do not look at the floor, ceiling, table top, or try to hide behind your notes or display material.

13. Try to be as relaxed as possible. Use a chatty delivery, as if you were describing something to a group of friends.

14. Speak in a clear, strong voice so all can hear you. Speak slowly so all can understand you. Hold your visual material so all can see it. Pause from time to time to allow an idea to reach the audience.

15. In presenting a new word or idea you will have to repeat it several times if it is to mean anything to your audience. Show a new word on a card rather than just repeating.

16. Conclude with a short summary.

PROCEDURE FOR MAKING A BIBLIOGRAPHY

A bibliography is a listing of all the sources that you have used in your research. You make a bibliography so that people who are interested in finding out more about your subject will know where to go for information. It is suggested that you keep the information needed for this as you go through your note-taking. The information for your bibliography is available on the title page of the source you are using.

This is the form to be used for all individual source books:

Author (last name first). *Title.** City of Publication: Publisher, Date of Publication. Pages used.

Example:

Gidal, Sonia and Tim. *My Village in England.* New York: Random House, 1963. Pp. 46-49.

This is the form to be used for all periodicals:

Author (if name is given, last name first). "Title of Article Used." *Title of Periodical,* Volume Number (month, year), page numbers of the article.

Example:

————"Britain: Life in the Old Bulldog." *Newsweek,* 81 (May 28, 1973), pp. 48–49.

This is the form to be used for all encyclopediae:

Author (if name is given, last name first). "Title of Article Used." *Name of Encyclopedia,* date of edition, volume, page numbers of the article.

Example:

————. "Greece." *Modern Century Encyclopedia,* 1972, 10, pp. 894–897.

---

*The titles of books, which appear in italics in this listing, should be underlined when a bibliography is typewritten or handwritten.

LEARNING CENTERS

Learning Centers can be set up around an elementary classroom or media centers for practice in social studies skills. The Centers can be used for reinforcement of a sampling of skills as they are needed, but they are most effective if they are centered around common conceptual learning or a few specific skills. The model for primary pupils which follows offers multisensory learning in the thinking skills of hypothesis formation and testing, generalizing from data, and drawing inferences that go beyond the data.

RUSSIAN FAMILY IN MOSCOW[6]

Introduce the Learning Center activities through these discussion questions:

1. What kind of clothing do we wear and where do we get it?
2. What kinds of food do we eat and where do we get them?
3. How do we travel to other places?

Begin to develop a retrieval chart to record the data and through questioning extend it to include other people previously studied, as in the chart which follows:

What We Need	Our Source	Early New England	Ashanti	Kibbutz
FOOD CLOTHING TRANSPORTATION				

Add another column with a culture about to be studied. For example: *Russian*. Ask:

1. How do you think a family in Moscow would get its food and clothing?
2. How do you think it would get to different places?

Divide the class into five groups. Assign one of the following questions to each group in order to gather data to complete the retrieval chart:

1. What kinds of food do people in Moscow eat?
2. Where do people in Moscow get their food?
3. What kinds of clothes do people in Moscow wear?
4. Where do people in Moscow get their clothing?
5. What do people in Moscow use to get from one place to another?

Tell the children that they are going to look at or listen to many different materials; many of these materials include information about many things, but they should only try to find information to help them answer their question. Also tell the children that some materials may not contain any information about their question. Set up five Learning Centers in different parts of the room with materials listed below from the accompanying media kit. Provide an opportunity for each research group to use the media at each Learning Center to answer the assigned question.

Learning Center A
Filmstrip 1: The City of Moscow

Learning Center B
Filmstrip 2: Recreation, Work and Celebrations

Learning Center C
Tape Cassette: My Day; Olga and Her Family

Learning Center D
Nikolai Lives in Moscow (Book)
Masha's Days (Book)
AYTO-Y-BAC (Russian Book)
National Geographic Magazine Moscow (Book)

Learning Center E
Russian Family Study Prints
Russian Recipes
Artifacts: Puppet, Khokhloma Spoon, Matroishka

Tell the members of each group that when they finish looking at or listening to the different materials, they should have enough information to answer their question and to help complete the retrieval chart. In addition, encourage each group to plan some unique way of sharing its information with the rest of the class. For example, a shopping group might act out shopping for food from different vendors and stores; the food group might plan a tasting party of Russian dishes and use the spoon; the clothing group might illustrate the changes that have occurred in clothing from that worn by the puppet and the rest of dolls to that worn today.

Once the groups have had the opportunity of sharing their findings and completing the retrieval chart, call attention to the completed chart. Ask questions such as:

1. What do you notice about the kinds of clothing people wear?
2. Why do you think people dress in these ways?
3. What does this tell you about the kinds of clothing people wear?

Record the children's generalizing statement on newsprint or the chalkboard.

Proceed in a similar manner with the other topics from the retrieval chart. Conclude by referring to the series of generalizations developed by the class and ask: What do these ideas seem to tell us about people?

Teachers can evaluate the level of thinking by judging the completeness of data on the retrieval chart and the type of generalizing statements proposed by children in their analysis of the data. Further evaluation would occur when children begin a new unit of study and are asked to apply their generalizations.

ROLE-PLAYING

Elementary teachers have long known the value of role-playing in learning social studies concepts and skills. According to Fannie and

George Shaftel,[7] whose method is summarized here, role-playing should begin under the direction of the teacher in a story or media presentation. First, role-playing is a spontaneous activity with the children responding in their own way to the presented situation. Play sessions, followed by sharing periods, help refine role-playing techniques to incorporate problem-solving skills such as the setting up of regulations and the assigning of tasks. Role-playing becomes both more meaningful and creative when it is enriched by discussion, research, and a wide range of media and personal experiences. Role-playing offers an open-ended way for young students to direct their own inquiries, pace their own learning, and grow in decision-making skills.

This role-playing model for primary social studies is from *One Plus One: Learning About Communities* (from the Macmillan social studies program, *Focus on Active Learning: Social Studies*).[8] The lesson includes activities for learning social-process and thinking skills.

DOGS AND PEOPLE

Read or tell the story "Dogs and People" (pages 111–115 in the student text, *One Plus One: Learning About Communities*).

"Dogs and People" tells the story of unleashed dogs who come to the playground. One day some dogs fight and a child nearby gets bitten. Parents organize a newspaper campaign for a dog leash law. They also hold meetings to urge that dogs be restrained. The town officers respond with a new regulation saying that all dogs must be kept at home during school hours and set a fine of $25 for anyone who breaks the law.

Discuss:

1. Why did parents get upset about the dogs at school?
2. How did the parents show they were upset?
3. How was the new town law passed?
4. How did the town officers make sure the law was obeyed?
5. Suppose the people had not become upset about the dogs, but the town officers had passed the law just the same. What might have happened?

Relate the question of freedom in the story "Dogs and People" to the students' freedom in school.

1. Can you do exactly as you wish in this classroom?
2. Is it right to limit your freedom at school? Why?
3. What kinds of limits on your freedom do you think would be unfair?

Prepare students for role-playing situation:

"Let's act out a meeting like the one we read about in 'Dogs and People.' Each person will have a card that tells you what part you will play, but not the exact words. You make up your own words."

Distribute *Role-Playing Cards* for the following roles: town officers, citizens, parents, teachers, dog owners, delivery men. (Role-Playing cards from *World of Communities Media System* or teacher-prepared cards like the ones on pages 100–103—Teacher's Edition of *One Plus One*.)

Record one role card on chart paper to show students how they can transfer the descriptions into words and actions.

Examples of role-playing cards:

1. "You are a town officer. You are called a selectman or mayor. You sit at a table facing the 'citizens.' You lead the meeting. You listen to people and ask questions."
2. "You are an older person. You had a dog when you were young. Now, sometimes dogs that are tied bark and disturb you. You think dogs should be free to run around."
3. "You are a parent and your child was bitten on the playground. You want dogs to be tied or kept at home. You want your child to be safe at school."
4. "You are a teacher. You have a dog and you like dogs. Some children in your class, who are afraid of dogs, won't go out at recess. You do not know what to do about it."
5. "You are a dog owner. You do not have any children. Listen to what all the others say and decide what you should do."

(There would be several of each kind of members at the meeting, representing many points of view.)

Arrange the room so that the town officers sit at a table facing the citizens.

Allow time for pupils to think about their responsibility at the meeting.

Set up rules for the meeting:

1. The chief town officer will open the meeting, call on citizens to speak, and announce the decisions of the officers.
2. Citizens will stand when they wish to speak and wait for the town leader to call on them.
3. Town officers ask questions when they don't understand what citizens mean, hold a brief conference when all members have spoken, and tell the citizens what they plan to do (dog leash law, further study, or plan no action).

Hold the meeting.

Discuss the meeting.

Discuss the substance and process of the simulation.

Help students evaluate the meeting and plan how they could improve their performance.

1. Did the town officers act as most of the citizens felt? If not, what can the citizens do?

2. Do you think citizens should call attention to laws that are needed? Is that a
   responsibility of a citizen?

For evaluating how well the students understood the concepts of civic rights
and responsibilities, the teacher could check their responses to a new situation:

Prepare sketches which would show steps citizens might take to get a traffic
light at a dangerous intersection (or study pictures on pages 116–117 in student
text, *One Plus One*). Check to see if pupils can arrange events in sequence, and if
they understand cause and effect.

Discuss:

1. Who lost freedom when the light was installed?
2. Did anyone have to give up some rights?
3. Did anyone gain any rights?
4. Do you think the light should have been put in?
5. Was there anything else the city officers could have done?

Show signs such as:

NO TRESPASSING	SPEED LIMIT—55
NO PARKING	ONE-WAY TRAFFIC
UNLAWFUL TO LITTER	EXIT THIS WAY

Assign a sign to each small group, which discusses the following questions and
presents findings to the class:

1. Who loses freedom as a result of your law?
2. Who gains freedom as a result of your law?
3. Why do you think the law was made?
4. How does your group feel about the law? Would its members always obey it?
5. What process do you think people went through to get such a law? How do
   you think people could get such a law changed, if they wanted to do so?

ISSUE DISCUSSION SEQUENCES

To gain competence in discussing social-ethical issues students must
develop the appropriate intellectual skills. One very effective procedure, "Issue Discussion Sequences," is presented in *People/Choices/
Decisions*, an upper elementary program.[9]

The "Issue Discussion Sequences" extend over several lessons and
provide strategies and resources to teach students useful skills for conflict resolution. Within the sequence, students are asked to:

1. take a position on a controversial problem;
2. support their position with relevant data;
3. support their generalizations with specific facts;

4. listen attentively to others' positions and respond to each specific statement;
5. identify areas where more information is necessary; and finally,
6. understand the dilemmas and the many points of view possible in conflict situations.

The model, which follows, shows the "Issue Discussion Sequences" in operation and provides activities for thinking, as well as group process skills. Obviously, this model is intended for several class periods.

A VILLAGE FAMILY

Introduce the Mexican village of Azteca and the Vega family by viewing the filmstrip, "Azteca," or use this summary of information:

The Vega family includes Felipe and Elena, the father and mother, Roberto, 18, Ester, 11, Carlos, 9, Pancho, 5, and Maria, the baby. Azteca (not a real village but representative of ones in this area) is located about 75 miles from Mexico City. The whole Vega family are farmers and have lived all their lives in Azteca. They raise corn and make rope to sell at the village market. The Vegas have little land and, as they can't afford to even rent oxen, do most of the farm work by hand. The land is dry and they can't afford to irrigate it. As the children are needed to work, they have attended school only a few years. Maria, the baby, is not healthy, and they are unable to provide proper health care for her. The Vega family love their village; they know all the people there; they are happy with the village celebrations; and they are devoted to their lovely old church, whose bells sound throughout the valley. It would be difficult for them to leave the life they have always known, though they work very hard and life is not easy for them.

One day Felipe receives a letter (page 53, student text; copy included on page 192).

The receipt of the letter can be a dramatic event. Instead of the letter being read from the textbook, a copy might be "delivered" in an envelope. It can be explained to the children that a letter from Uncle Cesar to Papa Vega has been intercepted. How many of you can guess its contents? The letter can then be read to the class and the discussion questions asked.

The children should be asked to suggest thoughts that might occur to Felipe or Elena when they consider moving. The statements may be general or specific, but they should be based on what the children know about the village. Examples might be given to insure that the class understands the activity. For instance, Felipe might think: "No rain again this year. Maria is ill because she does not have good food. Work in the fields becomes harder every day." Children could record their statements and, when ten or more statements have been recorded, they can be played back. Through discussion, the children can be helped to clarify their statements, eliminate duplications, and see why certain statements can be used to support either position.

Dear Felipe:

I hope that you and your family are in good health. How is Maria? Now that spring and warm weather are here, perhaps her sickness is gone? I send my best wishes that she get well quickly.

One night last week when I was returning from work, I met Miguel Marcial. Miguel now lives in Mexico City. He went to Azteca not long ago to visit his sick mother. He told me that things are not good in Azteca this year. The rains have not come and the land is very dry. He said that even the plums are small like peas.

Brother Felipe, I know that even in good years the land on the hill does not always give you enough to pay your debts and buy your food. Brother, you know in your own mind what is best for your family. It is not for me to tell you what you should do. But here in Mexico City, my family eats meat on many days and we have milk. Life is not easy, but we have things I did not have in Azteca. There is electric light. Soon I hope to buy a television set and pay for it a little each week. Manuel, my son, goes to school here every day and is writing this letter for me.

Perhaps you will think of coming to live in Mexico City. I will try to help you find work. I feel there is hope for a better life for your family in Mexico City.

Your brother,
César Vega

Play the recording, "Felipe Considers a Change" (script included from Teacher's Edition, pages 36–39). Students listen for the answers to the following questions:

1. Why is Papa so upset today?
2. What does Roberto think about moving to Mexico City?
3. Why does Elena urge Roberto to speak to Felipe?
4. Will Elena be able to convince Felipe to stay in Azteca?

FELIPE CONSIDERS A CHANGE (Recording Script)

Papa. Roberto! Carlos! The morning will be gone before we get to the fields. There is much work. Finish your tortillas.

Roberto. Sí, Papa. I am ready, but Carlos has gone with Ester to get water for the plum tree.

Papa. The plum tree! What's more important, the plum tree or the corn? Ah! Here is Carlos. Come, Carlos, it's getting late. Roberto, Carlos is here. Let's go to the fields. There is much work to be done.

Roberto. Sí, Papa.

Mama. Carlos! Roberto! Do not forget your tortillas!

Roberto. Sí, Mama, we have them. Papa, there are clouds, maybe there will be rain. The corn is dry.

Papa. Ah! Rain! There will be no rain. Yesterday, there were clouds and no rain. And the day before there were clouds and no rain.

Roberto. But there are many clouds today.

Papa. Ah! Roberto, you do not learn. Look at the sky. The clouds are white and thin. By noon they will be gone, and the sun will toast the earth and the corn. Now, go with Carlos to look for wood on the mountainside. If you work hard, you'll find all we need and maybe some for Mama to sell at the market. By mid-day come to the fields. There is much work for both of you.

Carlos. Papa is angry.

Roberto. He is not really so angry, he is just worried. If there is no rain, the corn will die. Then we'll have to buy corn at the market, but we don't have enough money for that. So, Papa will have to borrow some. Times are very hard, Carlos.

Carlos. Papa wanted to pay back Señor Gómez the pesos that he borrowed last year.

Roberto. It will be worse this year, if the rains don't come soon. Last year at harvest time, I worked for Señor Gómez in his fields. I made a hundred pesos. But this year, with no rain, even Señor Gómez will not need extra workers.

Carlos. If we are lucky, we will find the wood that we need for the house. But I do not think we will find enough wood for Mama to sell. And there won't be any plums to sell this year either.

Roberto. Without water nothing grows. Things are not good, Carlos. Maria is not well. She gets so little milk. Mama is worried about her. There is not enough money to buy all the milk and fruit she needs to get well. I heard Mama telling Papa about Rosa Garcia. The Garcias are moving to Mexico

City. I could find work and make some money for myself. But for Papa and Mama and Ester, it would be hard to leave. Here, Papa owns his own house and has his own fields. Mama knows everyone. Life is not easy, but they love Azteca.

Narrator. Felipe and the boys work all day. By noon the clouds are gone and the sun is hot. In the late afternoon, they return home for their supper. They eat a meal of tortillas and beans. After the meal, Felipe calls Elena, Roberto, and Carlos. And Felipe speaks to them.

Papa. Elena, today I have thought much in the fields. I can see there won't be much corn unless there is a miracle, and I do not expect a miracle for the Vega family this year. Elena, you know what is in my head: Mexico City. I have spoken today to Juan Garcia and he has heard there is work in Mexico City, a better life. In Mexico City I could work and earn a living for my family. Here we work and work and work and we have nothing.

Roberto. Papa! Mama does not want to go to the city.

Papa. I can't help it. I don't want to leave, either. But we cannot go on this way. The corn is struggling and could easily die. Then we will have to borrow more money to buy food and for corn seed to plant next year. What else can we do? I cannot let my family go without food. I know what must be. There is no reason to talk more today. I have to go to the village now to see Juan again. I'll be back later.

Mama. Roberto! You must talk to your Papa. Life is hard, but has always been hard.

Roberto. Papa is right. Things are very bad for us here. The corn is almost without life. Mexico City may be better—better food for Maria, too. Maybe there will be money to buy clothes and meat. I cannot argue with Papa because I think he is right. You must speak to him yourself, Mama.

Mama. You are young, Roberto. You do not know what it is to live in a strange place, to leave all the people of the village. I have lived in Azteca all my life. I have heard that people do not go to church in the city, and the priest does not know the people. Mexico City is a big place with many strangers. I'm too old to leave my home.

Roberto. There are many new things in the city, Mama. You would get to like it. The ways of the village are old.

Mama. But Roberto, you do not understand. We cannot leave Azteca. Roberto, you are the oldest son. You must talk to Papa and help him to understand. He will listen to you. We will be alone with no friends. We will be among strangers who will steal from us. Azteca is our home.

After listening to the recording, the children should be asked to take a position on whether they believe the Vega family should move to Mexico City or remain in Azteca. The teacher should try to legitimize independent position-taking by encouraging individuals, especially those who adopt the minority view, not to change their position merely because most or certain people in the class take the opposite position. One way to discourage children from emulating one another is to use a secret ballot where they simply write "move" or "stay" and pass it in to the teacher. It should be emphasized that even those individuals who are not certain should choose a position.

Children should then be divided into two groups: those who support staying, and those who support moving. One group can then be asked to offer one reason (statement of fact) supporting its position. After a few moments of discussion, the group decides on an initial argument, which it announces to the other side. The other group must respond directly to that statement with one supporting its own position. Its response is then announced, and then the groups alternate turns. It is the teacher's role to keep the discussion directed and to encourage the individuals to respond to one another. This strategy deliberately slows down the succession of arguments, and encourages consideration of the previous argument. The teacher does not engage directly in the argument; but he or she may wish to interrupt, if some of the arguments express statements that are unquestionably false, or if individuals fail to question even the most obviously poor reasons. The children should be able to recognize when an argument has little data to support it.

Evaluate:

Observe how well students:

1. Accurately describe situations.
2. Listen to the position of others in an argument.
3. Respond directly to a previous argument or statement.
4. Provide specific data to support general statements.
5. Evaluate the accuracy of data.
6. Categorize data.
7. Empathize with others and their problems.

Evaluate how well students understand the dilemma faced by the Vega family, and how well they can support positions they take on issues by doing selected exercises from pages 32, 34, and 35 from *A Village Family Activity Book* (examples of exercises follow):

1. Write statements about the Vegas' way of life in Azteca that would be reasons for their moving or staying:

REASONS FOR STAYING IN AZTECA   REASONS FOR MOVING FROM AZTECA

_____   _____

_____   _____

2. Write specific information for the following statements:

- The Vegas are a poor family.
- Felipe's land is difficult to farm.
- Mama Vega enjoys living in Azteca.
- The Vega children are not able to attend school regularly.
- There are many occasions which the Vegas enjoy in Azteca.

3. Arrange the statements below under the proper headings. Be sure the statements support the general heading truthfully:

REASONS WHY THE VEGAS   REASONS WHY THE VEGAS
SHOULD STAY IN AZTECA   SHOULD MOVE TO MEXICO CITY

- Everyone in the family works very hard, but there is not enough to eat.
- There are many activities in the plaza in Azteca.
- Felipe loves his land and Azteca.
- Ester has many friends in the village whom she enjoys.
- Felipe's land is difficult to farm and does not provide enough food.
- There was very little rain this year.
- The Vegas have more money than they need.
- Mama has friends she has known all her life in Azteca.
- Life has been getting harder for the Vegas each year.
- The Vegas can't afford proper health care for Maria.
- The Vega children have to work and can't attend school every day.
- There are people in Azteca who are richer than the Vega family.
- Felipe's brother promises a better life in Mexico City.

SOME CLOSING THOUGHTS

This author believes that with elementary students, decision-making objectives require social interaction. Therefore, programmed instruction units, workbooks, and skill kits have not received special treatment in this chapter. Elementary students and teachers seem to be already too burdened with these programmed types of materials, along with the ever-present ditto or "purple-passion" sheets in their language arts and mathematics programs. Many parts of skills kits and many pages of workbooks, however, will fit the conceptual framework and skill objectives of social studies programs. Many teachers use these materials eclectically. In an attempt to individualize programs, kits and workbooks are disassembled, laminated, and reassembled into meaningful learning experiences which fit the needs of a particular class.

HELPFUL TEACHER RESOURCES

For elementary teachers who wish to read further or need sources concerning decision-making skills, the following annotated list of publications is offered.

Albertson, D. Richard and Cecil J. Hannon. *Twenty Exercises for the Classroom.* Fairfax, Virginia: National Training Laboratory Learning Resource Corporation, 1972. This packet of lessons was designed to help elementary and secondary teachers use sensitivity and group processes. The lessons focus on discussing, listening, problem solving, decision making, consensus building, and leadership. Activities include brainstorming, role-playing, and problem analysis.

Dunfee, Maxine and Claudia Crump. *Teaching for Social Values in Social Studies.* Washington, D.C.: Association for Childhood Education International, 1974. This resource illustrates how different value clarification techniques relate to student self-image, prejudice, friendship, the environment, and self-government.

Fraenkel, Jack R. *Helping Students Think and Value: Strategies for Teaching the Social Studies.* Englewood Cliffs, New Jersey: Prentice-Hall, Inc., 1973. Chapters in this teacher text focus on subject matter selection, learning activities, teaching procedures to develop thinking and valuing, and evaluation. Each chapter includes objectives, a statement of abilities the teacher should develop, a presentation of the main theme, and a self-test. Key ideas are summarized in chart form, and teacher questions are systematically sequenced.

Furth, Hans G. and Harry Wachs. *Thinking Goes to School: Piaget's Theory in Practice.* New York: Oxford University Press, 1974. *Thinking Goes to School* is a practical guide to Piaget's theory. The book offers a vast number of "Thinking" activities. There are 179 games and exercises described for primary-age children. "Thinking Games" include: "General Movement Thinking," "Discriminative Movement Thinking," "Visual Thinking," "Auditory Thinking," "Hand Thinking," "Graphic Thinking," "Logical Thinking," and "Social Thinking." Content for the book is based on the program of the Tyler Thinking School in Charleston, West Virginia.

Lippitt, Ronald, Robert Fox, and Lucille Schaible. *The Teacher's Role in Social Science Investigation.* Chicago: Science Research Associates, 1969. A general guide for all social studies teachers, this book was written to accompany the *Social Science Laboratory Units*, a social psychology program for intermediate grades. The guide assists teachers in teaching the inquiry process to elementary students. The book discusses inquiry development, behavior specimens, techniques and skills of observation and data-gathering, interviews and questionnaires, and organizational designs for laboratory learning.

Selman, Robert L. et al. *First Things: Social Reasoning, A Strategy for Teaching Social Reasoning.* Pleasantville, New York: Guidance Associates, 1974. The teacher component for *First Things: Social Reasoning* series, three sound filmstrips, explains the social reasoning process and shows a teacher leading elementary students in discussions of interpersonal and intergroup dilemmas.

Smith, Lloyd L. and Joan E. Schreiber. *Social Studies K-6: A Guide for Curriculum Revision.* Des Moines, Iowa: Department of Public Instruction, 1970. This most comprehensive guide for social studies curriculum revision in Iowa is practical for any social studies teacher or educator involved in curriculum planning. It contains, also, examples of scopes and sequence designs, examples of teaching procedures, experimental programs and projects. A very complete appendix lists: five patterns for revision, social studies skills chart, taxonomy of map and globes for primary grades, diagrams of physical arrangements of elementary classrooms, a model for selecting instructional materials, a model for an instructional media center, and a selected bibliography for elementary social studies.

Shaftel, Fannie and George Shaftel. *Values in Action*. New York: Holt, Rinehart, and Winston, Inc., 1970. *Values in Action* is a series of 10 sound filmstrips and teacher's guide based on the "Role-Playing for Social Values" model of Fannie and George Shaftel. The series is produced as a complete kit containing open-ended filmstrip presentations and a teacher's guide that contains a rationale and detailed suggestions for conducting role-playing and discussions that lead to values clarification. The program helps students "examine their values and to realize that there are varied ways of solving their problems."

Simon, Sidney B., Leland W. Howe, and Howard Kirschenbaum. *Values Clarification: A Handbook of Practical Strategies for Teachers and Students*. New York: Hart Publishing Company, Inc. 1972. *Values Clarification: A Handbook of Practical Strategies for Teachers and Students* is a manual of 79 practical ways which students and teachers can use to clarify and actualize personal values. The book uses a values clarification approach which seeks to alleviate values confusion and conflict by helping students use the processes of choosing, prizing, affirming and acting. Most of the strategies can be used at any age level.

FOOTNOTES

[1]W. Linwood Chase and Martha Tyler John, *A Guide for the Elementary Social Studies Teacher* (Boston: Allyn and Bacon, Inc., 1972), pp. 55–65, 66–81. Used with permission.

[2]Helen McCracken Carpenter, ed., *Skills Development in Social Studies*, 33rd Yearbook (Washington, D.C.: National Council for the Social Studies, 1963).

[3]Paul R. Hanna, Rose Sabaroff, Gordon Davis, and Charles Parrar, *Geography in the Teaching of Social Studies: Concepts and Skills* (Boston: Houghton Mifflin Company, 1966).

[4]Bruce R. Joyce, *New Strategies for Social Education* (Chicago: Science Research Associates, Inc., 1972).

[5]Chelmsford Public Schools, *A Handbook for Preparing a Pupil Specialty on Europe* (Chelmsford, Mass. 1973). Used with permission.

[6]Charles L. Mitsakos, *Russian Family in Moscow (Family of Man: Social Studies Program)* (Newton, Mass.: Selective Educational Equipment, Inc., 1974), Teacher's Resource Guide, pp. 53–54. Used with permission.

[7]Fannie Shaftel and George Shaftel, *Role-Playing for Social Values: Decision-Making in the Social Studies* (Englewood Cliffs, N.J.: Prentice-Hall, 1967).

[8]Ruth MacDonald, *One Plus One: Learning About Communities*. Macmillan Elementary Social Studies, John Jarolimek and Bertha Davis, Senior Authors (New York: Macmillan Publishing Co., Inc., 1974), Teacher's Edition, pp. 98–103; Student Text, pp. 111–117; Workbook, pp. 94–102. Reprinted with permission of Macmillan Publishing Co.

[9]Harold Berlak and Timothy Tomlinson, *A Village Family (People/Choices/Decisions* program). (New York: Random House, Inc., 1973), Teacher's Edition, pp. ix, 31–33, 36–39; Student Text, 18, 53–55; pp. 34–35, Activity Book. Used with permission.

"... rational decision making is an attempt to plan the future. Indeed, it is impossible to have decision making without a future orientation! What are consequences of choices, if they are not expressions of the future?"

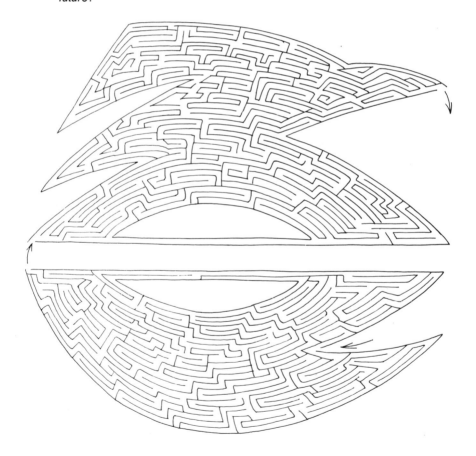

.7.
Kenneth Weeden

Teaching Decision Making
in Secondary Social Studies

*I have taught in high school for ten years. During that time I have given
assignments, among others, to a murderer, an evangelist, a pugilist, a thief, and
an imbecile.*

*The murderer was a quiet little boy who sat on the front seat and regarded me
with pale blue eyes; the evangelist, easily the most popular boy in the school,
had the lead in the junior play; the pugilist lounged by the window and let loose
at intervals a raucous laugh; the thief was a gay-hearted Lothario with a song on
his lips; and the imbecile, a soft-eyed little animal seeking the shadows.*

*The murderer awaits death in the state penitentiary; the evangelist has lain a
year now in the village churchyard; the pugilist lost an eye in a brawl in Hong
Kong; the thief, by standing on tiptoe, can see the windows of my room from the
county jail; and the once gentle-eyed little moron beats his head against a
padded wall in the state asylum.*

*All of these pupils once sat in my room, sat and looked at me gravely across
worn brown desks. I must have been a great help to those pupils . . . I taught
them the rhyming scheme of the Elizabethan sonnet and how to diagram a
complex sentence.—*ANONYMOUS

Let us imagine for a moment that our students are not third graders or
ninth graders or twelfth graders, but adults in their thirties and forties,
and the twenty-first century has just begun. We are retired; they have
families, jobs, and mortgages. How are they handling their lives? What
kinds of jobs do they have? Have they selected careers, or did they just
fall into something because they needed money? What kinds of con-
sumers are they? Do they seek information and compare before buying?
Can they budget money, or are they facing personal bankruptcy? Are
their views on worldwide population problems and food shortages reasoned? Do they vote? Are they even *registered* to vote? What will *they*

do about crime, decaying cities, problems not even known today? In short, are they as adult pawns moved about by events they hardly see coming, or are they planners, doers, who face personal and civic problems with a determination and an ability to resolve them?

The answers to these questions lie partially in whether or not as students they learned to make rational decisions. In fact, how well young people learn to make rational decisions determines whether they as adults will utilize the facts and concepts we teach them today or merely discard them as so much garbage. As a consequence, this chapter:

(1) outlines several teaching components of decision making,
(2) examines examples of classroom teaching strategies,
(3) suggests how to incorporate decision-making activities in your present program.

TEACHING COMPONENTS OF DECISION MAKING

There are several special ingredients of teaching decision making common and equally essential to all social studies courses. First, we as teachers must begin to think more about the "future" and in turn emphasize it more in our courses. After all, rational decision making is an attempt to plan the future. Indeed, it is impossible to have decision making without a future orientation! What are consequences of choices, if they are not expressions of the future? Yet, most people live mainly in the past and the present. Alvin Toffler asserts that this will have to change or our society will face continual instability, if not destruction. He maintains that presently we have two major problems:

> First: *Lack of future-consciousness.* Instead of anticipating the problems of the future, we lurch from crisis to crisis . . . Our political system is "future blind." With but few exceptions, the same failure of foresight marks our corporations, trade unions, schools, hospitals, voluntary organizations, and communities . . . Second: *Lack of participation.* Our government and other institutions have grown so large and complicated that most people feel powerless. They complain of being "planned upon" . . . Blue-collar workers, poor people, the elderly, the youth, even the affluent among us, feel frozen out of the decision process. And as more and more millions feel powerless, the danger of violence and authoritarianism increases.[1]

In order to cope with these problems, Toffler believes that citizens must begin now participating in what he calls "Anticipatory Democracy." He suggests that people attend their city councils or state legislatures to lobby for "foresight" clauses requiring government bodies to consider the impact of proposed legislation on future needs and desires. He recommends town meetings on what communities should be like in 1985 or 2000, so that planners can begin now to anticipate needs and alter programs already underway.

Such a forecast places a heavy responsibility on social studies educators to teach youngsters both how to make rational decisions and then to make them: to become part of an anticipatory democracy. Neither has received much attention in social studies curriculum planning. Book and multimedia publishers urge their futuristic products on us, but no one has shown how such interests properly fit into the context of present social studies concerns.

The traditional orientation of the social studies is relatively useless for teaching decision making. It either emphasizes citizenship through the inculcation of American values, or it teaches social studies as if they were watered down social sciences. Neither approach has ever considered the study of the future, since their emphasis has been on the past and the present. Even the inquiry approach, so in vogue over the last ten years, has not generally dealt with the future. True, inquiry-oriented teachers help students identify, clarify, and test hypotheses. True, they work on evaluating data, but the focus is again on the past and present. This is not sufficient for teaching decision making. Students need practice and training *now* in planning their personal futures and that of their community and nation.

It is fine for students to study water pollution in their community, for example. If the research is limited, however, to the crisis today and the values clarified are restricted to those of today, then what has been the purpose of the unit? Perhaps we have made students better readers of newspapers and news journals. Perhaps students are better discussants of this issue than before, but we have not helped them as much as possible to become citizens of an anticipatory democracy unless we also attempt to teach them to ask automatically about future needs and the consequences of present actions.

Naturally, the term "future" is vague, since it can mean anything from the next moment or year to the next fifty or hundred years or beyond. We have to decide what future time period is most practical or relevant to the issue under investigation. Indeed, helping young people to see next week's or next year's consequences of their present actions is often far more difficult and perhaps more important than getting them involved in the long-range forecasts about electronic gadgets, genetic engineering, and the like of the next one hundred years. Therefore, this proposal to integrate "the future" into our course work is not an attempt to teach science fiction or idle speculation about 2076 A.D.; it is, instead, a call to help young people recognize that lives extend beyond the plea-

STUDENT INVOLVEMENT

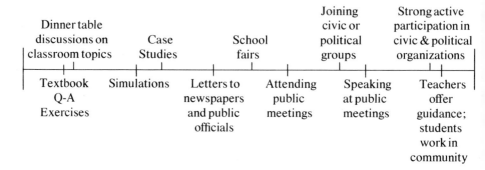

Dinner table discussions on classroom topics	Case Studies	School fairs	Joining civic or political groups	Strong active participation in civic & political organizations
Textbook Q-A Exercises	Simulations	Letters to newspapers and public officials	Attending public meetings	Speaking at public meetings	Teachers offer guidance; students work in community

sures and disappointments of the present. Actions taken either as private individuals or as citizens of a community *will* affect their future, tomorrow, next year, and beyond. Any decision-making teaching strategy which fails to communicate concern for the future is an inadequate approach to decision making.

A second responsibility is to help students become participants who act on their decisions, rather than merely talk about what someone else should do. This means that we have to encourage participation through creative assignments which involve students in solutions, not just in the problems themselves. Involvement, naturally, should cover a wide spectrum of activities in order to insure that all students—regardless of interests, maturity, or ability—can apply their learning outside the classroom. An indication of the range of activities possible in considering a civic problem is shown by the Student Involvement chart above.

For many teachers, involving students in learning activities outside the classroom appears to be too time-consuming and complex. Indeed, attempting to do too much too soon without the planning and self-assurance experience provides will prove to be disastrous. Therefore, begin by concentrating on one or two of these outside-the-classroom activities to accustom students to such procedures. As you develop experience and self-assurance with them, move on to other activities more challenging and even more oriented toward community involvement.

As an example, use the social science school fair. Remember the science fair? Try something akin to it with a major public issue or personal problem as the theme. Exhibits are excellent tools for teaching students how to inform and to persuade others about a topic of some importance to them. The school fair encourages public participation within the familiar walls of the school and does not provoke as much anxiety as a participatory activity in the community normally does.

Even that, teachers may feel, is too much to tackle at first. Why not then start with the standard group report to the class and develop it into a class presentation to another class or two, using audiovisual techniques, simulations, role playing, demonstrations, and model? Students could investigate the world food crisis, for example, by graphically explaining the problem today and the projections for the future. They might outline the various solutions that have been suggested, with the possible consequences of each outlined. At the end of the exhibit, students could vote on the alternative they chose, with the results being sent to their Congressperson and Senators in Washington. Students thus become teachers and learn that they can do more than just complain. From these class presentations, a school fair for the entire student body and PTA might be arranged.

There are, of course, many other ideas. An excellent source of creative teaching strategies encouraging student participation is the article by Ochoa and Allen.[2] Although about city living, their suggestions can easily be adapted to many other subjects. Four of their many suggestions follow:

1. Plan and produce a newspaper, a flyer, a photo essay that highlights some community problem. Circulate it to parents and the neighborhood in general.
2. Form a special interest community school club.
3. Develop student chapters of the various political parties and have them work in the election, supplying transportation and handing out literature.
4. Plan a school assembly to dramatize a community problem, inviting adults to participate. Have small group discussions (student-led) after the assembly to decide what can and should be done.

Thus far, we have discussed the need to incorporate a futuristic element into our courses and to develop a series of participation activities which teach students how to put their decisions into action. These changes alone, however, are not enough. It is essential, in addition, to bring students face to face with specific issues to which they can relate. Too often, we discuss mass transportation problems, poverty, racism, or drugs only in broad terms. We may duplicate copies of a speech or articles selected to show opposing viewpoints, throw in a movie or filmstrip, have a "rap" session, mention some "facts" from a book or newspaper article, have students do some library research, and call it a unit. Virtually all of us have done this; yet, more often than not, the results are that students really learn no more than a handful of facts and then only long enough to pass an examination.

Trying to teach decision making using this approach is very hard, since the values of individuals are either ignored or hardly mentioned. Instead, we need to involve students in a specific controversial case. In studying local mass transportation, for example, a particular highway route which displaces housing could be the focus, with emphasis on the conflict between highway proponents and subway proponents. In short, the answer lies in getting students caught up in a specific issue so that they develop empathy for the individuals and groups and feel a certain kinship with their likes, dislikes, goals and fears.

There are two successful techniques which can help us accomplish this goal: role playing and simulations. Role playing is a method of instruction in which individuals take on the roles of other people—real or fictitious—and act out their feelings, thoughts, and actions. It is a method of helping students understand public issues, as well as inter-personal conflicts, from the perspectives of others. The insight gained helps in understanding the problems and also in proposing solutions.

Naturally, the values of one generation are not necessarily those of another, and students must be made aware of this in order to prevent easy judgments from being made about people they do not know.

With role playing, the situation must be clear, specific, and relevant to students. Possibilities for selection are limitless and can be either historical or contemporary. Here are but three examples:

1. You are 15, new to a neighborhood, and at a party where everyone else is drinking. You want to be popular, yet you know that drinking is illegal and your parents would be upset with you. What do you do?
2. The year is 1942. You live in southern California, and your best friend is a Japanese American who is being picked upon on the way to school. Everyone else is calling her a traitor and can hardly wait until she and her family are removed to a relocation camp. What do you do?
3. You are an advisor to President Nixon in the winter of 1973 and discover that he is involved in the Watergate coverup. You enjoy the income and the prestige of working in the White House and know a year of experience will open to you lots of wealthy and prestigious law firms. A bright, ambitious young man, you think of yourself as basically honest and feel that you cannot continue to be indirectly aiding the President in lying to the public. You ask to see the President. What do you say?

In each of these situations, we are offering students the opportunity to identify with and become involved in conflict and the resolution of conflict to a far greater extent than possible through conventional textbook reading and question-and-answer homework.

Questions such as the following may be helpful to students involved in role-playing exercises:

1. What is the problem in the story?
2. How would you feel if you were_____? Why?
3. What alternatives does _____ have?
4. Which do you think_____ should do? Why?
5. What values are you supporting by that decision?
6. Which do you think is the worse alternative? Why?
7. What values are you supporting by that decision? Why?

The materials on role playing listed in the *Suggested Reading List* at the end of this chapter explain the process in detail and should be consulted before trying role playing for the first time.

A second useful technique is the use of simulations and games. Both are a more structured form of role playing, with fewer, more limited alternatives available. They are available for virtually every grade level and topic. The example, "Millersburg," examined later in this chapter, is typical of many simulations.

Both role playing and simulations are contrived situations developed in order to highlight one or a few very specific ideas. Neither fully replaces a study of real problems students face each day in trying to get along with others and in trying to make sense out of a very complex world. Both, however, are very helpful when used in conjunction with case studies. A case study focuses on a specific issue which is occurring or has occurred. It normally involves a wider range of complex factors, calling on students to gather and to evaluate evidence, to propose alternatives, and to make a decision supported by facts. Role playing and simulations are often useful as a part of a case study in order to articulate the feelings, thoughts, and beliefs of the various protagonists, as well as to provide feedback on the consequences of possible solutions. The *Public Issues Series* based on the Harvard Social Studies Project is an example of published case studies. We can, of course, create our own from stories on television or in newspapers, books, and magazines.

One very effective way of using the case study approach to teach decision making is through the preparation of position papers. Daily, people throughout government and business outline for their superiors the background of a particular problem, the various alternatives possible, their pros and cons, and a recommended course of action. The purpose of these papers, of course, is to provide top decision makers with information needed in order to set policy. All the skills of information gathering, analysis of evidence, writing, value clarification, and logical thinking are brought together into this one exercise. Naturally, not all students are capable of or interested in this assignment to the same degree, but the following outline for the position paper can be modified to fit individual needs:

TITLE

(Title should be in question form)
Example: Should the United States Seek Full
Formal Diplomatic Relations with the People's Republic of China?

I. *Statement of Problem*
This is a concise statement of the problem under consideration.

Example: Since the Communist revolution's success on mainland China in 1948, the United States Government and the People's Republic of China have refused to establish full diplomatic relations. President Nixon and Chairman Mao Tse-tung opened the door to informal diplomatic relations in the early 1970s. Presently, the two governments have low-level official representation in each other's capitals. Many people in the United States feel that this arrangement is unsatisfactory, and therefore seek complete diplomatic recognition and representation on the highest level. Others maintain that the consequences for the Taiwanese Government and the other governments in Asia and elsewhere who look to us to keep our defense treaties make the price of full diplomatic recognition too high.

II. *Background of the Problem*
This section should be a reasonably detailed account of how the problem developed, indicating the major factors contributing to the issues along with previous attempts to resolve it.

Example: This position paper on Sino-American diplomatic relations might appropriately cover such points as (1) U.S. position toward the Nationalist Government and the Communists during World War II; (2) economic policy of U.S. in the years immediately following World War II; (3) U.S. treaties and executive agreements with the Taiwanese Government; (4) the Korean War and other disputes between the two governments; (5) Chinese propaganda toward the U.S.; (6) Chinese rejection of the U.S. attempts to normalize relations; (7) secret Kissinger trips in the late 1960s and early 1970s; and (8) the Nixon visit.

III. *Alternative Policies*
At least three alternatives should be presented for dealing with the problem. These alternatives should cover as wide a spectrum of possibilities as feasible in order to prevent preconceived ideas from dominating the paper. The arguments pro and con for each alternative must also be presented and analyzed. The implications for the future of the United States—next year, five years, ten years from now—are also to be included.

Example: In the case of Sino-American relations, at least four alternative policies should be analyzed. (1) Continue present informal diplomatic relations. (2) Withdraw U.S. troops from Taiwan and renounce our defense treaty with her and cut off all diplomatic relations. (3) Maintain U.S. defense treaties with Taiwan, but cut off or reduce our level of diplomatic recognition and seek full recognition with the People's Republic of China. (4)

Maintain present relationship with Taiwan but increase economic aid to China, side-stepping the Taiwanese issue and pushing for a more advanced level of diplomatic relations short of full recognition.

IV. *Recommendation*
This section should indicate the policy that each student recommends. It could be one of the alternatives listed above in the "III" section, or it could be a combination of two or more of them. A full explanation of why the writer supports his recommendation above the others is necessary, along with an explanation of the values this particular recommendation supports.

In summary, then, there are several components of teaching decision making which should be integrated into the normal repertory of teaching strategies:

1. inclusion of the future in both personal and public issue topics we teach;
2. development of participatory activities which teach students how to act upon their decisions;
3. study of *specific* private and civic problems, not just general topics, through the use of role playing, simulations, case studies, and such normal activities as class discussions and textual readings.

TEACHING DECISION MAKING

Personal Decision Making

These principles also apply to decision making about personal problems, those which involve primarily one's self and immediate family. Topics such as these demonstrate this area of decision making:

1. What Careers Should I Choose?
2. Do I Want, Need Drugs?
3. Do I Really Want to Marry _____?
4. Am I Prejudiced Toward Others Based on Their Sex or Race?
5. Am I a Wise Buyer?

Note that each of the personal problems stated above could have been made into civic questions by dealing instead with broad topics, such as consumer laws, the changing job markets, drug abuse among teenagers, and the increasing divorce rate. The intent of these five questions, however, is not to study such problems; instead, they are intended to help students face and resolve specific personal problems in their lives.

Since *most* civic problems can be personalized, the question arises as to whether a problem should be dealt with on the public or the personal level. All students, regardless of ability, need to struggle with issues of world peace, poverty, and prejudice. As a practical matter, however, students not highly motivated by academic subject matter will have a greater degree of success learning decision making when they study issues which immediately affect their daily lives. More academically sophisticated students also need help in making personal decisions. We sometimes overlook the fact that they, too, are adolescents who suffer with self-doubt and are vulnerable to peer pressure and parental dominance. All issues, regardless of how cosmic in scope, must be decided ultimately on the personal level.

One very effective program in approaching personal decision making is developed in two booklets published by the College Entrance Examination Board. *Deciding*[3] for junior high school students and *Decisions and Outcomes*[4] for high school can be adapted to any number of topics, such as drugs, career education, or consumer decisions. These two manuals emphasize the roles that values, information, and strategies play in the decision-making process, and then relate these factors to students' own lives. The specific exercises reproduced below demonstrate their suitability for classroom use.

1. Value Clarification
   After having identified the values others express by their actions, students are directed to exercises A and B, which are reproduced below.
2. Information Gathering
   The exercise labelled C emphasizes the need to collect data from many sources. It shows the major roles that information plays in making decisions. It also shows that the alternatives selected are partially the result of the priorities of the decision maker.
3. Strategies
   The final example, labelled D, demonstrates the plan of action by which the decision maker combines his or her values and information together into a decision which will provide the greatest amount of satisfaction. Notice, too, that each of the strategies mentioned takes into account the consequences of each alternative. This, of course, is the way the future is incorporated into the decision-making process.

Exercises A, B, C, and D
Are on pages 211–217.

EXERCISE A[5]

Recognizing Personal Values

During the course of Mary's junior year in high school she did a lot of things. She made decisions (some that she thought about, others that she didn't). Mary, at age 16, had certain values. Can you identify them in order of importance based on the following information?

Mary registered for French, English, advanced math, social studies, art, physical education, and government. At the beginning of the year she joined a discussion group with eight friends. This was for the purpose of discussing future goals and behavior.

Mary frequently was absent from school, but was always there the day the discussion group met. When she stayed at home, she was painting, writing, or reading. She read a lot about mystical religions and hallucinogenic drugs. She also read broadly in many of the philosophical books, considered to be classics.

From this little information, what would you say were the five things Mary valued most?

During the evenings she would frequently go to the nearby university to attend lectures or plays. She went with graduate students of the university and would spend time afterwards talking about the plays or lectures.

Mary never dated any boy from her high school. Rather, she went on dates with college students or graduate students. She frequently wore the same dress to school, wore no make-up, and occasionally looked sloppy. She attended no school functions.

She fought with her mother, *talked to her father*, and spent time with her brother. Her mother and father wanted her to go to a prestige university. To do this, she would have to have mostly A's. She was getting C's and D's in several classes. She scored on an IQ test as a gifted child.

_____

_____

_____

_____

_____

Now, write your definition of a value.

_____

_____

_____

_____

_____

EXERCISE B[6]

Exploring Your Values

Values are the ideas on which people act. Earlier it was stated that the best way to know a person's values is to look at what he does. Try completing the chart below to see what it says about your values. Remember back to what you did last Saturday and Sunday. Fill in the chart from what you remember, stating the specific activities that took your time:

	SATURDAY	SUNDAY
8-9		
9-10		
10-11		
11-12		
12-1		
1-2		
2-3		
3-4		
4-5		
5-6		
6-7		
7-8		
8-9		
9-10		
10-11		
11-12		

List two or three values that are suggested
by how you spent your time during those two days: _____

_____

_____

EXERCISE C⁷

Al's Information-Seeking Game

Al is going into a new high school (as you may remember from the story on page 27). Below is a chart on which he, and you, can choose three pieces of information that will help him select the courses he needs for high school. You are to choose the three pieces of information that you think will help him get the information he needs most. The numbers in the chart refer to printed information on the next pages. (Don't look yet!) Circle the numbers of the three you think will be most valuable to him.

Sources of information	Kinds of information received (numbers refer to next page)		
	Risks involved	Short- and long-range objectives	Plans he might follow
Al himself—his own thoughts	1	2	3
Things Al might read; high school catalog, college guide, books about careers	4	5	6
Things Al might do; visit classes, visit a college, get a job	7	8	9
People Al might talk to; his parents, teachers, counselor	10	11	12

On pages 31-32 read *only* the three pieces of information you have chosen for Al to receive. Now, can you decide what courses he should take in high school?

Decision based on three pieces of information: _____

_____

Are you satisfied with this decision? If not, keep adding pieces of information until you feel ready to make a satisfying decision. Then write your new decision on page 32. _____

_____

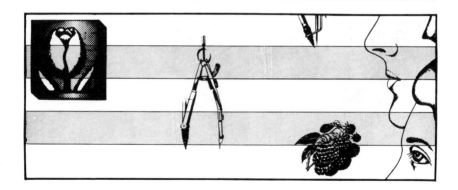

EXERCISE C[8]

Pieces of Information from which Al Can Make a Decision

1

"I don't want to risk getting poor grades in high school by carrying too heavy an academic load. But I'm not afraid of taking a chance for something important. My grades have been average and my test scores above average."

6

He reads that most students going into engineering have at least three options. One option is to take every possible math and science course in high school. A second option is to make sure they take English and social studies in high school so they are not without a humanities background, which they may miss in college engineering. A third option is to wait until college to do much specializing and to use high school to gain experience (such as visiting an engineer at work) so they are sure they want to become engineers.

2

"I would like to be eligible to go to an Ivy League or other highly selective college. However, I want most to be eligible to become an engineer after I graduate from college."

5

He reads that students can go to junior college and get basic courses before transferring to a four-year engineering college. It is good to have drafting and some machine shop before going into a full-fledged high-level engineering program.

7

Al gets a job in a machine shop making parts for a large engineering firm. He finds the work very boring and knows he doesn't want to put his life into this occupation. But he then visits a civil engineer in the city planning commission, and his job sounds a lot more to his liking.

3

"I can take a heavy academic course, which allows few electives; or take a medium heavy course with typing, band, and orchestra; or take the fewest possible college preparatory courses and still graduate from high school. I can play it safe and take courses in which I am most likely to succeed. Or I can take courses I really like (such as advanced calculus), but I'll have a greater chance of not getting a good grade. I can delay making my decision, but I don't like to. I can ask my parents and let them decide."

4

He reads that four years of math are recommended for all students wishing to go into engineering. Most good engineering schools require students to have at least chemistry and physics. In college students have less choice of courses as freshmen when they start in engineering.

8

Al's family uses the summer vacation to visit three big universities with engineering programs. Al reads their catalogs and visits the engineering buildings. He goes to the cafeteria and talks to some engineering students. He likes Tech. U. best.

EXERCISE C

12 Al's parents and counselor meet with him to look over the possibilities. They carefully outline three different plans for high school: one very heavy college preparatory with emphasis on math; one medium heavy college preparatory but with less language and social studies; one fairly light program including drafting and machine shop. He is left with the choice of deciding which plan makes most sense to him.

11 Al's parents and he talk about the economics of his going to college. His father offers to help him through college if he is willing to work part time. His parents feel he should ideally get work in something related to the career he wants, that is, engineering of some sort.

10 Al talks to his math teacher about how well he is doing in class and might do in advanced math. The math teacher says Al is good, but not the best, in theoretical math. His science teacher, however, very much encourages him to take more math. When he talks to his counselor, he urges Al to make sure he doesn't close his mind to other things besides engineering too early.

9 Al asks his counselor to arrange visits for him to the local engineering society. He wants to find out about the different types of engineers. After talking to members of the society, he decides to visit (with their help) a civil engineer, a mechanical engineer, a chemical engineer, and an aeronautical engineer. The aeronautical engineer's work is so interesting he asks for permission to work voluntarily at the man's plant during the remainder of the summer.

What decision do you think Al should make?
_____
_____
_____
_____
_____
_____

Which information was most influential to you in making this decision? _____
_____
_____
_____
_____

Do you think you had all the information you needed? _____
_____
_____
_____

What other information would you like to have? _____
_____
_____
_____

EXERCISE D⁹

Decision-Making Strategies

A strategy is a *plan of action*; strategy is sometimes called the science of planning. A decision-making strategy is the putting together of all the steps into a choice; it is the culminating act of the decision-maker.

Since all important decisions probably involve some risk or some uncertainty, how will the decision-maker finally choose in the face of these unknowns? The four most common *risk-taking strategies* are as follows:

Wish strategy	Choice of the alternative that *could* lead to the most desirable result, regardless of risk.
Escape strategy	Choice of the alternative that is most likely to avoid the worst possible result.
Safe strategy	Choice of the alternative that is most likely to bring success; has highest probability.
Combination strategy	Choice of the alternative that has both high probability and high desirability (multiply probability times desirability).

The Application of Strategy

Alice is now in her senior year in high school and is choosing a college for next year. She has been a good student and qualifies for admission to the prestige university in a neighboring community as well as for admission to the state university system and any of the state colleges. All high school graduates are eligible to attend her local community college.

Although her qualifications for the prestige university are minimal, she has been offered a scholarship there because she is a member of a minority race. Alice has applied to and been accepted at four colleges: Prestige University, State University, State College, and Community College.

She knows her decision is an important one and she must choose from four very clear alternatives. She wants very much to get a college degree, and her

greatest dream is to graduate from a prestigious college. This would make her family very happy and would make her feel very successful. What Alice dreads most of all is to drop out or to fail at college. She would feel humiliated by this.

She has information on her ability and her past performance, and she has looked at tables that helped her estimate her probabilities of academic success at each of the four alternatives. Her greatest chance for success in her major field of social science is at the State College, and the Community College runs a close second. The State University is a more distant third, and Prestige University ranks fourth with a high degree of risk. Now, how does Alice decide how to choose? Try applying the four strategies to her decision.

EXERCISE D

Wish

Using this strategy, Alice would attend Prestige University, in which there was the possibility that she would reach her desired outcome. Remember that this strategy does not consider risks or probabilities.

Escape

Using this strategy, Alice would probably attend the State College. However, if she wanted to *completely avoid* the worst outcome (instead of just minimizing it), Alice would have to decide *not to attend college.*

Safe

Using this strategy, Alice would clearly decide to attend State College, in which she would have the highest chance of succeeding. Remember, this strategy considers *only* the *likelihood* of success.

Combination

Using this strategy, Alice might decide to attend the State University because it might have the highest expected value—considering the high value to her of a degree from such a university. This strategy would require extensive data and personal analysis of Alice's values.

Alice's story illustrates how a decision-making strategy could be applied to the problem of deciding where to go to college. But this illustration is over-simplified. When a person is actually choosing a college, his decision is much more complicated. For instance, what about some of Alice's other values, desires, and objectives?

Maybe she wants to live at home.
Maybe she wants to major in anthropology.
Maybe she wants an active college social life.
Maybe she wants to live far from home.

Can you think of other factors she might consider? _____

_____

_____

_____

_____

_____

_____

_____

Can you think of other strategies she might use? _____

_____

_____

_____

_____

_____

_____

_____

Civic Decision Making

Let us now turn to civic problems, those which involve the community and the nation. American history, traditionally taught in both the eighth and the eleventh grade, contains many such issues.

How can history prepare people for the future? The answer lies in concentrating on what Oliver and Newmann, among others, term "public issues." Such issues have persisted in the past, exist today, and in all likelihood will continue as future conflicts. Problems such as "loyalty to one's government vs. legitimate authority," "competition vs. the public interest," "freedom of speech and press vs. an individual's right to a fair trial," and "limited government vs. government protection" are all issues which transcend time periods. We can utilize history to prepare students to deal with such basic issues of public policy by making decisions about them and then acting on those decisions.

Let us look at some teaching strategies using this approach. The material below is reprinted from *The American Revolution*, edited by Donald W. Oliver and Fred Newmann.[10] They suggest that students might concentrate on persistent issues such as these:

What is a proper government, and where does its power originate?

In what ways should people—as groups or individuals—be able to express themselves to constituted authority? And what responsibility do rulers have to listen?

When and how is authority to be challenged? Is there a precise measurement for the point at which dissent may turn to revolt? Is violence ever the "right" course?

The case of George Watkins highlights these questions:[11]

George took a table in the room reserved for the more prosperous, well-educated people. He ordered a mug of ale from the barmaid . . . He was bitter about the English. Ten years before, early 1763, George had put almost all his money into lands west of the Allegheny Mountains. He had expected to sell the land later at a good profit. Then the English announced the Proclamation of 1763, forbidding any Englishmen to settle west of the Alleghenies. . . . "I've been thinking," said Watkins, "our people in England just don't seem to understand our problems. . . . I wonder if this Sam Adams might not have something when he speaks about independence."

Dr. Johnson looked startled . . . "I certainly cannot go along with fire-breathers like Hancock and Adams. We should do what we must, calmly and legally. . . . We both know Hancock is a convicted smuggler who'll cut his country's throat just to save himself from jail!" . . .

"But Hancock was only forced to smuggle because England was worrying more about herself than about us." . . .

"If you're willing to defend a criminal, why not defend Sam Adams, too? You and I both know Sam Adams wants to fight England and turn this country into a slaughterhouse because he hates kings and noblemen. No matter what's offered him now, he'll never be satisfied . . . Sam Adams is powerful in the colonies because he tells the dissatisfied, the lazy, the idle that they're the only honest people. I tell you we can't have war, no matter what, because if men like Adams start running the show there won't be a decent businessman or doctor or lawyer or any man of property left in America. And the country will be governed by riffraff out of the gutters."

Watkins replied very slowly . . . "The English have not governed us very well. And I am not sure that they can govern well . . . The English government is corrupt. Enormous salaries, pensions, bribes, quarrels, padded accounts, illegal contracts, and illegal jobs—all using up the tax money. Maybe England is more of a stone around our necks than a protector of our rights."

"Open your eyes! Do you know what Sam Adams and his gutter crowd are doing? They have mobbed and beaten ministers, lawyers and doctors who have done nothing more than express their opinions. Yes, the finest men we've got have been thrown out of every town in the colony. Those rebels say they are fighting for freedom. Yet they do not permit anyone the freedom to disagree with them."

Watkins was puzzled and worried. He knew the need for a fair and reasonable government in this new world—government which understood the temper and desires of a new brand of freedom. But he wondered how such a government could be born out of the contempt for law . . .

We might begin by asking students to play the roles of Watkins and Johnson in this exchange of views, directing students' attention to questions such as these:

1. What is the problem Watkins faces?
2. How would you feel if you were Watkins? Why?
3. What alternatives does he have?
4. What do you think he should do? Why?

Individually, or in groups, students should brainstorm a list of as many alternatives as possible for George Watkins. It is important that no one judge any of the proposals. Students should be free to suggest anything they feel might be plausible.

The next problem is to identify values and to decide which values have priority over others. Go back over the story, having students articulate the values of the two men by pointing out the passages in the story which exemplify them. Another approach is to prepare a list of values such as freedom, wealth, self-respect, responsibility, lawfulness, equality, loyalty, and obedience, and have students find examples of them, jotting down the sentence(s) which demonstrate each. A values chart such as the following might help nail down the differences and the similarities between Watkins and Johnson, as well as clarify your own students' thinking about the issue.[12]

VALUES CHART

*Directions:*Below is a list of values commonly held by most people. Arrange them in order of importance for George Watkins, Dr. Johnson, and yourself. Place a "1" next to the one you believe the characters in the story would think most important and next to the one you believe is the most important. Continue until you have completed the chart with a "10" next to the value you think the characters would have regarded as the least important and also which you think is least important.

Values	*Watkins' Rating*		*Johnson's Rating*		*My Rating*	
Freedom						
Wealth						
Self-respect						
Responsibility						
Lawfulness						
Equality						
Loyalty						
Obedience						
Power						
Pride						

Often, however, a person cannot be sure in his/her own mind which value he or she truly believes is most important. In addition, many arguments between people pivot on conflicting values. Merely listing some values and asking people to choose often will be of little help. In such situations, there are three possible resolutions:[13]

1. Determine if the conflict is due to vague and/or emotionally loaded words. *Example*—Words such as justice, loyalty, and freedom seldom have the same meaning for different people. Perhaps consultation with a dictionary or group discussion will lead to consensus about the meaning of such words.

2. Determine if the individual or individuals can find a third value that they can both agree to.

Example—In a value conflict between respect for law and order and personal freedom, perhaps both persons could agree to support personal protection or welfare; or perhaps both individuals could agree to support a commonly agreed upon definition of human dignity.

3. Determine whether both individuals truly support their values by posing analogous situations which involve those values. Clarify the differences and similarities between the original situation and the new and contrived ones.
   Example—In a value conflict between personal freedom and loyalty to the group, suppose the principal of your school began a real crackdown on coming to school late and suspended people without really listening to their reasons. Would you still support the school rules in this case? If the United States is invaded, should you not join the underground?

There is no guarantee that any of these techniques will resolve the value conflicts either within a person or between individuals, but they are superior to simply saying, "Well, we each have our own opinion." We each do, of course, but the goal of thoughtful decision making is to select the alternative which truly advances our goals; this can't be done until we truly know what our goals or values are!

The role of the teacher in all of this is to guide the discussion so that it does not degenerate into a fight or go off on tangents. It is *not* the teacher's responsibility to comment on which values are superior or which alternatives are better. In addition, it is important to note that this exercise is only the introduction to a unit on the American Revolution. As the discussion progresses, the teacher needs to interject questions to help students see that more information is needed, that George Watkins or Dr. Johnson or someone else in another story may be exaggerating to win an argument. This initial discussion surrounding George Watkins' dilemma sets the stage for the inquiry portion of the decision-making process. Now that the students are involved in the issues, now that they have stated their values as they see them, now that they have made an initial decision, they have reason to do some research to determine the truth of conflicting statements about what went on.

After evidence has been gathered and evaluated, the process of helping George Watkins decide what he will do can begin again. Many students will alter their decisions, some will find new alternatives not listed earlier, and many will see the complexities of giving one value higher priority than another.

Is revolution relevant today? Of course it is, and students need to test any decision made about the American Revolution in light of contemporary and future problems. For example, a teacher might turn to the Vietnam demonstrations, the civil rights movement of the 1960s, the Red Power movement, or the women's lib movement for case studies. If these seem too overdone, then turn to the question of whether the

United States government should support with military and economic aid those nations which suppress their people. Focus on South Korea or Chile or South Africa. Is the Declaration of Independence just for us? Are there higher values to a nation than life, liberty, and the pursuit of happiness? Is military advantage over the Soviet Union more important than the fate of political prisoners in Chile or South Korea? Such questions help students to become familiar with these extremely difficult issues that surely will continue to shape American foreign policy.

What of the future? Students could select a pressing contemporary issue, such as discrimination against the American Indian, and develop a standard of conduct for themselves. What action by either the Indians or the Federal Government would cause them to protest nonviolently? What, if anything, would cause them to protest violently? Are there any circumstances under which they would join an underground movement to overthrow the United States government because of its treatment of a minority group?

History is so pervasive in secondary social studies that another example of the public issues approach may be helpful. This time the subject is European history, and the topic is the growth of modern science. Students have learned that, during the medieval era, the purpose of science was to ratify the teachings of the Church; truth independent of religious propriety was forbidden. Then during the sixteenth and the seventeenth centuries, the scientific method evolved and slowly the Church and science faced conflict. Today, most of us accept, without much comment, the value of scientific inquiry.

Young people could begin with the trial of Galileo and examine why the Church felt that his scientific theories endangered society.[14] Nearly all will agree with him against the Church, expressing the value that the search for truth is very important, perhaps on a par with the First Amendment's protection of freedom of speech and the press.

Students need to decide what Galileo should have done, or what the policy of the Pope toward scientific knowledge should have been. Either way, the value conflict is between the search for scientific truth and the protection of society as defined by those doing the protecting. But is the search for truth, as defined by the searcher, always paramount? Again, the use of an analogy proves to be a powerful teaching tool:

Example—Dr. Arthur Jensen advances the position that blacks average fifteen points lower than whites due to hereditary considerations. He has been met by very vocal protestors on college campuses attempting to stop him. Others have called for his dismissal. Public schools refuse to *seriously consider* his writings in class for fear that civil rights groups and the federal government might come down on them. Is Jensen's search for truth, *as he sees it*, worth this disruption to civil order he is causing?[15]

Example—Dr. R. D. Hotkiss finally unlocks the secret of creation and offers to the public the formula to determine the sex, color, height, intelligence, and special talent of a couple's offspring. Citizens in protest mob his laboratory and destroy everything. Was the mob correct in its action? Should Dr. Hotkiss be allowed to continue his research? Should he be allowed to sell his formula to the public?[16]

There are limitless other examples, but these demonstrate the practice of having students test their values in analogous situations. Do we truly value a search for truth regardless of the consequences? Perhaps within 25 years we will face the same dilemma the Church did in 1633. Will we respond as it did?

Geography is another major discipline in secondary schools. How can decision-making experiences be derived from it? Busing and school redistricting are major political issues today. A teaching strategy such as "Millersburg" can demonstrate decision making in political geography.[17] Students must draw high school district boundaries for the hypothetical city of Millersburg. The readings inform students that there are

MILLERSBURG

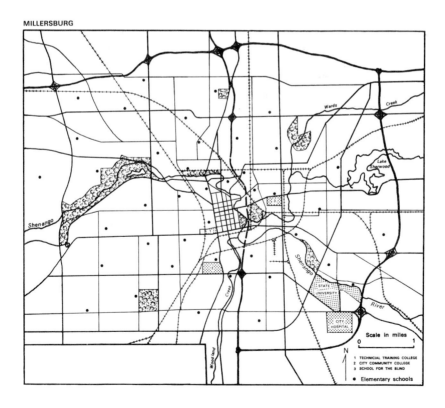

over 12,000 people of high-school age in the city, and that the number is expected to increase. Six new high schools are to be built, and the question is where, precisely, should the boundaries be drawn. Participants in this simulation are given information about family income, population density, ethnic composition of each area, industrial and commercial zones, transportation facilities, and locations of the elementary schools. Their basic problem is to determine what considerations should be taken into account in drawing these boundary lines. Citizen groups come before the board, each with different opinions. As board members, students must grapple with issues such as integration, busing, and future growth.

The considerations are actually value statements and, as such, need to be clarified by some of the techniques illustrated in earlier examples. Students should be asked to state explicitly what values they are supporting by the criteria they suggest for redistricting. They should further be asked to explain why.

Students are broken into groups representing the various lobbyists. There are four stereotypic individuals used. One such individual's profile follows:

Melvin Paine: Melvin Paine is left of center in his political and social convictions. At age 29 he is a regular contributor to the Sunday editorial page of the conservative *Millersburg Tribune*. He is the spokesman for the oppressed and downtrodden. A champion debater in college, he went on to spend two years with the Peace Corps in West Africa. He returned to his home town to take up the banner of social justice and to accept a low-paying job at the Community Center. Every civic group has felt Mel Paine's presence. Mel has begun to realize that change will occur only through political action, and he now has aspirations for city or state office. Mel fully realizes the consequences that can befall the minority group as a result of school districting decisions. He wants to do his best to protect their interests and perhaps to further his political career.[18]

After this simulation, students could gather information on the various groups in their own school district or one nearby that is facing redistricting and busing problems, study it, and propose their own school boundaries.

1. How many alternative plans can be created?
2. What values underlie each?
3. What is the present school plan?
4. What values underlie it?
5. Which plan would you vote for as a member of the Board of Education? Why?

6. How will future growth patterns affect your plan? Will they cause it to be changed?

The Millersburg simulation represents consideration of many types of values—lifestyle preference, money, ecological values, to name a few— whereas previous examples emphasize ethical values. As teachers, we need to stress that there are many criteria which compete for consideration. Deciding which criteria are most important in any given situation is essential to good decision making. Location theory, a major part of any geography course, emphasizes criteria other than ethical values.

Diagrams of hypothetical settlement sites provide a very simplified example of decision making in a geography course.[19] Students are asked: Where would you place a settlement in the year indicated for each of these drawings? What factors must you consider before you can answer this question? What information do you need which you do not have? These queries rather dramatically introduce students to location theory and once more give them practical experience in decision making.

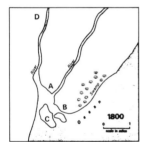 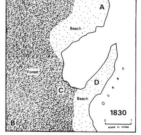 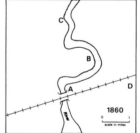

A more elaborate activity involving location theory is a simulation entitled, *Metfab*.[20] This activity uses role playing to demonstrate that decision making is a complex process involving many factors. Youngsters form management teams that are responsible for locating a new plant of the Metfab Corporation. Each group is made up of five officers of the company, each with a different responsibility. Their overriding concern, of course, is to locate their business in such a place that it will make as much money as possible. In arriving at this decision they will utilize economic information and will also draw upon environmental considerations, personal preferences, and their own specific area of expertise. Each member of the team must decide which set of factors is the most important, and then through group decision making they must decide which of the individual values the group will adopt. As with other simulations there is no one correct choice in selection; the objective is to articulate the process of decision making and to require students to investigate their own values. As with any simulation, the data available are incomplete and somewhat simplified; therefore, students must not be allowed to let their decision rest solely on it, but be encouraged to identify what additional information is needed.

The team is made up of the following people:

President—Gregory Williams, 53, is interested in locating the market area which will have the best long-range prospects for his company.

Sales Manager—Ralph McNeal, 45, is concerned with sales and is therefore most interested in present market conditions and shipping costs of the finished product.

Production Manager—Sam Dubrowski, 41, is responsible for production and therefore is concerned with productive labor force and minimizing the cost of raw materials.

Personnel Manager—Frank Greenstein, 37, is concerned with availability of inexpensive labor force and with attracting middle and upper management.

Treasurer—Stanley Engle, 48, wants to locate where good financial contacts and bank loans can be made at low interest rates and corporate taxes are also low.

This management team has narrowed the list of cities down to eight: Atlanta, Cincinnati, Detroit, Houston, Los Angeles, New Orleans, New York, and Pittsburgh.

An example of one role is Sam Dubrowski. He is in charge of purchasing steel, copper, and other raw materials. One of his major concerns is where to buy the company's steel, taking into account the transportation costs. In addition, he needs to consider where labor costs are least expensive and productivity is highest. In assuming the role of Sam Dubrowski, students must consult "Railway Freight Class Rates" tables and "Labor Productivity Index" tables, and consider the impact of the climate.

Once more it is important to emphasize to students the process of decision making that they are going through. Too often with simulations young people get so caught up in the game that after it is over they have a hard time explaining what they learned, or even what the purpose of it all was. Therefore, questions which outline the stages of the decision-making process might profitably be placed on the blackboard for student review during the simulation.

A follow-up to Metfab could stress the location of a specific store in the neighborhood of the school; for example, Dorothy Hughes owns 51 paint stores in the area. She is always looking for new sites. She knows that people travel no more than four miles to buy paint and wallpaper and that the amount of money people spend on these items is directly related to their income and size of home. Finally, the store must be in a shopping center with easy entrance and exit off a major highway.

Armed with detailed maps of their neighborhood, and demographic information from the Chamber of Commerce and the Census Bureau, students might find Ms. Hughes' 52nd store location.

Another follow-up strategy to the Metfab simulation would be to have students analyze why one store in their neighborhood failed, while another of the same type prospered. Of course, location is only one factor in the success or failure of a business, and this exercise can emphasize the danger of making decisions without all available information.

Even without these materials, traditional geography courses can still stress decision making. Suppose students are studying cultural-physical geography. Why not organize some of the material around a real decision, such as finding a suitable place to retire? With regard to retirement, what values will be most important to you? How would you rank the following: weather, number of hospitals, education facilities, crime rate, cost of living, public transportation, recreational facilities, housing, age of residents, and closeness to your children and grandchildren? Much of this information is available in statistical abstracts and in most large cities' telephone directories, which are on hand in major libraries. To simplify, you might make a list of ten large and ten small cities from which your students would make this selection. Another variation might be to plan the itinerary of a European vacation.

These examples represent how decision making can be incorporated in secondary level social studies. It obviously does not cover all subject areas—it need not, since the principles involved in each can be easily transferred from one topic to another. The bibliography at the end of this chapter, moreover, lists other materials which utilize or can be easily adapted to teach decision making.

INITIATING DECISION-MAKING INSTRUCTION
IN YOUR CLASSROOM

To a teacher who has never tried to teach decision making, the examples given may seem fine for other people's students but not for his or hers. This is only natural. With each year, the number and complexity of things we have to contend with seem to grow. It all seems like a rather large headache.

A few guidelines in how to get started might be helpful. First, plan the skills and affective content of your course in the beginning of the year or semester, just as the cognitive content of the course is planned. By habit, skills and values are treated as though they were stepchildren, an obligation not truly desired. This need not be so if students are tested in the beginning of the course and if we organize skill work as much as we do anything else. Each cognitive unit should teach some specific skill or set of skills which leads to the fulfillment of the course's skill and affective goals. Such initial planning needs to be done consciously and deliberately.

Student interest, ability, and maturity determine which steps are taught, in which order, how, and in what detail, naturally. If students are particularly intelligent or well prepared by earlier social studies courses, then it may be possible to teach research skills, inquiry skills, and value clarification along with the cognitive material of each unit. However, most students do not come to our classrooms so nobly equipped, and they need to work gradually into each of these skills.

Too often initial attempts to teach inquiry processes and decision making prove disappointing because students do not perform as do students in published dialogues who volunteer for extra work and come to class with all their homework finished and wanting to do extra reading. Too often writers seem to imply that teaching is easy and uncomplicated and that students have been sitting longingly for years waiting for just this opportunity to blossom intellectually. The truth is normally somewhat more modest. A chapter a week to memorize, a movie or two to break the routine, a ditto map along with a rap session now and then require little from students except patience. On the other hand, asking them to evaluate evidence, examine their values, research various alternatives, and analyze the truthfulness of evidence requires far more from them than they may be willing at first to give. Few people initially feel comfortable with new things; students are no different.

One method of introducing students to decision making is to begin by supplying students with all the information and all the values they need to consider. Perhaps with some groups it will even be necessary to suggest some of the consequences of the various alternatives. The important thing is to get students making decisions consciously and deliberately. Later in the same unit or the next, supply them with a less complete package. Perhaps leave out some of the alternatives or some of the value considerations, forcing them to begin to do some of the preliminary work leading up to the decision. Of course, each of us has to decide how fast this process can proceed. The important point is not to drown students in the decision-making process itself all at once. Students will not know what hit them; and we will end up feeling that we have wasted time. By beginning with the decision itself and working backward through the various skills outlined in the other chapters, we also demonstrate why value clarification and inquiry are important.

A second suggestion is that beginning teachers—both elementary and secondary—secure teacher's guides to well developed elementary school social studies textbooks. A program such as the Taba series carefully outlines what each lesson is about, what inquiry is all about, and how skills are taught. It also has some helpful types of questions which can get a class started on value clarification, developing generalizations, and comparing generalizations. Too often teacher's guides for the secondary level are not as complete or as specific, and, therefore, may leave the teacher new to the inquiry approach somewhat lost.

Finally, plan decision-making exercises as carefully as any other strategy. Used too often, such exercises will be as boring as a lecture a day or a movie every Friday. Select the issue you plan to have your students decide in terms of the time available, resources on hand, and the interests of your students. Nothing is more frustrating than to have spent a long time planning a unit only to find that students really do not grasp its significance, or that the quantity of research material available is too slim.

How we organize our classrooms physically, what relationships we have with our students, and the grading system we adopt, for instance, reflect our true commitment to teaching decision making. The way we run our classrooms can be as significant a learning activity as any topic we teach. Whether to do an assignment or not and how much time and dedication to spend on it are daily decisions students face, but probably seldom consciously, and formally deliberate over. We can help them do this by the way we organize the classroom, present the assignment, and ultimately grade them.

Decision making necessarily includes learning from past errors and having the self-assurance and determination to do a better job of it next time. This means we have to motivate, to encourage young people. Students required to sit alphabetically in lines of desks all facing the teacher's desk, only allowed to speak when called upon, and graded by a strict percentage average that does not reward improvement cannot be expected to acquire self-assurance or to feel a need for self-examination. There are several strategies which may be helpful:

1. Students decide where they will sit, next to whom they like, with the clear understanding that they will be moved if their behavior is disruptive.
2. Let them establish the membership of project groups and decide what each person's responsibilities will be, after having been briefed as to how to work in groups.

3. Assign them the task of setting part of the criteria for your evaluation of their work.
4. Have them set the due dates for their work, and then hold them accountable for those dates.
5. Encourage them to rewrite essays and redo projects by assigning a grade to the work and then explaining how it could be improved. They *decide* whether to accept the present grade.
6. Finally, and most importantly, help students see that each of these previous strategies is aimed at teaching them how to make decisions. For example, go through the steps in making a decision as to where to sit in the classroom, or whether to do an assignment. What are the consequences of each alternative? How important is it to sit next to a friend when it will, based on experience, lead to having to stay after school or otherwise be disciplined because they cannot keep from disrupting the classroom? Ask students who did not do an assignment why they did not. Why did they make that decision? What factors did they take into consideration? What values were they expressing? Obviously, their initial responses will include "I don't know," "It was too boring to do," "I didn't understand it." By working with individuals and groups on the various alternatives open to them and the values each reflects, we are teaching decision making.

After stumbling a few times—we must resist the temptation to step in and tell our students what to do and how to do it—they will begin to think in terms of consequences and values: "I could have turned this essay in last Friday, when due, but I needed more time to do it correctly," "In evaluating our project, we wasted too much time because you didn't check up on us enough. We didn't do it until the last moment," "I value goofing off more than I value getting a good grade." Whether this last student does a better job next time is problematic, but at least he knows that he has made a decision in light of a set of values. Was it a good decision? That is up to him. What we have done as teachers with this strategy is to help him face that question. Naturally, each classroom and each student is different, and consequently not all students will respond to these strategies. They work far more often than not.

Experiment in teaching decision making to your students by introducing it into your course content and also into your classroom management. You will find that the time and energy spent will be worth it.

SUGGESTED READINGS

This list is by no means comprehensive. It reflects additional materials the author has used in his classes or has run across in writing this chapter, other than those listed in the footnotes. It is a good starting point in gathering your own favorite items. Good luck!

I. Decision-Making Readings and Materials

Center for Humanities. *Hard Choices: Strategies for Decision Making*. (Slide-Sound) White Plains, New York: Center for Humanities, 1975.

_____. *Deciding Right from Wrong: The Dilemma of Morality Today*. (Slide-Sound) White Plains, New York: Center for Humanities, 1975.

_____. *Clarifying Your Values: Guidelines for Living*. (Slide-Sound) White Plains, New York: Center for Humanities, 1975.

Nelson, Jack. *Introduction to Value Inquiry*. Rochelle Park, New Jersey: Hayden Press, 1974.

Raths, Louis et al. *Values and Teaching*. Columbus, Ohio: Charles Merrill, Inc., 1967.

Shaver, James P., and A. Guy Larkins. *Instructor's Manual: The Analysis of Public Issues Program*. Hopewell, New Jersey: Houghton Mifflin Company, 1973.

II. Future Studies

La Conte, Ronald T. *Teaching Tomorrow, Today: A Guide to Futuristics*. New York: Bantam, 1975.

Toffler, Alvin. *Future Shock*. New York: Random House, 1970.

_____. *Learning for Tomorrow*. New York: Random House, 1974.

World Future Society. *The Futurist:* A Journal of Forecasts, Trends and Ideas. Washington, D.C.: World Future Society, 1976. (This Society publishes this journal bimonthly, along with many other pamphlets and newsletters. It also has an introductory slide presentation on the future, cassettes on various topics, and selected books on the future. For more information, write to: World Future Society, P.O. Box 30369, Bethesda Branch, Washington, D.C., 20014.)

III. Role Playing

Chester, Mark, and Robert Fox. *Role Playing Methods in the Classroom*. New York: S.R.A., 1966.

Klein, Alfred. *How to Use Role Playing Effectively*. New York: Association Press, 1959.

Shaftel, Fannie and George Shaftel. *Role Playing for Social Valuing*. New York: Prentice-Hall, 1967.

IV. Secondary-Level Instructional Materials

Amherst Project. Brown and Halsy (eds.). Reading, Mass.: Addison-Wesley Publishing Co., 1970–1974. *Hiroshima; What Happened on Lexington Green?; Thomas Jefferson, the Embargo, the Decision for Peace; The Rights of Americans: The Changing Balance of Liberty, Law and Order*.

Banks, James (ed.). *Teaching Ethnic Studies*. Washington, D.C.: National Council for the Social Studies, 1973.

Barger, Harold. "Judging the President's Decisions: A Critical Citizenship Skill," *Social Education* 40 (October, 1976), pp. 379–384.

Beyer, Barry. "Conducting Moral Discussions in the Classroom," *Social Education* 40 (April, 1976), pp. 194–202.

Elder, Charles. *Making Values Judgments: Decisions for Today*. New York: Charles E. Merrill, 1972.

Fenton, Edwin. "Moral Education: The Research Findings," *Social Education* 40 (April, 1976), pp. 188–193.

Fisher, Roger. "A Negotiation Exercise: Should the Tea Be Landed in Boston?", *Social Education* 38 (February, 1974), pp. 137–152.

Fraenkel, Jack (ed.). *Crucial Issues in American Government*. Rockleigh, New Jersey: Allyn and Bacon, Inc., 1976.

Gillespie, Judith, and Stuart Lazarus. "Teaching Political Participation Skills," *Social Education* 40 (October, 1976), pp. 373–378.

High School Geography Project, Macmillan Publishing Company. *Geography of Cities; Manufacturing and Agriculture; Habitat and Resources; Cultural Geography; Political Geography.*

King, David et al. "Using Case Studies to Teach About Global Issues," *Social Education* 38 (Nov./Dec., 1974), pp. 657–663.

Metcalf, Lawrence (ed.). *Values Education*. Washington, D.C.: National Council for the Social Studies, 1971.

Muessig, Raymond (ed.). *Controversial Issues in the Social Studies: A Contemporary Perspective*. Washington, D.C.: National Council for the Social Studies, 1975.

Oliver, Donald, and Fred Newmann, (eds.). *Public Issues Series*, Middletown, Conn.: American Education Publications, 1970 (A selective list). *Limits of War; American Revolution; Railroad Era; Religious Freedom; The Immigrant's Experiences; The New Deal; Nazi Germany; Privacy; Black in America; Our Polluted World; The Penal System.*

Patrick, John J. "Making Decisions About Participating in Elections," *Social Education* 40 (October, 1976), pp. 366–372.

Roger, Vincent (ed.). *Values and Decisions*. 1972 (A selective list). Middletown, Conn.: 1972. *Colonial Defiance; The Constitution; Neutral Rights; Conquest; Impeachment; Confrontation.*

Rosenzweig, Linda. "A Selected Bibliography of Material About Moral Education Based on Research of Lawrence Kohlberg," *Social Education* 40 (April, 1976), pp. 208–212.

Ubellohde, Carl, and Jack Fraenkel, (eds.). *Values of the American Heritage: Challenges, Case Studies, and Teaching Strategies*. Washington, D.C.: National Council for the Social Studies, 1976.

Wass, Philmore. *We Are Making Decisions*. Lexington, Mass., Ginn and Co., 1972.

Wisniewski, Richard (ed.). *Teaching About Life in the City*. Washington, D.C.: National Council for the Social Studies, 1972. (Especially chapters 5–8.)

FOOTNOTES

[1]Alvin Toffler, "What Is Anticipatory Democracy?", *The Futurist*, Volume IX, No. 5 (October, 1975), p. 224. Used with permission of World Future Society, Washington, D.C.

[2]Anna S. Ochoa and Rodney F. Allen, "Creative Teacher-Student Learning Experiences About the City," in *Teaching About Life in the City*, Richard Wisniewski, editor. 42nd Yearbook (Washington, D.C.: National Council for the Social Studies, 1972), pp. 151–154.

[3]H. B. Gelatt et al., *Deciding* (New York: College Entrance Examination Board, 1972).

[4]H. B. Gelatt et al., *Decisions and Outcomes* (New York: College Entrance Examination Board, 1972).

[5]*Deciding*, p. 11. Reprinted with permission from *Deciding* by H. B. Gelatt, Barbara Varenhorst, and Richard Carey, copyright © 1972 by the College Entrance Examination Board, New York.

[6]*Ibid.*, p. 14.

[7]*Ibid.*, p. 30.

[8]*Ibid.*, pp. 31–32.

[9]*Ibid.*, pp. 41–42.

[10]Donald W. Oliver and Fred Newmann, eds., *The American Revolution* (Middletown, Conn.: American Education Publications, 1967), p. 4. Special permission granted by *The American Revolution*, published by Xerox Education Publishers, 1967.

[11]*Ibid.*, pp. 9–12, in excerpts.

[12]The idea for this chart comes from "A Value Clarification Exercise: Values You Care About," in "Teaching About the American Revolution," Nona Lyon, ed., *Social Education*, Vol. 38, No. 2 (February, 1974), p. 156.

[13]These techniques are explained more completely in James Shaver and A. Guy Larkins, *Instructor's Manual, The Analysis of Public Issues Program* (Hopewell, New Jersey: Houghton Mifflin, 1973), pp. 375–378.

[14]Donald Oliver and Fred Newmann, *Science and Public Policy* (Middletown, Conn.: American Education Publications, 1969), pp. 7–12.

[15]*Ibid.*

[16]Suggested by *Using Science To Modify Men, ibid.*, pp. 42–44.

[17]High School Geography Project, "Political Geography," *Geography in an Urban Age* (New York: The Macmillan Company, 1970), pp. 1–5.

[18]*Ibid.*

[19]High School Geography Project, "Geography of Cities," *Geography in an Urban Age* (New York: The Macmillan Co., 1970), p. 15.

[20]High School Geography Project, "Manufacturing and Agriculture," *Geography in an Urban Age* (New York: The Macmillan Co., 1969), pp. 20–21.

"The problem of specifying skills in a general skilled process like decision making is much like the problem of defining a concept or the problem of breaking down a general objective into specific behavioral objectives. One must ask what it is that is essential to define or demonstrate the larger idea."

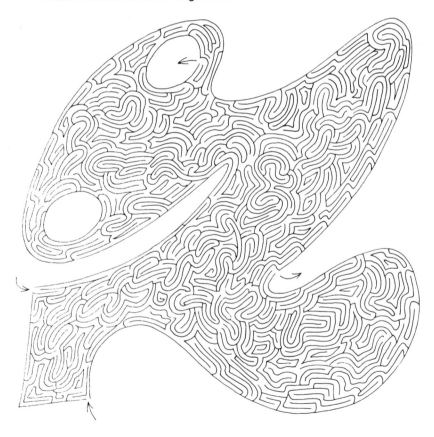

.8.

Celeste P. Woodley and Laura A. Driscoll

A Model and
Suggestions for Evaluating
Decision-Making Skills

This chapter presents a conceptualization of the decision-making process as a series of nine skill statements. Each skill statement will be defined; criteria against which to test the mastery of the skill will be presented; examples of student products demonstrating the mastery of the skill will be offered; and suggested evaluation techniques for each skill will be given. Before the skill statements with accompanying evaluation suggestions are presented, however, the rationale for the decision-making model and some general evaluation principles will be described. Following the presentation of skill statements and evaluation ideas, some suggestions regarding data management and use of evaluation data will be made. The final section will deal with the evaluation of group-process skills in conjunction with the evaluation of decision-making skills.

A DECISION-MAKING EVALUATION MODEL

To talk with any sense about diagnosing and evaluating skills inherent in the decision-making process, one must start with a precise notion of what those skills are. It is impossible to jump from a broad goal statement like "students will know how to make good decisions" to valid assessment statements. Broad aspects of decision making like "clarification of the issue" or the three major aspects identified in Chapter

One certainly help narrow the field of observation for the teacher-evaluator. They do provide good clues as to what the skills might be; but these steps, phases, or aspects are not skills. They do not tell us what the skills are. Skills must be derived from those steps, and the skill must be explicated in behavioral terms before evaluation can take place. To say it another way, we cannot see a decision-making skill. We must infer it from something the student says, writes, or does. The characteristics of that student product must match the generalized attributes of the skill concept which we hold in our minds. Those generalized attributes are the criteria against which we judge the quality of the student's decision-making skills. Teachers need to be familiar with those criteria in order to assess the specific skills inherent in the decision-making process. A major aim of this chapter is to present a set of criteria for each specific skill.

The problem of specifying skills in a general skilled process like decision making is much like the problem of defining a concept or the problem of breaking down a general objective into specific behavioral objectives. One must ask what it is that is essential to define or demonstrate the larger idea. To answer the question, one first must limit or define the idea—the objective, the concept, the skill, the process. To some extent, the definition will be subjective, tentative and arbitrary, but it will serve to communicate the field of focus and the logical criteria against which are tested further specifications.

Let us go to the immediate task as a working example: we are to write about ways to evaluate skills inherent in the decision-making process. We cannot begin to talk about evaluating until we know or invent the appropriate skills. What skills are decision-making skills? To answer that question we can go to the literature on decision making or we can construct a definition of the decision-making process and proceed to derive steps and skills statements. We have done a little of both to give a definitional basis from which to begin.

We define the decision-making process as a series of cognitive acts focused on choosing that begins with the identification of the occasion for decision and ends with reflection on the products of the process—the decision, the action, and the consequences. From that definition, arbitrary as it may be, we can go directly to the specification of the cognitive acts that logically make up that process. The requirement laid on by the definition is that these acts must be focused on or oriented toward choice or choosing. The requirement of logic is that the acts specified must be discrete and must collectively describe a process that begins with identification of the occasion for decision and ends with reflection on the products. The climactic act in the process is the act of deciding, but in our definition it is not the final act. We have arbitrarily extended the definition beyond the act of deciding to include acting on the decision and reflecting on the decision, action, and consequences.

We can proceed directly from the definition of the process to the cognitive acts that define the skills in decision making or we can take an intermediate step and identify general steps or stages in the process, each step usually encompassing more than one skill. Many curriculum writers have chosen the latter course and imply skills without specifying them. Commonly those steps or stages are designated something like: clarifying the issue, choosing from among alternatives, tracing the consequences of each alternative, evaluating the consequences of each alternative, and making the decision. Sometimes the steps are broader: identifying alternatives, evaluating alternatives, making a choice. In Chapter One three stages of decision making were identified:

(1) Identifying decision occasions and alternatives.
(2) Examining and evaluating decision alternatives.
(3) Deciding and reflecting on the decision.

Eventually stages or steps, however stated, must be translated into skill statements that contain a verb form representing a cognitive operation and an object that has been defined in terms of the decision-making process.

The verb-object interaction is crucial to the demonstration of the skill. To be able to do what the verb requires but to an irrelevant object is not to demonstrate the skill. To be able to discuss the relevant object in a way other than the verb requires is not to demonstrate the skill either. For example, if the skill is "evaluating alternatives," then the student must evaluate alternatives, not sources of information. Conversely, the student must evaluate, not describe, alternatives. To be precise in specifying what is expected of the student requires some definitional and analytical rigor on the part of the teacher-evaluator. We need to know what we mean by each verb form and each object.

The purpose in analyzing each skill statement is to more precisely define the competency—to set the criteria that indicate to the student and to the teacher what it is that the student must do to qualify his or her behavior as skilled. With both operational elements specified, we know the limits or criteria of the product. The product of the application of thinking to content is the overt indication of the existence of the skill. The product may be a verbal or written statement or a demonstrated act, depending on the skill and the task. It is that product that can be assessed or evaluated. Evaluation will be made in terms of the criteria contributed by the verb in the skill statement, the object in the statement, and the application of the former to the latter.

The model we suggest for evaluation of decision-making skills can be graphically shown in the diagram below.

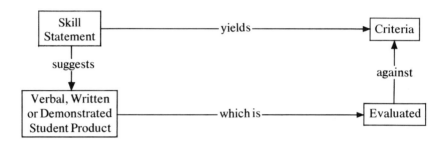

Decision-making skills treated in this chapter were selected and worded on the basis of our expanded definition of the decision-making process, some of the literature on decision making, and some of the current curriculum materials on citizenship. We have designated nine skills in the decision-making process. They fit rather closely the three stages of decision making identified in Chapter One.

    I. **Identifying the occasion for a decision.**
   II. **Recognizing the values implicit in a decision situation.**
  III. **Seeking and finding alternatives.**
  IV. **Creating alternatives.**
   V. **Predicting consequences of alternatives.**
  VI. **Weighing alternatives and selecting one course of action.**
 VII. **Determining appropriate action to implement decision.**
VIII. **Taking action to implement the decision.**
  IX. **Reflecting on the decision, action, and results.**

Each of the skill statements contains the two factors that together establish the criteria for judging attainment of the skill. The two factors are: (1) the verb form that describes the cognitive operation required, and (2) the object of the verb that describes what it is that the student must identify, recognize, seek, find or create, predict, and evaluate. The skill statement, then, describes the skill and gives a general guide for establishing the criteria against which a student's demonstration of the decision-making skill can be tested. The criteria for each of the skill statements are specified and examples of student products that meet those criteria are given in the section entitled *Criteria, Product Examples, and Evaluation Suggestions*.

EVALUATION

The evaluation of the decision-making process is multifaceted. The major evaluation questions that pertain to instruction in any subject area and for any age group also pertain in the evaluation of the attainment of decision-making skill objectives. Those questions—"Were the instructional objectives met by the students? How well or to what extent did the students master the objectives? What aspects of the instruction need to be revised or reviewed? What grades do the students deserve?"—are not answered easily or quickly. The appropriateness of the evaluation techniques that can be used will depend upon the purposes of the evaluation, the specific questions for the evaluation, and the "givens" of the decision-making situation (i.e., the role of the students, the age level of the students, the ability level of the students, and the content area to which the decision-making exercise is applied).

The role that evaluation plays in the teaching of decision-making skills is seen, generally, by the placement of the "Evaluation" box in the flowchart on page 238. Note that "Evaluation" is dependent upon "Criteria." Evaluation questions and techniques cannot be specified without the pre-specification of the characteristics (criteria) of the product and the characteristics (criteria) of the group-process skills. The identification of those characteristics depends, in turn, upon the description of both the cognitive operation and the object of the decision-making skill. The characteristics or criteria of the products have the most influence on the evaluation specifications, since they are, in effect, the necessary attributes of the products. The list of criteria for each product actually constitutes a checklist against which the product can be quantitatively and qualitatively rated. Since it is the overt product, rather than the underlying and covert processes that result in the product, that can be observed, the checklist of necessary attributes for the product is crucial in the attempt to evaluate whether or not the skill has been mastered. Likewise, a list of the characteristics of the group-process skills that are associated with the decision-making objectives provides a checklist for the evaluator to use in assessing the adequacy of that aspect of the decision-making process when it is conducted in a group setting.

A variety of evaluation techniques is available to teachers as they play the role of evaluators of their students' progress and of the efficacy of their own instructional methods and materials. Most teachers are familiar with standardized tests, teacher-made tests, and informal observation of students as ways of making diagnostic and attainment judgments. In regard to the evaluation of decision-making skills, specifically, the results of standardized achievement and aptitude tests will be of little use to teachers. Although such tests provide valuable information about the general ability levels of students, they rarely contain the kind of items that assess attainment of particular skills in decision making. Teacher-made tests and observational methods are of more direct use to teachers in the evaluation of instruction and learners because of their specificity and relevance to the context of the learning situation.

Suggestions for ways to evaluate the attainment of decision-making skills objectives will be presented for both informal and formal evaluation settings. Informal evaluation differs from formal evaluation in purpose, use to which the results are put, time in which the evaluation takes place, and most appropriate or frequently-used technique. Most teachers will find both types of evaluation useful and informative.

Informal evaluation has as its main purpose the immediate (post-instruction) evaluation of the students' products. The results of such evaluation will be used to make decisions about the efficacy of the instruction employed in teaching decision-making skills. The focus here is on finding out if the students have mastered the material presented to them during teacher instruction, so that the instruction can be revised or extended accordingly. This type of evaluation can be characterized as formative and continual; that is, it is ongoing during instruction and used primarily for teacher feedback. In many situations, the teacher will make a quick judgment, based on his/her impressions of the students' written or verbal statements, of the extent to which the skill has been mastered. In other situations, the teacher might want to use a simple rating scale or checklist to judge the quality of the products. Observation and analysis techniques will be appropriate in those cases where the students work in groups to demonstrate the skills; here, in addition to checking the product against the criteria for the decision-making skill, the teacher will want to rate the students on ability to work effectively in groups.

Formal evaluation is intended primarily for the evaluation of the learners rather than for the evaluation of instruction. The techniques that belong in this category will yield data that can be used for diagnostic purposes or for assigning grades to students. The methods used in formal evaluation tend to be pre-planned and more carefully constructed than those used in informal evaluation. The time for the evaluation is usually pre-specified so as to coincide with the end of a teaching unit and a time deemed reasonable for the attainment by most students of the objectives of instruction. The most commonly-used technique for formal evaluation of decision-making skill objectives is the teacher-made test. Paper-and-pencil tests can, of course, be constructed in a variety of ways and can consist of many different types of questions. The age level of the students and the depth of content coverage that should be tested will help determine the test specifications. Questions written at several different cognitive levels—knowledge, comprehension, application, analysis, synthesis, evaluation—will be needed in order to determine if students have grasped the meanings of the concepts inherent in the skill objectives, know what the criteria for the decision-making skills are, can apply the right cognitive tasks in unfamiliar situations, can analyze decisions according to the skill components, and can evaluate the worth of the decisions. The tests can consist of objective test items and/or essay questions, although objective items tend to be more reliable than essay questions.

Measurement techniques applicable to formal evaluation are not limited to paper-and-pencil tests. The teacher could, for example, request the students to again engage in the activities that led to the decision-making skill products during instruction, only to do so under test conditions—without teacher intervention and using a decision context not previously discussed by the class. The difficulty with such a technique comes in the scoring of the products. Checklists or rating scales with categories representing discernible differences in the degree to which the criteria of the products are met will be needed in order to make comparative judgments of the learners' attainment levels.

The evaluation suggestions that appear in the next section, after the description of each step in the decision-making process, are categorized according to the role of the students, the age of the students, and the evaluation setting. The different roles that students can assume in instructional activities associated with decision-making skills are decision-maker, role-player, and analyst. The type of decision-making activity that students are asked to complete will usually determine the appropriate role. That is, if students actually go through the process of making an original decision, they are decision makers; if they simulate decision-making situations of the past, they are role-players; and if they concentrate on sorting out and reflecting upon the steps taken by previous decision makers, they are taking the role of analyst. Ways to evaluate decision-making steps according to student role are not always distinct; i.e., more than one role can often fit within the same evaluation context.

The age of the students will certainly be a determining factor in the design of evaluation activities. Secondary-level students will be able to produce more sophisticated products, which will require more elaborate evaluation schemes, than will elementary-level students. The evaluation suggestions that are offered for the elementary level are probably most useful for the upper-elementary grades.

The suggestions that appear under "Informal" settings and "Formal" settings in the charts in the next section are not meant to be entirely exclusive to the setting under which they are subsumed. There will be times, for example, when the teacher will aggregate some of the impressions gathered informally and combine them with the formal data before assigning grades; that is, he/she will be using informal evaluation results in addition to formal evaluation results in making final judgments about students' level of mastery. The informal evaluation results can aid in providing valuable continuous diagnostic information about the learners. And the results of the formal evaluation can provide feedback to the teacher that can help in the planning and revision of instruction. The breakdown of suggestions according to the two settings is a general one and certainly not meant to be absolute for all teachers in all instructional situations.

Finally, a word is needed about the ideas presented under the formal evaluation setting. The items that appear under "Formal Evaluation" are examples of the types of item that could comprise end-of-unit tests on the decision-making steps. The examples do not constitute suggested tests in their entirety. The test item examples are intended, in part, to emphasize that test items can vary in format.

CRITERIA, PRODUCT EXAMPLES, AND EVALUATION SUGGESTIONS

I. **Identifying the Occasion for a Decision**

A. *Cognitive Task:* Identification
B. *Object of the Cognitive Task:* Occasion for Decision
C. *Prior Conditions Necessary for the Demonstration of the Skill:* Must know meaning of the concept "Occasion for Decision" and what the necessary and sufficient conditions are; must know what "Identify" means.
D. *Criteria Against Which To Test Products or Behavior Which Demonstrate Skill:* The student must pick out, describe, or define the following aspects of a decision occasion:
    1. The need for choice between two or more courses of action;
    2. The short- or long-run need for action following the choice must be at least implicit;
    3. Existence of personal or group goals as a basis of the choice between action alternatives;
    4. Identification of the decision maker(s).
E. *Product Examples:*
    1. TEACHER: Can you describe a situation where a decision is called for?
        STUDENT: Well, when you have to choose a book to read in the library.
        OTHER STUDENT: When people have to decide whether to evacuate their homes or stay and risk being drowned.
        OTHER STUDENT: It's any time there are two or more ways to do one thing and only one can be chosen.
    2. TEACHER: By the spring of 1974 it was obvious that there was public distrust of the President, and there were accusations of dishonesty,

illegal entry, invasion of privacy, incompetence, etc. made against government officials. Name as many decision situations as your group can think of that might have existed in the spring of 1974.

GROUP: (1) The Congress would have to decide whether to investigate the accusations.

(2) The President would have to decide what to tell the American people.

3. TEACHER: Imagine that you are Edmund Ross, a Republican member of the House of Representatives during the administration of Johnson. It is the year 1868 and Johnson's impeachment trial is underway. The Republicans are exerting pressure on you to vote with the majority of your fellow party members—that is, for conviction. You are not at all convinced that Johnson is really guilty of the offenses that he has been accused of.

Describe the decision situation that you, as Edmund Ross, find yourself in.

STUDENT: I have to decide whether to vote as the Republicans tell me to vote or to make up my mind independent of the party's position.

F. *Informal Evaluation Suggestions:*

	ROLE OF STUDENT*	LEVEL OF STUDENT
1. Teacher judges student responses (products) against the criteria; teacher questions students if products are incomplete or vague; for example, since criterion "3" is likely to be absent explicitly, the teacher would want to ask such questions as, "*Why* would you want to read a book about sports instead of a book about science? or *Why* would you want to read a book about science instead of a book about sports?"	D-M	Elem.
2. Teacher administers questionnaire:[1]	D-M	Elem.

	Yes	*No*
a. Do you ever decide with whom you will play at recess?	____	____
b. Do you ever decide what books to read for an extra-reading assignment?	____	____
c. Do you ever decide what movie to go to?	____	____

etc.

This questionnaire is designed to elicit "yes" responses primarily (since many of the actions students take are the results of their own decisions, at least partly or some of the time); the teacher should interview students regarding any "no" an-

*D-M = Decision Maker; An = Analyst; R-P = Role-Player.

swers they give to see *why* they aren't recognizing the decision occasion. This should help the teacher become aware of the "missing ingredient" in the student's product.		
3. Teacher uses rating scales or checklists to judge the extent to which the skill is demonstrated. The rating scales or checklists pertain to the students' written or verbal products (one product per group, if it is a group activity).	D-M An R-P	Sec.

a. When students are asked to list a number of decision situations, their listing can be rated on the following scale:

1	2	3	4	5
lacks any decision situation		contains several decision situations		is complete; contains all possible decision situations

b. In describing a decision situation, the decision maker is:
____ identified explicitly
____ identified implicitly
____ not identified at all

c. In describing a decision situation, alternatives in the decision occasion are:
____ explicitly mentioned
____ implicitly identified
____ missing entirely

G. *Formal Evaluation Suggestions:***

1. Which of the following are times when a decision is called for?	D-M	Elem.

                                           Yes   No

a. Your teacher shows you how to do an arithmetic problem.   ____ ____

b. Your mother asks you if you want to go to the beach or to the park.   ____ ____

c. You like two TV shows that come on at the same time.   ____ ____

**These are examples of the types of items that could comprise end-of-unit tests on the decision-making steps. The examples do not constitute suggested tests in their entirety.

	D-M	Elem.

2. Which of the following is *not* a time when you must make a decision?

    _____ Your brother wants you to lend him your bike.

    _____ Your father gives you $1.00 to spend on anything you want.

    _____ Your grandmother comes over to your house to eat dinner with your family.

    _____ Your teacher tells you to write a story about some fun thing you did during the summer.

	An	Elem.

3. Each of the following paragraphs is about someone who must make a decision. Finish writing the last sentence of each paragraph by naming two choices that the person has.

    a. Mrs. Long wants to make a cake. She can make a _____ cake or a _____ cake.

    b. It is Saturday afternoon and Billy has finished all his chores. He could _____ or he could _____.

    c. The house next door burned down. Your family wants to help the people who lived there. Your family could _____ or _____.

    (This question calls for teacher judgment; responses should be considered acceptable if two clearly different and feasible choices are given.)

	An	Elem.

4. The jury has just heard both sides of a case that was presented in court. A man was accused of stealing some tires from a gas station. The man said that he did not take the tires. A worker in the gas station said that he saw the man take the tires. The tires were found in the man's back yard.

    a. Who is/are the decision maker(s) in this situation (check one)?

    _____ the lawyers

    _____ the gas-station worker

    _____ the man

    _____ the jury

    b. What is the main issue in this situation (check one)?

    _____ whether the gas-station worker took the tires

    _____ whether the man took the tires

    _____ whether the jury needs more time to think about the case

    _____ where the tires were found

   c. What two choices are there for the decision maker(s) (check two)?

      ____ the man is guilty

      ____ the man did not take the tires

      ____ the gas-station worker and the man need to talk to the jury

5. Which one of the following statements does *not* indicate that a decision was made?   An   Sec.

      ____ The rescue operation involved the volunteer fire departments from three cities.

      ____ The school has a new cafeteria.

      ____ The children were awakened by the sound of the thunder.

      ____ The teacher took the students on a field trip to the museum.

6. A high school principal allows a group of students to form a committee to recommend how the $1,000.00 in the school-renovation fund will be spent. The principal has assured the committee that its recommendations will be followed.   An   Sec.

   a. Who is/are the decision maker(s) for the use of the $1,000.00?

      ____ the principal

      ____ the students on the committee

      ____ the majority of the student body

   b. The students make up a list of possible ways to spend the money. The list includes:

     1. a new scoreboard for the football field

     2. work tables for the chemistry lab

     These two choices represent (choose one):

      ____ differences in decision situations

      ____ differences in goals

      ____ differences in the interpretation of the task of the committee

7. Read the following conversation. Then answer the questions that follow.   An   Sec.

   STAN: I don't understand how anyone could even consider voting for the Republican Presidential candidate! Why, the Republicans want to take this country back to the 19th century! I'm not going to waste my time listening to what the Republican candidate has to say.

   MARY: That's a closed-minded attitude! How can you judge a candidate without listening to what she has to say? I'm glad that most people don't feel the way you do!

a. From what Stan says, it is clear that (choose one):

_____ he must make a decision regarding whom to vote for

_____ he has chosen some other candidate instead of the Republican candidate

_____ the Republican candidate does not represent an alternative for him

b. What decision occasion is implicitly referred to in the conversation?

_____ the election of a President

_____ the worth of the electoral system

_____ whether Mary or Stan is the more open-minded person

_____ no decision occasion

II. Recognizing the Values Implicit in a Decision Situation

A. *Cognitive Task:* Inferring

B. *Object of the Cognitive Task:* Values and/or value conflicts implicit in a decision situation.

C. *Prior Conditions Necessary for the Demonstration of the Skill:* Must know the meaning of "value" and "value conflict"; must know what the differences are between facts and values; must have had practice with inferring.

D. *Criteria Against Which To Test Products or Behavior Which Demonstrate Skill:*

1. The items named as values must be logically derived from the decision occasion; that is, must plausibly attach to goals or means alternatives, to persons making or affected by the coming decision;

2. The items named as values must qualify as values; that is, as central beliefs about how one ought or ought not to behave, or about some end-state of existence, worth or not worth attaining.

The naming of the values and/or the identification of real or potential value-conflicts must be more than wild guesses. To show inferencing, the student must be able to associate the value with the characteristics of the situation or person(s) in the situation that suggested it.

E. *Product Examples:*

1. TEACHER: We know that we need to decide what our class is going to do with the money we made on the bake sale. John has suggested that we spend the money on an aquarium for our classroom. Mary has suggested that we sponsor a Christmas party for the children in the Orphans' Home. Can someone tell me what the different *reasons* for spending the money in these two different ways might be?

STUDENT: Well, we'd like to spend the money on something that we can use in class and that would be fun and interesting for us. We'd also like to use the money to do something nice for someone else.

TEACHER: So does the choice involve differences in what is considered important by different persons in the class?

STUDENT: Yes. If we buy the aquarium, it's because we would rather have something for ourselves than give something to someone else.

TEACHER: Okay, we are agreed that the money will be spent on the Christmas party. . . . In deciding whether to serve cookies or cake, are we involved in a choice between two different values?

STUDENT: No. This choice is between two things that are very much alike. We could just toss a coin. . . .

2. Students simulate a Congressional session in which federal tax monies will be allocated. Before the role-playing activity begins, the students will list the values implicit in major alternatives (those already mentioned in Skill #1, Identification of the Occasion). The list could include:
- environmental concerns
- international influence (power)
- care for the poor, elderly, etc.
- concerns about the quality of education

F. *Informal Evaluation Suggestions:*

	ROLE OF STUDENT*	LEVEL OF STUDENT
1. Teacher judgment required to assess whether or not students can name a value in response to the question, "What is considered most important to the person who suggests this choice?", and whether or not they can recognize the presence of real or potential value conflicts in decision occasions.	D-M An R-P	Elem.
2. The teacher can present (orally) a list of opposing choices for a decision occasion and ask students to name the value implicit ("What is considered important by the person if he/she chooses this?") for each choice. Sample set of alternatives:	An	

a. John can:
_____ spend his allowance on a new toy, or
_____ give his allowance to the March of Dimes.

b. The Congress can:
_____ increase taxes to pay for more roads, or
_____ leave the taxes the way they are.

c. The City Council can:
_____ allow some apartments to be built on mountain land, or
_____ prevent any new buildings from being constructed on mountain land.

d. The School Board can:
_____ hire one new teacher, or

---

*D-M = Decision Maker; An = Analyst; R-P = Role-Player.

_____ buy new sports equipment and football uniforms.

3. The teacher can give students a simple values inventory to fill out. For example:[2]   **D-M   Elem.**
Check whether you agree or disagree with each statement. If you cannot decide, put a check under "Can't Decide."

	Agree	*Dis- agree*	*Can't Decide*
a. Big cities are better places to live than small towns.	_____	_____	_____
b. The space program is more important than providing health care to the poor.	_____	_____	_____
c. We need more parks instead of more roads.	_____	_____	_____
etc.			

The teacher should question students about their "Can't Decide" responses, to make sure that they understand the issues and to try to get them to make choices. An inventory like this one can help the teacher know the extent to which students' values are clarified in their own minds.

4. Teacher judgment is required to check the sufficiency and accuracy of a list of values specified by the students as being implicit in a decision occasion. For each product (group or individual), the teacher tabulates the number of values listed for the decision occasion, and compares this number to the number on a list compiled by the student. Also to be assessed is the quality of the lists; i.e., whether or not the concepts listed are values and whether or not they are consistent with the decision occasion.   **R-P An   Sec.**

5. The teacher can ask the students (orally), "Think of some value that is important to you. Then tell me how it might affect your decision regarding what you will do after you graduate from high school." Teacher judgment is required to judge the consistency between the stated value and the stated alternative. Each student's statement could be categorized as follows: **D-M   Sec.**
   • Incomplete (does not contain a value and/or an alternative)
   • Inconsistent (contains both an alternative and a value, but the two are not logically linked)

- Complete, consistent (contains both a value and an alternative that are logically linked)

G. *Formal Evaluation Suggestions:*   An   Elem.

   1. Bob wants to get a job after school so that he can have more spending money. Neither his mother nor his father wants him to get a job. His mother wants him to study after school. His father wants him to join the swimming team.

      a. Which one of the the following does Bob consider most important in this decision situation?

        ____ sports
        ____ money
        ____ education

      b. Which one of the following does Bob's mother consider most important in this decision situation?

        ____ sports
        ____ money
        ____ education

      c. Which one of the following does Bob's father consider most important in this decision situation?

        ____ sports
        ____ money
        ____ education

   2. For each of the following sets of choices, tell whether or not there is a values-conflict: An   Elem.

	Yes	No
a. choosing between eating a peanut butter sandwich and eating a cheese sandwich	____	____
b. choosing between playing checkers and playing a card game	____	____
c. deciding if you will let a girl join the boys' baseball team	____	____
d. choosing between skipping school to go skiing or going to school	____	____
e. choosing between reading a school book or watching cartoons on TV	____	____

   3. When asked the question "What do you consider to be the most important thing in your life?", Mr. Smith said, "My job." Mr. Blake said, "My family." Tell one thing that you think each man might choose to do on a Sunday afternoon that would go along with what he considers most important.   An   Elem.

Mr. Smith: _____		
Mr. Blake: _____		
(Teacher judgment is required to assess accept-ability of response. The answers should logically derive from the values stated in the question.)		
4. Which one of the following is a value statement that might be mentioned in connection with a legislature's decision regarding gun control?	An	Sec.

4. Which one of the following is a value statement that might be mentioned in connection with a legislature's decision regarding gun control?

_____ Guns are inexpensive

_____ Freedom to own guns is not guaranteed in many countries

_____ Freedom to own guns is a right that should be protected

_____ Our forebears said that guns were necessary

5. Which one of the following pairs of values would most likely be in conflict in a governmental decision regarding desegregation?

_____ health—power

_____ money—equality

_____ individualism—equality

_____ money—individualism

III. Seeking and Finding Alternatives

A. *Cognitive Task:* Looking for, gathering, categorizing, and interpreting information relating to and within the limits of the decision occasion.

B. *Object of the Cognitive Task:* Choices of action in addition to, or more specific than, the two or more that originally defined the decision occasion.

C. *Prior Conditions Necessary for the Demonstration of the Skill:* Must know that resources exist; must know how to use resources; must understand the general relationship between the decision situation and the type of information likely to be found in specific sources; must have had prior experience with categorizing information and interpreting data. Chapter 3 deals extensively with the information-gathering skills.

D. *Criteria Against Which To Test Products or Behavior Which Demonstrate Skill:*

1. The student must have looked for ideas for an alternative action (one not defined in the original decision occasion);

2. The student must have either found ideas for an alternative action (one not defined in original decision occasion) or have become convinced that there are no other alternatives to be found;

3. The student must present an alternative that makes sense for the situation; that is, it is another plausible goal or means to a goal for the decision maker(s). If the student is convinced that there are no other alternatives to be found, then she/he must present evidence of having sought but not found other alternatives.

4. The student must have referred to a variety of resources to get ideas for alternatives.
5. The student must know when to quit looking for ideas and start creating ideas.

E. *Product Examples:*
  1. The group is trying to decide what to do to repair a leaky boat. Two alternatives have been suggested: Line the bottom with plastic, or replace some of the boards. A student goes to a manual on boat-building and maintenance and finds out that a pine-tar product can be used effectively as a sealing agent. Another student asks a neighbor who owns a boat, and she suggests a commercial caulking product.
  2. The veterinarian says that the injured cat must (1) have its leg amputated, or (2) be put to sleep. The student reports that there are no other alternatives. He/she has checked with several other vets, and also has gone straight to some primary sources (i.e., animal husbandry books). All of the sources yield the same information: For this type of injury, there is no other solution.
  3. A group of students are role-playing the decision situation that resulted in the dropping of the atom bomb on Hiroshima in 1945. The alternatives identified during step #1 (Identification of the Occasion for Decision) were: "Drop the bomb on Hiroshima" and "Don't drop the bomb on Hiroshima." The group members seek additional information by checking historical accounts of the original decision-making process, and then list all other alternatives that were available to the decision makers at that time.

F. *Informal Evaluation Suggestions:*

	ROLE OF STUDENT*	LEVEL OF STUDENT
1. Teacher judgment is required to rate the list of alternatives on dimensions related to the criteria. Sample rating scales and checklists: a. Sufficiency of sources	D-M An R-P	Elem.

1	2	3	4	5
no sources cited		list of sources incomplete		list of sources complete

  b. The alternatives found:
  _____ are plausible
  _____ match the goals of the decision occasion
  _____ include some reference to source(s)

2. Teacher observes the students (or asks the librarian to observe them) as they seek information in the school library. Teacher (or librarian) uses a checklist to record the extent to which they use	D-M	Elem.

*D-M = Decision Maker; An = Analyst; R-P = Role-Player.

common or appropriate sources. Sample check-list:[3]

_____ Uses *Reader's Guide to Periodical Literature*

_____ Uses card catalogue

_____ Uses bound volumes of journals

_____ Uses encyclopedia

The observer could complete a checklist for each student, or could tabulate the number of students who use each source on one checklist.

For a specific product, the checklist should include sources that are relevant to the particular decision occasion around which the product is constructed.

3. The teacher could also conduct an informal survey of the students, to determine their familiarity with commonly-used sources and to determine the extent to which they would be inclined to go to various sources in seeking different kinds of information. The teacher could also check with the school librarian to find out, approximately, the extent to which students of various age groups use the available resources in the library.   [D-M]   [Elem.]

Secondary teachers will find all of the above valuable, as well as: [Sec.]

4. The teacher asks each student to complete a form while she/he is seeking information. The headings of a sample form are as follows: [D-M] [An] [R-P]   [Sec.]

Source	Information Sought	Information Found	Alternative

Teacher can use the completed forms to assess the students' range of knowledge about available sources, their ability to find information in specific sources, etc.

G. *Formal Evaluation Suggestions.*[4]

1. If you wanted to know about different ways of travel that early American settlers might have used, which one of the following would you look in?   [An]   [Elem.]

_____ dictionary

_____ atlas

_____ history book

_____ book about trains

2. If you wanted to find a book in the library about different sources of energy, in which one of the following places would you look first?   [An]   [Elem.]

____ card catalogue ____ the shelf with the newest magazines ____ an encyclopedia ____ a dictionary		
3. Suppose that you want to find out about how you and your class can help the victims of a flood near where you live. Which one of the following would be the *best* place to go (or call) to find out what you can do to help? ____ a hospital ____ the City Council ____ the Red Cross ____ the library	An	Elem.
4. The Chief of Police wants to present some ideas to the Police Board for ways to reduce the crime rate. Which one of the following would be the *best* place for the Chief of Police to gather information that would help him/her come up with a list of possible ways to reduce crime? ____ survey the Chiefs of Police in cities of a similar size ____ read a book on famous criminals ____ write to the U.S. Department of Labor and ask for statistics on crime rates ____ interview some prison guards	An	Sec.

IV. **Creating Alternatives**

The distinction between seeking and creating alternatives is made by the kind of thinking called for. Seeking is defined as looking for and gathering specific given or remembered information, relevant to the decision situation. Creating requires the student to independently generate alternatives by constructing new relationships, by integrating ideas within a new frame of reference, or by seeing new possibilities in the given information. Creating, in short, requires the student to think in terms of what is possible rather than what is actual. Seeking requires a systematic search for and gathering of what is actual and available.

A. *Cognitive Task:* Thinking divergently.[5]
B. *Object of the Cognitive Task:* Choices of action in addition to, or more specific than, the ones that originally defined the decision occasion and the ones that were found in Skill # III, Seeking and Finding Alternatives.
C. *Prior Conditions Necessary for the Demonstration of the Skill:* Same as for "Seeking Alternatives"; also, must have had some opportunity to brainstorm, to think divergently, to create new thought products.

D. *Criteria Against Which To Test Products or Behavior Which Demonstrate Skill:*
   1. The student generates a choice possibility that makes sense given the conditions of the decision situation and that, as far as the student is concerned, is not an obvious or given option;
   2. The student generates a choice possibility that represents new ways of integrating facts and/or other alternatives.

E. *Product Examples:*
   1. The decision makers for the highway project are considering two alternative routes through the city; both are ground routes through residential sections. Created alternatives include: (1) elevating the freeway; (2) building a beltway around the city; (3) building a subway instead of a highway; (4) building bike-paths instead of a highway.
   2. The desk will not fit through the doors of the building. Movers are considering removing the legs, cutting out the doorways, or trying a window.

F. *Informal Evaluation Suggestions:*

	ROLE OF STUDENT*	LEVEL OF STUDENT
1. Teacher judgment is required to rate products on such dimensions as creativity and feasibility. Sample scales and checklists:	D-M	Elem.

   a. number of alternatives created: _____
   b. flexibility:

1	2	3	4	5
all created alternatives are the same type		created alternatives represent several different types		created alternatives represent great diversity in type

   c. originality:
      _____ the alternatives are ones not previously mentioned in class
      _____ the alternatives represent new ways of integrating ideas given or obvious
   d. practicality:
      _____ the alternatives are feasible
      _____ the alternatives match the goals of the decision occasion

   Secondary teachers will find the above valuable, as well as: Sec.

---

*D-M = Decision Maker; An = Analyst; R-P = Role-Player.

2. A classification and analysis of teacher-student verbal interaction can be made, using a system such as the *Aschner-Gallagher Classification System* (Aschner et al., 1965). Student responses could be classified as follows:[6]

   EL—Elaboration: structured or free (s. or f.). Building upon a point already made; filling out or developing a point, but not shifting to a new point, often by concocting new instances or examples.

   DA—Divergent Association: (s. or f.). Constructing a relationship between ideas, casting the central idea into sharper and often unexpected perspective, by comparison, analogies, etc.

   IMP—Implication: (s. or f.). Extrapolation beyond the given, projection from given data—typically, by antecedent-consequence or hypothetical construction—to new point(s) of possibility.

   SYN—Synthesis: Spontaneous performance, tying in, integrating the current central idea with an entirely new point or frame of reference. May be a variation or reversal of a previous conclusion.

   The use of a classification system such as this one requires that the teacher (or other observer) listen to student responses (either live or taped) and categorize them. Student responses will often involve a combination of two or more of the categories. Although such categorization is tedious, it can aid the teacher in determining the limits of students' ability to create new alternatives.

   (D-M, An, R-P — Sec.)

G. *Formal Evaluation Suggestions:*

   1. Your baseball team wants to get some uniforms. Every team member has been asked to think of a way to get the uniforms. The team has no money right now, so the members would have to first get the money if they are going to buy the uniforms. List as many ways as you can think of to get the uniforms.

   (D-M — Elem.)

   _____

   _____

   _____

   _____

   _____

(Teacher judgment required to score responses. Tabulate the number of responses and consider as unacceptable two or less. Qualitatively rate the responses on flexibility, originality, and practicality using scales such as the ones presented under "Informal Evaluation.")		
2. Imagine that you are the Governor of your state. The Director of Health Services has just resigned, and you must appoint another person to this position. You are being pressured by several special interest groups (e.g., women's groups, the American Medical Association, the National Urban League). Each group wants you to appoint a different person (someone sympathetic to the particular interest). Which one of the following alternatives is the *most* creative alternative?	R-P	Sec.

_____ appoint the person recommended by the AMA, assuming that that person knows the most about health

_____ let representatives of each group meet and make the decision

_____ appoint a representative from each group to a Board of Health Directors, thus substituting the sole Directorship with a Board.

V. Predicting Consequences of Alternatives

A. *Cognitive Task:* Analyzing, inferring, explaining, identifying probabilities.
B. *Object of the Cognitive Task:* Probable relationships between an action or actions proposed or implied in an alternative and the hypothesized impact of the action(s) on one's self or others or the reaction(s) by one's self or others.
C. *Prior Conditions Necessary for the Demonstration of the Skill:* Must have had experiences with relationships, including cause-effect relationships; must have had experience anticipating probable results; desirable to have had experience with formulating and testing hypotheses.
D. *Criteria Against Which To Test Products or Behavior Which Demonstrate Skill:*
   1. The related elements, one in the alternative action and at least one in the impact or reaction statement, must be identified in or obvious from the context;
   2. The consequences named must be reasonable, plausible—not idle threats or wishful thinking;
   3. The list of predicted consequences should include some reference to all the important aspects of alternatives, and include mention of both the short-term and the long-range probable consequences;

    4. Where appropriate, evidence should be presented of having formulated and tested hypotheses in conjunction with the consequences of alternatives.

E. *Product Examples:*
    1. "My mother won't like it if we do that."
    2. "If you tax salt, the people will become more resentful."
    3. "We can't jump the ditch; we will surely fall in."
    4. "If the accused kidnapper gets too much adverse publicity, she will not be able to have a fair trial."

F. *Informal Evaluation Suggestions:*

	ROLE OF STUDENT*	LEVEL OF STUDENT
1. Teacher should check to see if students understand what hypotheses and cause-effect relationships are. Have students generate as many consequences as possible for some action that they might engage in; e.g., If you never went to school, then:	D-M	Elem.

_____

_____

_____

etc.

Teacher can ask students which of the possible results presented above are likely to be actual *effects* (rather than just relationships).

	ROLE OF STUDENT*	LEVEL OF STUDENT
2. Teacher judgment is required to determine the extent to which students' products include plausible consequences for the alternatives previously identified. Products can be rated on sufficiency, plausibility, and relevance to the alternatives and the decision situation. Sample rating scales and checklists (for each alternative, separately):	D-M	Elem.

    a. Sufficiency: The number of predicted consequences is:
    _____ inadequate
    _____ adequate
    _____ more than adequate
    b. Plausibility: The predicted consequence(s) is/are:

1	2	3	4	5
not at all plausible		remotely plausible		extremely plausible

Secondary teachers should find all of the above suggestions useful as well.   Sec.

---

*D-M = Decision Maker; An = Analyst; R-P = Role-Player.

G. *Formal Evaluation Suggestions:*

1. You are faced with a decision about what to do   R-P   Elem.
   during your summer vacation. On the left is a list
   of choices. On the right is a list of the things you
   might gain. Match each choice with its *most likely*
   gain.

Choices	*Gains*
● go to camp	● a new skill
● get a baby-	● healthier body
sitting job	
● take sewing	● money
lessons	

2. Imagine that you are Abraham Lincoln. It is the   R-P   Elem.
   year 1862. You are thinking about what might happen if the slaves in the South are given their freedom. Write down as many possible results as you
   (in your role as Lincoln) can think of.

   _____

   _____

   _____

   _____

   _____

   (Teacher judgment is required to rate responses.
   Use the criteria of sufficiency, plausibility, and
   relevance. Scales and checklists can be used.)

3. Which one of the following would most likely oc-   An   Sec.
   cur if a large scientific research organization decided to locate in a small farming town?:
   _____ land value would decrease
   _____ unemployment would increase
   _____ school attendance would not change
   _____ retail sales would increase

4. The Presidential nominee for the Democratic Par-   An   Elem.
   ty has narrowed his/her choices for a running mate
   to three persons. Which one of the following is the
   question that he/she should ask in trying to predict
   the consequences in terms of the decision situation?
   _____ Which person could help me most to win the
         election?
   _____ Which person could help me win friends in
         Congress after I am elected?
   _____ Which person would get along best with the
         Republican candidates?

5. Below is a list of "predicted consequences" that   An   Elem.
   pertain to the decision choice to revoke the draft
   of young people into the military:

(1) the number of volunteers will increase
(2) the number of "draft evaders" will decrease
(3) enrollment in colleges will decrease
(4) the cost of recruiting men and women into the
    military will increase
a. Which one of the predicted consequences
   above is an assured *effect*?
   ___ 1   ___ 3
   ___ 2   ___ 4
b. Which one of the predicted consequences
   would be of most concern to a military budget
   committee?
   ___ 1   ___ 3
   ___ 2   ___ 4

VI. Weighing Alternatives and Selecting One Course of Action

A. *Cognitive Task:* Analyzing, identifying, matching, comparing, contrasting, synthesizing, judging in terms of one's own and the public's criteria.
B. *Object of the Cognitive Task:* The alternatives with all their characteristics and implications, including value loadings.
C. *Prior Conditions Necessary for the Demonstration of the Skill:* Must have had opportunity to make relative judgments about merit of two or more items; must know how to compare and contrast two or more ideas or actions.
D. *Criteria Against Which To Test Products or Behavior Which Demonstrate Skill:*
   1. Equal analysis of nature and consequence of each alternative;
   2. Comparison across alternatives on basis of one or more elements;
   3. Contrast across alternatives on basis of one or more elements;
   4. Consideration (either implicit or explicit) of the values associated with each alternative in the comparisons and contrasts of costs and benefits;
   5. Summary into single statement of the essence of each alternative's costs and benefits;
   6. Ordering and justifying of the alternatives in terms of decision maker's values, analyst's values, values of society;
   7. Selection of the alternative with the highest order in the ordered list to be the alternative of choice.
E. *Product Examples.* A statement of comparative judgment and justified choice of alternative action:
   1. Alternative A is not as good as Alternative B in terms of public cost over a short time period; but in the long run, Alternative A will bring ten times the benefit in environmental quality for the public. I select Alternative A because it is compatible with my own feelings about the environment— I'm willing to sacrifice, tighten my belt—and because it fits the long-range goals of this society for improving the quality of life.

2. If we go on a field trip to the new space museum, we will be able to see lots of things that we've studied about in science class, but we will all have to pay some of the transportation cost. If we spend our free day helping with the city's "Clean Up the Parks" campaign, we will not have to spend any money and we will be doing something good for the community. I would rather go to the museum, but I think that the "Clean Up" idea is better for most of the class—a lot of kids don't have any extra money to spend and, besides, a lot of them aren't really interested in science.

F. *Informal Evaluation Suggestions:*

	ROLE OF STUDENT*	LEVEL OF STUDENT
1. To aid students in comparing and contrasting alternatives (in terms of costs and benefits), give them sets of choices and ask, "How are these choices the same (what are the same things that you'd get and what are the same things that you'd have to give up)?" and "How are they different?" Students could fill out a chart to help them see the similarities and differences.	D-M	Elem.
2. Teacher judgment is required to assess the quality of the ordering and justifying of the alternatives. The teacher will want to make both an objective rating and a subjective rating of the student's products. The objective ratings will be made in terms of the criteria for the product; the subjective rating will be a judgment of the worth of the ordering and justifying in terms of the teacher's own (or relevant others') values.	D-M	Elem.
3. Teacher judgment is required to assess the adequacy of the product. A sample checklist follows:	D-M An R-P	Sec.

Sample chart:

PROBLEM[7]

	Choice 1	*Choice 2*
costs		
benefits		

(item 2 continued)
For a sample checklist for the objective rating, see the suggestions listed for secondary students. The subjective ratings should be discussed with the students.

(item 3 continued)
_____ personal costs are considered for each alternative
_____ societal costs are considered for each alternative
_____ personal benefits are considered for each alternative

*D-M = Decision Maker; An = Analyst; R-P = Role-Player.

_____ societal benefits are considered for each alternative

_____ both long- and short-term costs and benefits are considered for each alternative

_____ costs are compared

_____ costs are contrasted

_____ benefits are compared

_____ benefits are contrasted

_____ alternatives are ordered

_____ the ordering is justified

_____ one alternative is selected

4. Students could complete a chart (similar to the one appearing under suggestion #1, with elaborations):

	D-M
	An
	R-P

| | Sec. |

PROBLEM

	Choice 1	Choice 2
Person(s) affected		
Name:	cost_____	
	benefit_____	
Name:	cost_____	
	benefit_____	

Have students fill in the blanks with the costs and benefits of each alternative to the person(s) affected by the decision. Then have students put a "+" next to those costs and benefits which are consistent with the person's values. For example, a "+" would appear next to "it would cost a lot of money" under "costs" if the person(s) identified to the left of that item is *not* concerned about spending money for that reason; a "+" would belong next to "I would be able to spend more time with my family," if that aspect was identified as a "benefit" and it was something valued positively by the person(s) to whom it referred.

The teacher then asks students to rank order the choices and justify the ordering—by stating whose values are considered most important, for example. The justification should be based on an integration of the information in the chart and a personal judgment.

G. *Formal Evaluation Suggestions:*

1. Here are some things that you might think about doing if you wanted to learn how to ski:

   • read a book about skiing

   • see a movie about skiing

   • take a free lesson from a friend

| | R-P | Elem. |

- try to teach yourself how to ski
- take some lessons at a ski school

a. Circle the choice that would probably cost the most money
b. Circle the choice that would probably be the most dangerous to you
c. Underline the choices for which you would not have to go where there is some snow

Now tell which *one* of the choices you would make for yourself. Tell *why* you choose the one you do. Be sure to say what it is about that choice that you think would be best for you.

_____

_____

_____

(Teacher judgment is required to score the last section. Use a checklist similar to the one in section F—suggestion #3.)

2. Imagine that you are a member of a state legislature in 1919. The 18th Amendment (prohibiting the manufacture and sale of alcoholic beverages) has been proposed by the Congress. Now it is up to the states to ratify it. An argument is taking place in your legislature among several other members. Here is the dialogue which you are listening to:

R-P   Sec.

MR. LONG: This amendment, if passed, would restrict individual rights. I am opposed to the government interfering in the private lives of the citizens.

MR. SMITH: But it is morally wrong, in my opinion, to drink alcoholic beverages. Don't we have a responsibility to strengthen the moral atmosphere of our country?

MRS. PARKER: I don't think we should even consider the moral issue—that's *not* our responsibility! But I'm *for* this amendment for a different reason. I think that alcoholic beverages are a threat to the physical well-being of the people.

a. Which one of the following is a value held by Mr. Long?
____ health   ____ money
____ individualism   ____ power

b. Which one of the following is a value held by Mrs. Parker?
____ health   ____ money
____ individualism   ____ power

c. What is a perceived *benefit* to the people of the U.S. implied in Mr. Smith's statement calling for the acceptance of the amendment?
—freedom of expression
—decrease in alcohol abuse
—decrease in cost of alcohol
—decrease in governmental interference

d. Suppose that you believed that drinking alcohol was morally wrong; and yet when it is time to vote on the amendment, you vote against its ratification. Which one of the following benefits did you probably place greater emphasis on than any of the costs when you weighed the alternatives?
_____ physical health and well-being
_____ freedom from governmental interference
_____ your own moral convictions
_____ the government's regulation of interstate commerce

3. Below is a list of alternatives for the decision occasion, "Where should I send my child to school?" Imagine that you are a middle-class white parent, living in a big city that uses busing to achieve integration of the public schools.   R-P   Sec.

(1) send child to expensive, all-white private school, located close to your home

(2) send child to public school, which will involve having child bused across town.

a. Name one cost to you in each alternative:
(1)_____
(2)_____
(sample answers: (1) money; (2) control over child's educational environment)

b. Name one benefit to you in each alternative:
(1)_____
(2)_____
(sample answers: (1) proximity of child's school to home; (2) exposure of child to children of other races)

c. If your top priority in life is saving your money for leisure activities, retirement, etc., which alternative would be more attractive to you?
_____ (1)
_____ (2)
_____ both are equally attractive

VII. **Determining Appropriate Action to Implement Decision**

A. *Cognitive Task:* Matching concrete behaviors with semantic abstractions (translation of semantic content of decision into discrete, sequential and appropriate anticipated behaviors).

B. *Object of the Cognitive Task:* Ideas and actions inherent in decision.

C. *Prior Conditions Necessary for the Demonstration of the Skill:* Must be able to follow directions; must have had opportunity to put steps of some activity in logical sequence; must know what the general dimensions of most activities are (e.g., who, what, when, where, how much, etc.).

D. *Criteria Against Which To Test Products or Behavior which Demonstrate Skill:*

1. Shows an accurate matching of the components in the decision with appropriate implementation components;
2. Shows recognition of time considerations necessary to carry out phases of the decision;
3. Incorporates behaviors faithful to the spirit or intent of the decision;
4. Designates tasks of relevant persons;
5. Recognizes if the decision made is so complex that the appropriate action is more decision making, rather than other types of behaviors.

E. *Product Examples:* An outline of separate actions arranged in time sequence and described by purposeful relationship to decision intent:

1. Having decided to try to arrange a compromise with the enemy, we will:
   a. Identify opposition leaders;
   b. Designate a team leader;
   c. Set a time and place for the meeting;
   d. Draft an agenda;
   e. Gather together necessary materials;
   f. Meet with opposition leaders.

2. TEACHER: Now that the family has decided to move from the farm to the city, what steps must be taken in making the move?
   STUDENT: They must sell or rent the farm to someone else and buy or rent a house in the city. They also must choose a moving day and get a truck or hire some movers. Before they can actually leave, they will have to pack up all their things at the farm. The last action will be to leave the farm and travel to the city.

3. TEACHER: By 1776, several of the most influential colonists had decided that they should be independent of Britain. Once this group had made this decision, what were the actions that they needed to take to carry out the decision?
   STUDENT: Well, they had to win the war.
   TEACHER: But before they could even fight a war, what did they have to do?
   STUDENT: They had to start the war.
   TEACHER: But starting the war was not necessarily part of the original decision, was it?

STUDENT: No. The decision was to become independent. So the next step was to tell the other colonists and the British what they had decided. That was the Declaration of Independence.

TEACHER: Right. The first step in the act of becoming independent was to declare the independence. Voicing the intent to be independent of Britain was an appropriate action to take to implement the decision.

F. *Informal Evaluation Suggestions:*

	ROLE OF STUDENT*	LEVEL OF STUDENT
1. Teacher judgment is required to assess whether or not students are able to determine the appropriate action. A checklist such as the following can help the teacher rate the students' products.	D-M An R-P	Elem.

    ____ the action specified is consonant with the decision

    ____ the action specified is a realistic way of implementing the decision

    ____ the steps specified as ways to take action are inclusive

    ____ the steps follow a logical sequence

    ____ if there are several "appropriate" actions, that fact is recognized by the students—as well as the fact that a recycling through the decision process is required

Secondary teachers, as well as elementary teachers, should find the above useful for informal evaluation.   Sec.

G. *Formal Evaluation Suggestions:*

1. You have decided to read a book about airplanes for a class reading assignment.   An   Elem.

    a. Where could you find a book about airplanes?

    _____

    b. Who might help you find it?

    _____

    c. How long do you think it might take you to read the book?

    _____

    d. Which one of the following books would be a book that would best fit your decision?
    —*Famous Inventors*
    —*The History of the United States*
    —*All About Birds*
    —*A History of Flight*

*D-M = Decision Maker; An = Analyst; R-P = Role-Player.

2. Your class has decided to have a bake sale at the school fair. The fair is next week. Everyone has said that she or he will do something to help with the sale.
  a. Which one of the following is the most important decision that must be made next?
    ____ when to have the fair
    ____ who will bring what food to sell
    ____ who will buy the food at the sale
    ____ whether you want to have a bake sale or not
	An	Elem.

3. You have decided that you want to learn how to play chess. Name two other things that you must now do or decide before you can start to learn. _____ _____ (Sample answers: When you will learn, how you will learn, who will teach you, how you will find a teacher, where you will get a chess set, etc.)	An	Elem.

4. Having decided that a new highway is needed, which one of the following would be the appropriate action for the State Department of Highways to take?
    ____ draw up specific plans and itemize costs
    ____ survey the people to find out if they want a new highway
    ____ consider alternatives to a new highway
	An	Sec.

5. What is the most appropriate first step to take after deciding to run for President of the Student Body at your school (choose one)?
    ____ write your acceptance speech
    ____ find out what the job of Student Body President entails
    ____ announce your plans to seek the job
    ____ decide whether you really have the time to run for President
	D-M	Sec.

VIII. **Taking Action to Implement the Decision**

A. *Cognitive Task:* To do something overtly that is specifically related to and forwards progress toward the decision goal, or to identify the overt actions taken by a decision maker to implement a decision.

B. *Object of the Cognitive Task:* Ideas and actions inherent in implementing the decision.

C. *Prior Conditions Necessary for the Demonstration of the Skill:*
 1. Must have had the opportunity to translate an idea for action into actual action, or
 2. Must be able to determine, from written or verbal accounts, what action, if any, took place.
D. *Criteria Against Which To Test Products or Behavior Which Demonstrate Skill:*
 1. The student must make an observable move (or report one already taken) that is consonant with the implementation plan; or specifically identify an action taken and explain its relationship to decision implementation;
 2. The student must be able to explain why the action fits the decision need;
 3. If appropriate, the student must repeat the action consistently in some pattern of his/her life.
E. *Product Examples:*
 1. Having decided to actively support the Greenpeace "Save the Whales" effort, the student picks up petitions to take to the supermarket.
 2. When Edmund Ross voted for Johnson's acquittal, he took the logical action to fulfill his earlier decision—he cast his vote against conviction.
 3. When Harold sold his car to get money, he showed that he was serious about paying his own way through college.
F. *Informal Evaluation Suggestions:*

	ROLE OF STUDENT*	LEVEL OF STUDENT
1. The teacher must observe the student's actions and make judgments regarding the sufficiency, appropriateness, and consistency of the action. A checklist of behaviors could be filled out for each student. Sample checklist: ____ behavior is appropriate for the decision ____ behavior represents reasonable amount of follow-through ____ behavior is consistent The teacher should also check to see if students can explain why the actions they take are the appropriate actions. Interviews with the students will help the teacher make these judgments. The teacher should ask such questions as: "Why did you do what you did? How did you know where to go? How did you know when to stop?", etc.	D-M R-P	Elem.
2. Teacher judgment is required to answer the question, "Can the students identify the action taken in situations in which they were not involved that fulfilled the requirements of the decision?" The teacher could orally drill the students, using situations like those presented under "Formal	An	Elem.

*D-M = Decision Maker; An = Analyst; R-P = Role-Player.

Evaluation Suggestions,'' and ask students to
name the action(s) that indicated that the deci-
sion(s) had been carried out.

Secondary teachers should also find the above sug-   Sec.
gestions useful.

G. *Formal Evaluation Suggestions:*

1. Abraham Lincoln in 1862 decided to free the slaves in the states which had rebelled. Which one of the following actions did he take to carry out that decision? ____ he talked to Southern leaders about the results of freeing the slaves ____ he issued a proclamation that all such slaves would be free as of a certain date ____ he spoke with lots of people to see how many of them wanted to free the slaves	An	Elem.
2. Think about the last time that you and your friends decided to play a certain game. What action did you take to carry out that decision (choose one)? ____ you talked about whether you wanted to play the game or not ____ you talked about which game you wanted to play ____ you played the game	D-M	Elem.
3. After considering possible alternatives, Nixon decided, in the summer of 1974, to resign from the Presidency. What one main action did he take to implement that decision? ____ he checked with his advisers to see if he could avoid leaving office ____ he talked with his lawyers about his chances of winning an impeachment trial ____ he told the country that he was stepping down from office ____ he asked his family if it thought he should resign or not	An	Sec.

IX. **Reflecting on the Decision, Action, and Results**

A. *Cognitive Task:* Identifying the outcomes (results) of the action taken and
comparing outcomes, action taken, action determined, and purpose with
each other to judge the worth of the decision purpose; making a judgment,
based on personal values, of the worth of the decision, action taken, and
outcomes. (Analyzing, verifying, evaluating.)

B. *Object of the Cognitive Task:* The decision, implementing actions, results—separately and in interaction.

C. *Prior Conditions Necessary for the Demonstration of the Skill:* Must know how to delineate purpose, action determined, action taken, and outcomes in the completed decision situation; must be able to make a judgment.

D. *Criteria Against Which To Test Products or Behavior Which Demonstrate Skill:*
   1. Judgment of whether the outcome followed from the decision and action;
   2. Judgment of how closely the outcome matched the expectations implicit in the decision;
   3. Expression of worth or quality of decision, action, results;
   4. Analysis of why the outcomes do or do not match the purposes, actions determined, actions taken.

E. *Product Examples:* Verbal or written statements that judge the validity of outcomes against the implications of the decision and the action; judge the worth of the decision and/or outcome against the premises of the occasion, including the values of the affected person(s):
   1. The violent reaction of the crowd was not what had been anticipated when the mayor read the decision of the City Council to sell the mountain park land. It appears that the members of the City Council did not weigh the alternatives in terms of a sufficient number of criteria—they might have forgotten to consider popular public opinion. Or, perhaps they did not have enough information to identify an alternative that would have been more acceptable to the people.
   2. There was nothing wrong with my decision to go to college; I just chose a school that was too tough for me.
   3. I think that the President's decision to send more troops to Vietnam was a bad decision. He did not take into account the public's attitude about the war. The amount of disruption and chaos that the war led to in this country was not worth the attempt to save South Vietnam from communist rule.

F. *Informal Evaluation Suggestions:*

	ROLE OF STUDENT*	LEVEL OF STUDENT
1. Teacher judgment is required to assess the logical consistency, sufficiency, and worth of the students' products. A checklist such as the following can be used to rate the products according to the logical consistency and sufficiency criteria: ___ consideration of both short- and long-term outcomes ___ consideration of unexpected side effects ___ comparison of outcome(s) with steps in the decision-making process ___ detection of inconsistencies among steps and outcomes	D-M	Elem.

*D-M = Decision Maker; An = Analyst; R-P = Role-Player.

____ judgment made of worth or usefulness of decision and of decision in terms of outcomes		
2. Give students a situation in which several different undesirable outcomes for a decision are possible. List (verbally or on paper) the possible desirable outcomes and ask students to answer the question, "What went wrong that led to this result?" for each outcome. Judge answers to be acceptable if they pinpoint one or more possible deviations in the process following the decision, or possibly failings in earlier steps. Sample:	R-P	Elem.

Your family decided to plant a vegetable garden in the back yard. Tell me what might have gone wrong for each of the following things to happen:

a. The garden never got planted.

   (Sample answers: Nobody planted it; nobody organized it.)

b. The garden was planted, but winter came before any vegetables were ready to be picked.

   (Sample answers: The time chosen for planting was wrong; nobody had accurate information about when to plant.)

c. The garden was planted, but bugs destroyed all the vegetables.

   (Sample answers: Nobody remembered to spray for bugs; nobody looked into the problem of bugs before they made the decision to have the garden; it was an unpredictable consequence—a completely new phenomenon for the type of soil, the climate, etc.)

Secondary teachers should also find the above ideas useful.		Sec.

G. *Formal Evaluation Suggestions:*

1. Suppose that you decided to build a model airplane for a science project. You bought all the materials that you needed, but you could not build it. When you told your teacher, he said, "That's a fine idea, but since you can't complete it, I'll have to give you a low grade."	R-P	Elem.

   Which one of the following did you most likely *not* do that caused this problem?

   ____ choose a project that your teacher liked

   ____ take all the steps necessary to carry out

your decision to make the airplane
_____ think carefully about what you would do
with the airplane after you build it
_____ buy the materials

2. In 1215, King John of England signed the Magna
Carta. The signing was the action which implemented a decision made by King John. The Magna
Carta guaranteed the rights of the nobles to be
represented in governmental decisions regarding
taxation. The alternative which King John had rejected had been *not* to grant the nobles this right
and face the consequence of uprisings by the nobles. The Magna Carta had great impact on the
nature of both the English and the American systems of government. It is considered to be one of
the foundations of the U.S. Constitution.

                                                   D-M   Sec.
                                                   An
                                                  R-P

a. If you lived in England in the 13th century and
you favored an autocratic governmental structure, would you have considered King John's
decision to be a good one?
_____ yes
_____ no
_____ I don't know

b. Suppose that you lived in England in the 13th
century and you thought that the Magna Carta
was too extreme an idea, but you also thought
that *something* had to be done to prevent the
nobles from rebelling. Which steps in the decision-making process would you have wanted
to concentrate on (choose one)?
_____ identifying values associated with the alternatives
_____ seeking or creating alternatives
_____ predicting consequences of alternatives
_____ taking action on a decision

c. Reflecting back *now* on King John's decision,
what is its most important long-range effect?
_____ it prevented the nobles from rebelling
_____ it showed that compromise could lead to
peace
_____ it set a precedent for the guaranteeing of
rights to representation
_____ it established a monarchy in England

DATA MANAGEMENT AND USE

The nine decision-making skills we have identified are assumed to be equally significant to the decision-making process. We have also assumed that all nine are vital to the fulfillment of the process. To be able to demonstrate only some of the skills would indicate a partial understanding but not mastery of the process of decision making. Is it important to know the degree of mastery attained by students? Is it worthwhile keeping track of which skills are demonstrated and when? Is it worth knowing whether a student can go through the whole process once? Is it important to determine whether the student can engage the process at any point and move forward or backward from that point?

We think that the answers to the above questions are all affirmative. If decision-making skill is a collective skill, dependent on the mastery of several component skills, then we do have to keep a record of the student's progress and performance. Otherwise we can tell the student nothing about his or her attainment of the critical ability to make and judge decisions. Furthermore, we will not know whether our instruction has been effective.

When we keep track of skills acquisition and mastery, we can find out for ourselves and for teachers who will work with the student in the future where the weak spots are. We can work with the student to assure that he or she does acquire the basic skills of good decision making.

The attainment of the complete set of skills can make a big difference in the way one eventually lives. Most of us know people whose ability to make humane and effective decisions for themselves or others is flawed because they lack one or another of the decision skills. The person who consistently misses opportunity may simply not recognize an "occasion for decision." The principal who decides to interrupt classes with administrative announcements may always be puzzled at faculty irritation if he or she is unaware that values are implicit in a decision situation. The high school graduate who chooses to do what a best friend does without seeking other alternatives may do himself or herself a great disservice. We are familiar with the person who can carefully reach a considered decision, yet cannot make one move to implement the decision. The armchair decider is a decision maker in the narrow definition, but he or she changes nothing if no action is taken.

It may be that decision-making skills are the most neglected of the skills taught in school. An additional benefit of keeping records of student decision-making skills may be to point out to faculties the need for opportunities for students to practice skills of deciding, determining action, taking action, and reflecting on action and consequences.

Record keeping is a tedious business, even when one is convinced that it is worth the time. The technique suggested here is meant to yield a lot of information about the student but to require a minimum of teacher time. Ditto enough copies of the following matrix so that each student may also keep a record of progress.

DECISION-MAKING SKILLS: OPPORTUNITIES/DEMONSTRATION

Skills	As Analyst	As Role-Taker	Decision Maker
Identify Occasion			
Recognize Values			
Seek/Find Alternatives			
Create Alternatives			
Predict Consequences			
Weigh Alternatives			
Make Decision			
Determine Action			
Take Action			
Reflect			

Student's Name_____

You may use the cells in this matrix to indicate—by a slash—that a student has had an opportunity to demonstrate a particular skill in the various role modes. That opportunity may have come from written exercises, such as those suggested earlier in the chapter, or from oral discussions in the classroom. It may be useful to indicate the date on which these opportunities were given so that you can check on opportunity frequency. When the student has demonstrated his or her command of the skill, mark the cell with an X and the date. It seems unlikely, given a class of twenty-five or thirty students, that it would be possible to fill in every cell for each student. You may find that giving students an opportunity either to analyze decisions already made or to role-play a decision maker is sufficient to help in conceptualizing the process and a particular skill. It would not be difficult to record student performance on skills for just one or the other of these "practice" categories. The student's prowess as analyst can be indicated by a written analysis of a case study that involves decision-making. The case study given in Chapter One about the Browns' decision to buy a home is an appropriate case study for older students. For younger children, the following situation may suggest an appropriate stimulus.

Rick's mother looked at him closely at dinner. "How come you seem so happy tonight?," she asked. "Something good happened today," Rick answered. "Our teacher announced that the field trip to the museum was all set for next Thursday—all day. She said that anybody who couldn't go could work in the library that day. Well, I knew I probably could not go because I'm on safety duty at noon and after school. The principal made us promise never to miss unless we are sick."

His mother interrupted, "But, Rick, why didn't you tell your teacher? She would have made it O.K. with the principal." "I thought about that, but I didn't want to get her into it. I thought of asking the principal myself, but I figured he would get mad. Then I thought that I would make arrangements with my safety partner to get a friend to take my place." "Don't do that! You could get all of you in trouble," his mother warned. "Well, I didn't. I had just about given up trying to go on the trip. Then today at noon while I was on duty, the principal came out of the building and walked right up to the crosswalk where I was. He said, 'How's it going?' and smiled at me. That's when I decided to tell him, 'Not so good,' and I told him about the field trip." "Well, what did he say?" his mother asked. "He just said to come in to his office tomorrow and he would work something out so I could go. He wasn't mad at all. Boy, am I glad I decided to tell him about it."

From an episode like this the teacher can ask students to analyze or sort out the situation and the decision-making process. The students can identify Rick's skills or lack of them. Did Rick recognize an occasion for decision? Did he consider some alternatives? What made him change his mind about talking to the principal? Was it a good decision for him?

The students' answers to these questions will not tell you whether the students can apply particular decision-making skills. Their answers will indicate, however, whether they comprehend the meaning of the skill(s). Both opportunity and demonstration of understanding can be marked accordingly in the matrix in the column "Student as Analyst."

To determine whether the student has internalized skill meanings and can apply particular skills in real situations the teacher needs to use a little ingenuity. Any time an occasion for decision exists, the teacher can observe the skills of some students. For example, any time a teacher gives options for activities or reports, the student must decide on one topic or activity. Most of the time all the decision-making skills are inherent in the choice situation, and it only requires observation or debriefing to determine whether the student has applied the skill. Is there someone in the class who does not recognize the decision situation; that is, that there is a choice to be made among topics or activities?

Does a student verbalize values while considering choices? "I already wrote a report on Lewis and Clark. I want to do something different." "If I choose the dried foods activity, then I'll be in with a lot of girls."

The teacher can ask students why they made the choice they did and get an idea of the selection process each student used. Were alternatives considered? From what points of view? Did the student take action on the choice of activity? Did he or she actually interview a senior citizen, for example, or build a model city, or write a report on ancient cities of the Sahara? Finally, the teacher can ask each student to write an evaluation on his or her choice after the consequences—grade on report, activity outcome—are known.

For high school students in an elective class, one might ask for an analysis of the decision making that led to the choice of that particular course. What was the decision situation? What were the considerations in making the choice? What were the alternatives? We know the decision and the action taken—the student did elect to take the course and is presently enrolled. Ask the student to reflect on the decision and the consequences. Was it a good choice?

The entire episode as recalled and assessed by the student will yield some information by which to evaluate the student's skills as a decision maker. Both the assessment and the criteria for assessing should be shared with the student. A worthwhile extension of this activity might be to let the students sound out alternatives for next semester or after high school with their peers. Ask the students to use a criteria sheet to check one another's decision-making skills and to rate the quality of the decision. As students become aware of the characteristics of decision-making skills through the use of their own and others' examples, they begin to understand the skill, to acquire and apply it.

GROUP PROCESS SKILLS IN DECISION MAKING

In group decision making, interpersonal skills or group dynamics skills become important variables in determining the quality of the group decision. Specific group process skills have been treated in Chapter Five. The authors of this present chapter believe that the more students are involved, with direction, in observing the process by which groups make decisions, the better they will contribute to effective group decisions. Let students observe and rate group process and the resulting decisions when you are evaluating groups for your own assessment purpose. We find the following activity to be instructional and interesting for intermediate level students, but it can work as well for older students.

Given an occasion to choose some activity or object for the class, the teacher divides the class randomly into groups of five. One member (or two, if necessary) becomes the observer for each group and keeps a record of the following variables:

(1) Frequency of talk. Every time a member makes a verbal entry into the discussion, make a single tally next to that person's name.
(2) Kind of comment. The comment of each participant is classified as C (Closing), S (Sustaining), or E (Extending). A Closing comment is one that tends to thwart or shut off further exploration. "That's a dumb idea!" or "I don't have anything to say." A Sustaining comment keeps discussion open. "What do you think, Mark?" "Maybe we can think of some other ideas." An Extending comment is one that encourages, adds new ideas, probes for more information, leads to a new stage of development. "Tell us a little more about your idea, Connie." "What do you think would happen if we did that?" "Let us look at the disadvantages of each of these ideas."
(3) Role of Each Participant. The kind of role generally played by each participant can be described as Initiator, Facilitator, Blocker, Non-contributor. An Initiator (I) brings up new ideas, gets things going. A Facilitator (F) keeps the conversation going, brings in those who are not talking, helps to clarify comments. A Blocker (B) makes negative comments, quarrels, is stubborn or dogmatic. A Non-contributor (N) is silent, passive, reluctant to comment or take a position.
(4) Time it takes to reach a decision. Record in total number of minutes.
(5) Quality of decision. Quality might be rated according to predetermined criteria for the issue in question. For example, if the students are trying to choose a piece of equipment for the whole class to use that costs less than $15.00, then cost and utility criteria are implicit. The decision might also be rated as Poor, Fair, or Good on the basis of the decision-making skills demonstrated by the participants. Refer to the nine skills described earlier in this chapter to derive criteria such as: group understands decision situation; group recognizes value considerations; group seeks alternatives; group weighs alternatives; etc.
(6) Participants' feeling about the decision. With 1 indicating a very poor decision and 5 designating a superior decision, ask participants to indicate on a continuum of 1 to 5 their evaluation of the quality of the decision.
(7) Participants' feeling about their own participation in the decision making. Ask the participants to indicate on a scale of 1 to 5 how they felt about their own participation in the group. Have 1 designate Very Dissatisfied, and 5 Very Satisfied.

The one or more group observers then summarize their data individually for their respective groups and report the summaries to the total class. A summary sheet might look like this:

SUMMARY FOR GROUP #1

Student	Talk Frequency	Kind of Talk	Role in Discussion
J.H.	/	C	Non-Contributor
R.S.	///////	S	Facilitator
L.L.	////	E	Initiator
K.C.	///	C	Blocker

Time to reach decision: 16 minutes
Quality of Decision: Fair
Participants' feeling about decision: Mean 2.3 or "Just Fair"
Participants' feeling about participation: Mean 3.0 or "Satisfied"

Another summary sheet from the same class might appear:

SUMMARY FOR GROUP #2

Student	Talk Frequency	Kind of Talk	Role in Discussion
L.R.	////	E	Initiator
T.M.	//////	S	Facilitator
C.C.	/////	E	Initiator
O.R.	///	S	Facilitator

Time to reach decision: 9 minutes
Quality of decision: Good
Participants' feeling about decision: Mean 4.0 or "Good"
Participants' feeling about participation: Mean 4.5 or "Very Good"

What will be of interest to the class are the relationships between the variables for the various groups. The teacher can ask what things seem to go along with a decision rated Good by the observer and what things seem to contribute to a Poor or "Just Fair" decision.

These group discussions can also be counted as opportunities for individual students to demonstrate specific decision-making skills. The teacher, student teacher, or an aide might assess individual demonstrations of skills during these discussions.

CONCLUSION

The chapters of this Yearbook have affirmed the thesis of the opening chapter—that decision making is the essence of social studies education. Learning to make humane and socially effective decisions brings together and applies knowledge, intellectual and interpersonal skills, and values. In this chapter we have identified the special skills that make possible the bringing together and applying of knowledge, skills, and values in situations requiring choice of action. Our purposes have been to provide a model for evaluation of decision-making skills, the criteria against which to assess the products of skill application, examples for use in informal and formal evaluation, and some suggestions for managing the data on student performance.

REFERENCES

Banks, James A. with Ambrose A. Clegg, Jr. *Teaching Strategies for the Social Studies*. Reading, Massachusetts: Addison-Wesley, 1973.

Citizenship Decision-Making Instructional Materials. Citizenship Development Project, Richard C. Remy, Director, Columbus, Ohio.

Dunkin, Michael and Bruce V. Biddle. *The Study of Teaching*. New York, N.Y.: Holt, Rinehart and Winston, 1974.

Effective Thinking in the Social Studies, 37th Yearbook, NCSS. Washington, D.C.: NCSS, 1967.

Experiences in Decision Making, Elementary Social Studies Handbook. Province of Alberta, Canada: Department of Education, January, 1971.

Experiences in Inquiry. Association of American Geographers and American Sociological Association. Boston, Massachusetts: Allyn & Bacon, Inc., 1974.

Ten Brink, Terry D. *Evaluation: A Practical Guide for Teachers*. New York, N.Y.: McGraw-Hill Book Company, Inc., 1974.

FOOTNOTES

[1] Adapted from Unit I *Citizenship Decision-Making*, Roger LaRaus and Richard C. Remy (Columbus, Ohio: The Mershon Center, Ohio State University), p. 6.

[2] Adapted from *Experiences in Decision Making*, Department of Education, Province of Alberta, January, 1971, p. 41.

[3] Adapted from *Evaluation: A Practical Guide for Teachers* (New York: McGraw-Hill Book Company, Inc., 1974), p. 274.

[4] Also see the SRA "Sources" subtest of the SRA Achievement Test series and the reference skills subtest of the Iowa Test of Basic Skills.

[5] Dunkin and Biddle cite Guilford's definition of "divergent production" or "divergent thinking" as "the kind that goes off in different directions. It makes possible changes of direction in problem solving and also leads to a diversity of answers, where more than one answer must be acceptable." Michael Dunkin and Bruce Biddle, *The Study of Teaching* (New York: Holt, Rinehart and Winston, 1974), p. 247.

[6] *Ibid.*, p. 248.

[7] Adapted from *Experiences in Inquiry*, Association of American Geographers and American Sociological Association (Boston: Allyn and Bacon, Inc., 1974), p. 121.